LONGMAN LINGUISTICS LIBRARY
Title no 23
MODALITY AND THE ENGLISH MODALS

LONGMAN LINGUISTICS LIBRARY

General editors
R. H. Robins, University of London
G. N. Leech, University of Lancaster

Modality and the English Modals

F. R. Palmer

Professor of Linguistic Science
University of Reading

LONGMAN

LONDON AND NEW YORK

LONGMAN GROUP LIMITED LONDON
Associated companies, branches and representatives throughout the world
Published in the United States of America by Longman Inc, New York
© Longman Group Ltd 1979

First published 1979
Cased ISBN 0 582 55109 9
Paper ISBN 0 582 55108 0

British Library Cataloguing in Publication Data
Palmer, Frank Robert
    Modality and the English modals—(Longman lin-
guistics library; no. 23).
    1. English language—Verb 2. English language—
Modality
I. Title
425   PE 1315.M/   78-40698
ISBN 0–582–55109–9
ISBN 0–582–55108–0   Pbk

Typeset by CCC and printed and bound at
William Clowes & Sons Limited, London and Beccles
Printed in Great Britain at The Pitman Press, Bath

Preface

There is, perhaps, no area of English grammar that is both more important and more difficult than the system of the modals. After considerable dissatisfaction with my own work as well as that of others, I decided that the only way to make any approach to a solution was by a careful investigation of an extensive set of written and spoken texts. This book is a result of that decision.

The texts are taken from the Survey of English Usage in University College London. I am deeply indebted to all those who have prepared the Survey, and, in particular, to Randolph Quirk for not merely allowing me free access, but also welcoming me into the offices of the Survey and providing space in which to work over a considerable period of time.

I also wish to thank those who have commented on an earlier draft of the book, especially Michael Garman, Arthur Hughes, P. H. Matthews, R. H. Robins and Herman Wekker and, finally, my wife who has spent so much time reading and correcting both copy and proofs.

University of Reading   F R P
February 1979

Contents

To Nicola and Jonathan

Chapter 1

Introduction

The title of this book is designed to indicate that it will be concerned with the semantic concept of modality, but only to the extent to which it is signalled by the English modal verbs. It will not be directly concerned with modality in general, or with other expressions of modality in English.

1.1 Modals and modality

We must first consider what is meant by 'modal' or 'modal verb' and by 'modality', and how the two concepts may be related.

I.I.I Form and meaning

An investigation of modality and modals inevitably raises problems concerning universal grammar and the relation between form and meaning. For it is clearly one of those semantic-syntactic categories that, as Jespersen (1924: 56) says, 'Janus-like face both ways, towards form, and towards notion'. If we decide to approach it exclusively either from form or from meaning we run into difficulties.

A purely formal approach is unsatisfactory, or even, perhaps, impossible. It would confine us to looking for the formal patterns of a single language, for there can be no identification of such patterns from one language to another. Not only would this fail to say anything of interest about language in general; we would also be unable to make use of familiar grammatical and semantic concepts. Unless there is some semantic, non-language-specific, basis, there can be no justification for using a term such as 'modality', since this term implies that the semantic characteristics that it denotes are already known and understood.

A purely semantic approach also runs into difficulties. For it is not at all clear how, precisely, modality should be defined in semantic terms, and any precise definition may well exclude a great deal of what we wish to describe in actual languages. In particular, if the semantic system is presented as a logical system, it will have little in common with natural languages. Logical systems do not 'underlie' natural language, but are essentially languages themselves that can, with varying degrees of success, be translated into a language such as English.

We are forced, then, to do as Jespersen suggested, to take into account both form and meaning. There clearly must be some kind of semantic basis to the concept of modality, yet at the same time precisely what is to be handled within that concept will depend on the formal features of the language being described.

In this sense the formal analysis is the more basic; it allows us to set some fairly clear limits. Yet a formally defined category will contain some semantically heterogeneous items. If, for instance, we define modality in English in terms of the modal auxiliaries, we shall, by including WILL, have to include within the system of modality both futurity, which seems to belong more to the system of tense, and volition, which has little in common with the more obvious modal concepts of possibility and necessity (1.1.6), but belongs more with the verbs of wanting, hoping, etc, which are essentially lexical rather than grammatical in English. Similarly, in German, the formally defined modals WILLEN and SOLLEN include within their semantics what is said to be true. This must be accounted for in any study of German, but would be quite irrelevant for English.

1.1.2 Von Wright's modes

Von Wright, in what was a pioneering work on modal logic (1951: 1–2), distinguishes between four modes. These are:

[i] The alethic modes or modes of truth.
[ii] The epistemic modes or modes of knowing.
[iii] The deontic modes or modes of obligation.
[iv] The existential modes or modes of existence.

Von Wright admits that the last, which belongs to quantification theory, is often not regarded as a branch of modal logic, but adds that there are essential similarities between it and the other modes. He sets them out in a table, and we are to assume, presumably, that the horizontal arrangement is significant:

Alethic	Epistemic	Deontic	Existential
necessary	verified	obligatory	universal
possible		permitted	existing
contingent	undecided	indifferent	
impossible	falsified	forbidden	empty

These are, however, essentially a logician's set of categories and von Wright's purpose in setting them up is, openly, to investigate their formal structure in terms of truth tables etc, as for quantification theory. In contrast, the aim of the linguist must be simply to investigate the kind of modalities that are clearly recognizable in language and the systems which they exhibit.

Alethic modality has been the main concern of logicians, but it has little place in ordinary language. It is true that MUST may be used to indicate alethic necessity as in:

John is a bachelor, so he must be unmarried.

Yet it would be no less natural not to use MUST and to say *so he is unmarried,* and it seems likely that no clear distinction is recognized by native speakers between this alethic use and the epistemic use of MUST.

Linguists have used the term 'epistemic' to refer to the use of the modal auxiliaries MAY and MUST, as in *He may be there, He must be there.* Von Wright notes that the word *possible* is used in ordinary language in an epistemic sense, yet in his system 'possible' belongs to the alethic mode, and the term in the epistemic mode is 'undecided'. This is related to the fact that epistemic modality in language is usually, perhaps always, what Lyons (1977: 792) calls 'subjective' in that it relates to an inference by the speaker, and is not simply concerned with 'objective' verifiability in the light of knowledge. Epistemic necessity, indicated by MUST, is thus not to be paraphrased as 'In the light of what is known it is necessarily the case that ...', but by something like 'From what I know the only conclusion I can draw is ...'.

Deontic modality, too, has a place in ordinary language. The modal verbs are used to express what is obligatory, permitted, or forbidden. But like epistemic modality, it is usually subjective in that the speaker is the one who obliges, permits, or forbids. Von Wright's modality is 'absolute', but he recognizes that it can be 'relative', *ie* to some moral code or some person. Deontic modals are, thus, usually performative in the sense of Austin (1962: 4–7) (see 2.4.3, 4.1).

The existential mode is, as von Wright says, a matter of quantificational logic and is more concerned in ordinary language with *some, any, all* than the expressions of modality. But it is of interest to us for two reasons. First, CAN is used in an existential sense to mean 'some' (though more commonly 'sometimes') *eg Lions can be dangerous* (8.3). Secondly, the rules for logical equivalence with negation in existential modality are closely paralleled in the other modalities, especially the epistemic (1.1.5, 3.5.5).

In a footnote von Wright (1951: 28) also recognizes dynamic modality which is concerned with ability and disposition as in *Jones can speak German.* It is undoubtedly true that CAN is used in English to refer to ability. But no very clear distinction can be made between what one is able to do and what it is possible for one to do. I shall use the term 'dynamic modality', therefore, to refer generally to the modality of events that are not conditioned deontically (and both dynamic and deontic modality are distinct from

epistemic modality in that they are modalities of events, while the latter is
the modality of propositions). Under dynamic modality, therefore, we shall
consider not only 'possible for', but also 'necessary for' (where there seems
to be no deontic source, the necessity arising only from circumstances or
possibly the subject's own disposition) and, in addition, the 'volitional'
sense of WILL (7.1).

1.1.3 Modality and factuality

Lyons (1968: 307) defines mood 'in relation to an "unmarked" class of
sentences which express simple statements of fact, unqualified with respect
to the attitude of the speaker to what he is saying'. He continues 'Simple
declarative sentences of this kind are, strictly speaking, non-modal
("unmarked" for mood)'. In a more recent book (Lyons 1977: 848) he has
insisted on the distinction between 'mood' and 'modality', where mood is
essentially a grammatical category. But he does not define modality except
to distinguish it from the descriptive function of language (725). He had
previously noted (1968: 308) three 'scales' of modality, those of 'wish' and
'intention', of 'necessity' and 'obligation', and of 'certainty' and 'possibility'.
Although he gives a Latin example for the first and English examples for the
other two, he provides no evidence that these are clearly marked
grammatically, in any known language, as distinct 'scales'. The second two
pairs are clearly what von Wright calls 'deontic' and 'epistemic' modality,
and it is with these that Lyons is mainly concerned in the later book. 'Wish'
and 'intention' are dealt with only in a discussion of 'non-factives', and
although it is clearly implied that factivity is related to modality, there is no
indication of the precise way in which the basic notions of possibility and
necessity will relate to 'factive', 'contra-factive' and 'non-factive'. Nevertheless the basic distinction is clear: 'mood' is a grammatical term, while
'modality' is a semantic term relating to the meanings that are usually
associated with mood. The relation between mood and modality is thus like
that between tense and time.

On the one hand, then, we observe that languages have grammatical
categories, which we may call 'moods', that relate to a whole variety of non-
factual expressions. Some of these may be different from those we have
already noted. For instance, in some languages there are grammatical ways
of expressing what is said to be so. One such language is German, as we
have already noted (1.1.1); another is the American Indian language
Menomini (Hockett 1968: 237). Menomini also includes in its system of
mood reference to unexpected events and to unfulfilled intentions, as well as
statement and question.

'Modality', on the other hand, is a semantic term, and I shall use it in this
book to refer to the meanings of the modals. It is not necessary to define
precisely what kinds of meaning are involved. We take the formal category

as our starting-point, and it is sufficient for our purpose that the meanings involved are such as to justify characterizing them as 'modality'.

Since we have established the set of modal verbs as the grammatical category with which we are concerned, we do not need the term 'mood', though in theory there would be no obvious objection to describing each modal as one of the 'moods' of English. But 'mood' is usually reserved for inflectional categories that exhibit modality – the subjunctive, optative, etc, as opposed to the indicative. Zandvoort (1962: 64, 86–9) uses 'mood' to distinguish between the subjunctive and indicative in English (marked by the absence or presence of final -s with the third person present tense form of the verb), and criticizes the Oxford English Dictionary's definition of *auxiliary* as 'a verb used to form the tenses, moods, voice, etc, of other verbs'. He suggests that the proper term here is not 'mood' but 'modality'. This is rather confused; the distinction being made is not between grammatical mood and semantic modality but, as far as we can gather, between the two grammatical-semantic categories of modal verb and mood. But if that is so, it is not clear why he did not equally object to the term 'tense' and distinguish the time characteristics of the auxiliaries from the inflectionally marked tenses of English, past and present. It is, moreover, debatable whether the distinction between subjunctive and indicative is useful here, whether English has, in this narrow sense, any moods at all.

1.1.4 Modality and tense

Lyons (1977: 809) points out that it is possible to treat tense as a modality and to include tense-logic in modal-logic. This is not in itself of great interest to the linguist, but more important is the fact that philosophers have for a long time debated whether the future can ever be regarded as factual, since we can never know what is going to happen. This is of relevance to the study of languages because there is so often a close connection between, or even identity of, forms used to refer to the future and forms used for various kinds of modality. 'Reference to the future ... is often as much a matter of modality as it is of purely temporal reference' (Lyons 1977: 816). In an article that is one of the classics of linguistics, Fries (1927), arguing against talking about the English 'future tense', shows how, in a whole variety of languages various verbs and forms, 'devices which naturally looked to the future for fulfilment', have been used as future tenses – verbs of wishing, possibility, having, etc. In the same spirit Lyons points out that in most of the Indo-European languages future tenses have been created from forms that originally expressed not futurity, but non-factivity, especially from the subjunctive and words indicating intention or desire. Synchronically, he notes (1968: 310) that the French future tense may indicate probability and the Russian imperfective may signal futurity, intention, or determination, while for Greek and Latin '(i) in certain contexts the future may replace the subjunctive, and (ii) there is no "future subjunctive" form in either language'. (*Cf* also Ultan 1972.)

In English the relationship is no less obvious:

[i] The modal verbs WILL and SHALL (clearly definable as modals – 1.2) are used to indicate future time as well as what is more obviously modality. In traditional grammar, of course, they are said to form the future tense.

[ii] The modal verbs, even in their present tense forms, often refer to future events (see 3.5.2, 4.5.3, 5.3.4, 6.3.4). Indeed there is no way of marking them formally for future, because they cannot occur with preceding WILL or SHALL, or with any other form, *eg* BE GOING TO, that is used to indicate future time.

Less obvious is t.`   ̄elationship between modality and past time. We find in English:

[i] SHOULD is essentially an independent modal, with no past time reference, yet it is formally the past tense of SHALL (and for MUST and OUGHT as 'past tense subjunctives' see Curme 1931: 413).

[ii] The past tense forms of English have two functions. They mark both past time and 'unreality'. Thus we can compare:

John comes/came every day.
If John comes/came, he will/would stay.

In the first the past tense form indicates past time. In the second it does not; it indicates present unreality. Joos (1964*b*: 121) indeed suggested that they are both essentially 'remote', the one in time, the other in reality.

[iii] *Could* and *would* can be used for past time reference but not if there is reference to a *single* completed action. We cannot say (see 5.3.3, 7.4.3, 9.1):

*I ran fast and could catch the bus.
*I asked him and he would come.

(Yet in both cases the negative forms *couldn't* and *wouldn't* would be perfectly acceptable.)

It is also important to note that there are some languages that do not have temporal systems at all in their grammar but rather have 'grammaticalized' modal distinctions (Lyons 1977: 816). Thus, in the American Indian language Hopi (Whorf 1956: 57–64, 207–19), there are three 'tenses' which Lyons (1968: 311) suggests might be more appropriately described as 'moods'. The first is used for statements of general truths, the second for reports of known or presumably known happenings, and the third for events still in the reach of uncertainty. The second and third would seem to be clearly contrasted as non-modal and modal, but it is also the case that past time events will normally be referred to by the second, and future events by the third. Indications of time in this language are essentially derived from indications of modality.

I.I.5 **Modality and logic**

Even if there are some correspondences between von Wright's modes and the modal systems of English, it would be quite wrong to assume that the English systems or those of any other languages follow any absolute set of logical rules or fit into a rigid logical framework. For logical systems are idealized systems, while natural languages are notoriously untidy. What logic they have is likely to be fragmentary and inconsistent.

Nevertheless, there are some relations of a logical or semi-logical kind within the semantics of modality in English (and possibly of other languages). We can, for instance, find a relationship involving negation with possibility and necessity in that, without being ambiguous, the first sentence below can be seen as the negative of either of the other two:

He can't be working in his study.
He may be working in his study.
He must be working in his study.

The essential point is that the first sentence can be seen either as negating the modality expressed by MAY (possibility) or as negating the proposition (2.3.1) with the modality expressed by MUST (necessity). Thus it can be interpreted as either 'He not-may be working in his study' or 'He must not-be working in his study'.

This is very similar to what is found with the quantifiers *some* and *all* in that *No one came* may be seen as the negation of either *Someone came* or *Everyone came,* depending on whether it is the quantifier or the verb that is negated ('Not-someone came' or 'Everyone not-came').

We find, then, that with negation there are equivalences not only for the quantifiers, but also for the modalities of possibility and necessity. We can express the equivalences for the quantifiers as:

$$\sim\exists \equiv \forall \sim \quad \text{(Not-some} \equiv \text{All-not)}$$
$$\exists \sim \equiv \sim\forall \quad \text{(Some-not} \equiv \text{Not-all)}$$

Similarly, for the modalities, we have:

Not-possible $\equiv$ Necessary-not
Possible-not $\equiv$ Not-necessary

There is yet a further point of resemblance. We have seen that *No one came* can be treated as the negation of either *Someone came* (ie $\sim\exists$, Not-some) or *Everyone came* (ie $\sim\forall$, All-not) and that *can't* similarly relates to both *may* (ie 'Not-possible') and *must* ('Necessary-not'). These are, of course, explained by the logical equivalences. However, there are quite distinct forms for the other pairs of equivalences. For we have two forms, both *Some did not come* and *Not everyone came* to correspond to the logically equivalent ($\exists \sim \equiv \sim\forall$). The same is true of the other equivalence in the modality system. For we again have two possibilities:

He may not be working in his study.
He needn't be working in his study.

It would be reasonable to see the first as 'possible-not' and the second as 'not-necessary', though the status of *needn't* within the epistemic modal system is debatable (3.5.3).

Similar, but rather less strict, equivalences seem to hold for other kinds of modality too. (See 2.3.2, 3.5.3, 4.5.1, 6.3.1.)

In view of this it is not, perhaps, surprising that one of the modals used for possibility sometimes indicates 'some' (8.3). There is some relevance in von Wright's treatment of the 'existential mode' along with, and parallel to, his other modes (1.1.2).

1.1.6 Possibility and necessity

I shall take as my starting-point the assumption that the basic notions of modality are those of possibility and necessity (*cf* Lyons 1977: 787). Discussion of possibility and necessity go back, not surprisingly, to Aristotle, though Aristotle's view of their interrelations is not always clear (*cf* Hintikka 1973: 40–61). We shall see, however, that although the 'possibility' modals can often be paraphrased in terms of the English word *possible, necessary* seldom, if ever, provides an accurate paraphrase for necessity (3.2.1).

There are obviously different kinds of possibility and necessity as is clear from von Wright, and some of these are indicated in natural languages. Natural languages often also include other notions that can be described in terms of possibility in a looser sense, in that they are merely non-factual. It is this that would allow us to reconcile Lyons's account, which includes 'wish' and 'intention', with that of von Wright. It would also allow us to treat reported speech as modality in German, since there is no guarantee by the speaker of the factual nature of what is said. But possibility and necessity are central to our discussion; they are the 'core' of the modality system.

1.2 The formal system

Although some scholars have questioned whether the modals should be placed in a category separate from that of the other verbs that have verbal complements (Ross 1969, Huddleston 1974, 1976b), there can be no doubt that there are formal criteria that clearly distinguish WILL, SHALL, CAN, MAY, MUST and OUGHT TO, and to a lesser extent USED TO, DARE, NEED and IS TO, as modal verbs. I shall not go into detail here; the facts are not in dispute and are well known. I shall merely give a brief summary of the position (for details see Palmer 1974: 18–29), but for the theoretical issues see 9.4.

To begin with, we may take the criteria used by H. E. Palmer (1939: 122-5) for his anomalous finites and by Chomsky in the four transformations that are particularly related to the auxiliaries (Chomsky 1957: 61–9). These place the modals in the same class as the 'primary' auxiliaries (Palmer 1974: 15) BE, HAVE and DO. They are:

[i]   Inversion with the subject. (*Must I come?*)
[ii] Negative form with *-n't*. (*I can't go*)
[iii] 'Code'. (*He can swim and so can she*)
[iv] Emphatic affirmation. (*He will be there*)

In similar functions all other verbs require the 'empty' or 'support' verb DO. These Huddleston (1976b: 333) refers to as the 'NICE properties', Negation, Inversion, Code, Emphatic affirmation.

There are further specifically 'modal' criteria:

[v]   No *-s* form for 3rd person singular.
[vi] Absence of non-finite forms. (No infinitive, past or present participle.)
[vii] No cooccurrence. (No **He may will come.*)

WILL, SHALL, MAY, CAN, MUST and OUGHT TO fit all these criteria with the exception that MAY has no *-n't* form in the present. MUST and OUGHT TO differ from the others in having no past tense forms, while OUGHT TO is the only one that requires *to*.

USED TO may meet many of the criteria in some people's speech, but in standard spoken English has none of the 'NICE' properties, but occurs, like non-modals, with DO, except in negation where, although *usedn't* is less likely, *used not* is quite common.

DARE and NEED occur both as non-modals (with DO) and as modals with the first two of the 'NICE' properties. But the modals occur only where the contexts actually require these properties (*eg Dare he go? He daren't go*, but not **He dare go*).

IS TO has the 'NICE' properties, but this is also true of the verb BE when it is not an auxiliary (Palmer 1974: 152–4). However, IS TO also meets criteria [vi] and [vii] unlike non-auxiliary BE. Because there are no non-finite forms, it is not appropriate to refer to it as BE TO; *be to* does not occur. It differs from the other modals in one respect only, that it has all the finite forms of BE, *am, is, are, was* and *were;* this is contrary to [v].

Had better and *would rather* also require consideration. The characteristics of *would rather* can be explained in terms of *would* as a form of WILL. A similar solution is not available for *had better;* it cannot simply be treated as a form of HAVE or HAVE TO, because it may be followed by an infinitive without *to* (*had better go, cf had gone, had to go*). But it fits criteria [v], [vi] and [vii], with no *-s* form, no non-finite forms and no cooccurrence with other modals.

It has been noted by a number of scholars that these characteristics of the modals are essentially formal features of English. They are not, for instance, to be found with the modals of German, which are otherwise very like those of English and historically related to them. (For a comparison see Jenkins 1972: 10.) Huddleston (1976*a*: 213, 1976*b*: 334) even objects to the use of the 'NICE' properties as criteria for the modals on the grounds that they are idiosyncratic and not universal. Such an argument should lead us to conclude that there is no more significance to these characteristics than to those of the nouns that have internal inflection, MOUSE, GOOSE, FOOT, etc. But these formal characteristics of the modals form a complex set and it is plausible to suggest that they have been retained in the language only because native speakers are aware of the modals as a set, and it is not difficult to show that, in fact, the modals have a great deal in common semantically. (For a detailed discussion see 9.4.)

1.3 Previous semantic proposals

Let us now look briefly at some of the proposals that have been made to deal with the semantics of the modals. We shall not, however, discuss the different syntactic models that have been employed (*eg* the transformational approach of Jenkins (1972) and the stratificational account of Johannesson (1976)). The choice of model is largely a matter of general linguistic theory and presentation, and does not greatly affect our discussion.

1.3.1 'Basic' meaning

Ehrman (1966: 10) distinguishes between 'basic meaning' and 'overtones'. The basic meaning is the meaning 'that applies in all its occurrences', and is 'in a sense the lowest common denominator of all the occurrences', whereas the overtones are 'subsidiary meanings which derive from the basic meaning but which add something of their own'. Thus the basic meaning of CAN, for instance, is 'nothing in the state of the world prevents the predication' with overtones that include 'there are certain positive qualities of the subject such that he is cleared for the predication' and 'no lack of permission prevents the predication'.

The idea of the basic meaning is a familiar one. Joos (1964: 5), with his 'signals grammar', assumes that 'signals will have consistent meaning'. The most extreme statement is that of Bouma (1975: 314) who, quoting Jakobson for support, argues that 'a grammatical form has a basic meaning that is invariant in all its uses'. This is pure dogma with no very obvious theoretical justification and no empirical basis.

It can easily be shown that Ehrman runs into difficulties. For instance, although she has a single meaning for CAN, she argues that MAY 'is defined in terms of a continuum characterized by two dimensions of meaning', dimensions that she calls 'circumstance' and 'occurrence' (they correspond roughly to dynamic (or non-epistemic) and epistemic possibility). This is, in effect, to admit that there is no one basic meaning and the continuum model could with advantage be applied to other modals.

Leech, too, (1969: 276) points out that her definition of WILL as 'the occurrence of the predication is guaranteed' fails because (a) it does not show the difference between WILL and MUST, HAVE TO, etc, which equally guarantee the predication; (b) it does not allow the WILL of willingness where the predication is not guaranteed; (c) it does not account for the oddness of WILL in contexts where the predication is guaranteed, eg ?*The sun will rise every morning*.

Such objections are inevitable with a 'basic meaning' approach. Nevertheless Ehrman's account is the best so far, partly because of the detailed exemplification and discussion and partly because her theoretical claims are relatively modest.

However, such critical comments must not be taken to imply that we cannot look for a fairly generalized common meaning or a set of closely related meanings for each modal. It is only when precision is demanded or invariance postulated that the notion of a basic meaning becomes unrealistic.

1.3.2 Matrix analyses

Because there is a fairly clearly defined set of modals in English, it is natural to attempt to arrange them in a semantic framework. The most obvious and, *prima facie*, attractive way is to place them within a multi-dimensional matrix, with each dimension indicating some set of related semantic features. Such analyses are familiar in linguistics and date back at least as far as Sapir's (1925) 'Sound patterns'.

The application of such an analysis to the modals is made even more plausible by the fact that the primary system of the English verb (involving the inflected forms and forms with HAVE and BE) can be very easily handled in a formal-semantic matrix of four dimensions, tense, aspect, phase and voice, each with two possibilities, yielding sixteen different forms ($2^4 = 16$) (Palmer 1974: 33–4). It is tempting to arrange the modals in a similar way.

Among modern linguists Twaddell (1960: 11) was the first to make such an attempt. He set out the eight modals in a two-dimensional matrix with three terms in each dimension and one cell left empty:

	Prediction	Possibility, capability, permission	Necessity, requirement, prescription
Absolute, unrestricted	WILL	CAN	MUST
Contingent, inconclusive	SHALL	MAY	NEED
Morally determined		DARE	OUGHT

His reasoning is that 'the fact that the modals do not cooccur suggests that there are elements of incompatibility in their meanings', which is very reminiscent of Trubetzkoy's (1939: 30) notion of opposition. But Twaddell

obviously came to recognize that his analysis was unsatisfactory since he did
not repeat it in the second edition of the work (Twaddell 1965). However,
we do not know whether his dissatisfaction was with this particular analysis
or with matrix analysis in general.

Joos (1964) has a much more ambitious plan. For him the eight modals
are to be arranged in a three-dimensional matrix forming a 'semological
cube' ($2^3 = 8$). The distinctions are between casual (WILL, SHALL, CAN, MAY)
and stable (MUST, OUGHT TO, DARE, NEED); adequate (WILL, CAN, MUST,
DARE) and contingent (SHALL, MAY, OUGHT TO, NEED); assurance (WILL,
SHALL, MUST, OUGHT TO) and potentiality (CAN, MAY, DARE, NEED). An
analysis of this kind assumes, of course, that there are 'basic' grammatical
meanings as discussed in 1.3.1. Joos backs his classification with detailed
and often amusing arguments, but there are three fundamental objections to
his analysis and to any similar analysis.

[i] There is no reason to believe that the modals fit into such a matrix, even
if they are a distinct set. The analogy with phonology is a false one, because
the phonological features are based ultimately on clear physiological and
acoustic features; but there are no similar, readily available, semantic
features.

[ii] The categories are clearly based on purely idiosyncratic judgments.
Some are greatly at variance with my own, *eg* those concerning adequate
WILL and contingent SHALL (*pp* 177–8, 238–9), even though Joos was
describing British English. Moreover, the fact that others have produced
quite different analyses shows that we are in an area of highly subjective
judgments.

[iii] Even if Joos's analysis could be justified by academic arguments, it
would not explain how the native speaker succeeds in using the modals, for
the categories bear little relation to any judgments that the native speaker
seems to make; they completely lack any naturalness and fail in 'descriptive
adequacy' (Chomsky 1964: 28–9). (It is to be noted that in the same year
Diver (1964) analysed the English modals in terms of a single dimension of
'scales of likelihood'.)

The greatest danger with analyses of this kind is that the investigator can
convince himself of the correctness of his solution simply on account of its
neatness and simplicity. We feel that there has to be a neat system and so set
about creating one. Moreover, we may well come to believe that the system
we have established after a great deal of fairly abstract thought is after all
not merely the system for this language, but for all languages. This is sadly
what Bouma (1975) seems to have done. For he began by analysing the
semantics of the German modals (Bouma 1973). When he attempted to deal
with English (Bouma 1975), he started with the German system that he had
established:

	Imminent	Biased	Precarious
Objective	MUSS	SOLL	DARF
Subjective	WILL	MAG	KANN

He then proceeded to apply the same analysis to English with the resulting:

	Imminent	Biased	Precarious
Objective	MUST/HAVE TO	SHALL/SHOULD/OUGHT TO	MAY
Subjective	WILL/WANT TO	WOULD LIKE TO	CAN

He even suggests that 'the basic semantic notions involved are very probably universal in nature'. Yet it is painfully obvious that his system is based on a formal German set (just as Joos's was based on a formal English set), and that the semantic categories chosen were those that best fitted the matrix established for German. The reason that they can be applied to English or may even appear to be universal is, quite simply, that they are vague and that any variations can always be explained away. For instance, Joos's precarious modal indicates 50:50 probability. Yet it is possible for a speaker to use such a modal 'in a situation in which both speaker and hearer understand that the event will almost certainly be realized'. Modals have quite specific meanings, apparently, but they need not always have these meanings! Moreover, if we were to accept Bouma's analysis, we should have to admit that German was more rational than English, since its formal and semantic categories coincide; that, in itself, is a cause for suspicion.

There is no limit to the variety of analyses of this type that can be thought up; others that may be noted are that of Marino (1973) with three binary features and, for German, the even more complex, but symmetrical, model of Calbert (1975).

1.3.3 Componential analysis

A rather different approach is that of Leech (1969: 202–38), who offers what he calls a 'structural and componential description'. This involves seven systems:

Causation – 'causes'; 'is caused by'
Actuality – 'actual, real'; 'non-actual, unreal, hypothetical'
Constraint – 'weak' (eg 'permission'); 'strong' (eg 'obligation')
Authority – 'has permission/is obliged to'; converse
Volition – 'wishes'; 'is wished by'
Ability – 'is able to'; converse   .
Probability – 'probable'; 'improbable'

I have used the term converse to indicate, for Authority and Ability, a relation similar to that of passive for Causation and Volition. Leech symbolizes the Causation pairs as → CAU and ← CAU, but whereas he glosses

$(x) \rightarrow$ CAU (y) as '(x) causes (y)' and $(x) \leftarrow$ CAU (y) as '(x) is caused by (y)', he
switches the order of the variables for AUT and ABLE, $(x) \rightarrow$ AUT (y) being
glossed as '(x) has permission/is obliged to (y)' and $(x) \leftarrow$ AUT (y) as '(y) has
permission/is obliged to (x)'. There is, in addition, a further dimension
relating to the involvement of speaker and listener.

Leech's features do not form a matrix; they are not plus and minus binary
features (like those of, for instance, Marino 1973). The different systems
interrelate, but in no very systematic way, and there is no overall symmetry.
(One always can, of course, convert such a description into a matrix, but it
would be enormously more complex and not very illuminating.)

The main objection to Leech's analysis concerns its theoretical justification. For he argues that we must take note of 'the underlying logical
relationships', which he compares with the 'bone structure' of the human
body. But there is no reason at all to believe that there are such underlying
logical relationships in any rigid sense, and certainly not in a way
comparable to the bones of the body. It is ironic indeed that he criticizes
another scholar (Lebrun 1965) for relying on '*a priori* philosophical
categories' (277). Yet Lebrun's distinction of 'physical possibility', 'moral
possibility' and 'logical possibility' seem to be better founded on actual
observation than Leech's own categories.

A complete criticism of Leech would depend on a detailed analysis, for
his categories provide him with sufficient flexibility to be able to account for
the data. But it is often difficult to see why he chooses a particular analysis,
or why a particular formula should suggest the meaning intended.

The greatest weakness of the analysis is that it is more concerned with
classification than explanation. To account for 'ability', for instance, by
simply introducing $\leftarrow$ ABLE and $\rightarrow$ ABLE does not show that ability is
possibility that is linked to the subject; similarly there is no attempt to
account for the distinction between epistemic and non-epistemic modality
('possible that' and 'possible for'), but merely the suggestion that the
difference between *The pound may be devalued* and *The pound can be
devalued* is to be indicated by a formator system $\pm\tau$, to represent
'theoretical'/'practical' (within the predication, not the modality). Admittedly, there can be no simple analysis or simple explanation for the modals,
but the presentation of formulae does not in itself solve any of the problems.
Given enough binary distinctions, it is always theoretically possible to
classify any set of data, and if new data or counter-examples are found, there
can always be modifications of, or additions to, the distinctions. Yet Leech's
account is full of interesting observations and insights.

1.3.4 Speech acts

Boyd and Thorne (1969: 57–74) propose an analysis of the modals using a
notion of speech act that is adapted from the work of Austin (1962). They

take from Katz and Postal (1964: 74–9) the suggestion that imperative sentences contain the element imp and reinterpret this in the light of their understanding of Austin to argue that the semantics of both *You will go* and *I order you to go* are represented by:

I imp you You go.

This leads them, after some modification to their earlier suggestion, to the view that we can interpret *Shall I open the window?* as:

I imp you You state whether You imp me I open the window.

(This has been simplified to correspond with the earlier formalization, and ignores a controversial interpretation and formalization of *you*.) Insofar as this interpretation brings out the performative nature of some of the modals, it is helpful and illuminating but it runs into difficulties of both a general and a particular kind.

To begin with, the suggestion that there are in the semantics (or possibly the deep structure) performative verbs such as IMP or ORDER is unhelpful, and even misleading. For it is obvious that *Go* and *You will go* are not in any way identical with *I order you to go*. The essential difference is, of course, that the latter contains *I order;* the fact that an order is being given is actually stated. It is misleading to argue that the other also contains the same or a similar verb. The thesis becomes even more unhelpful when we find that statements are interpreted in terms of *I state . . .*, for this becomes utterly redundant. (For the *reductio ad absurdum* of this see Ross (1970) and the review of Matthews (1972: 128–32). Unfortunately, Austin partly fell into the trap himself, in that he first clearly distinguished performatives such as 'I promise . . .' from the 'constatives', and yet finally concluded that perhaps even constatives were performatives.) The simple point is that there are different sentence types, declaratives, imperatives, interrogatives, and that these have to be marked as such. But nothing is gained by assigning to all of them the same kind of semantic or deep structure. In particular, nothing is gained by assigning to imperatives and interrogatives a semantic or deep structure that is essentially a declarative one. Yet this is what is done by interpreting *Go* as 'I order you to go'. For there is no more reason to reinterpret imperatives as declaratives than vice versa; they are simply distinct sentence types and neither is more basic. Nevertheless there is virtue in the analysis, insofar as it shows that, for instance, *Shall I open the window* is a request (which involves the speaker asking the hearer to act) for permission from the hearer (*ie* for the speaker to act).

More particularly Boyd and Thorne's analyses lead them into difficulties. They see the difference between *He goes to London tomorrow* and *He will go to London tomorrow* as:

I state He goes to London tomorrow.
I predict He goes to London tomorrow.

But they are forced to admit that 'the illocutionary force of the utterances is the same, or nearly the same'. This paradox is explained by saying they have different 'illocutionary potentials', but 'almost identical illocutionary force'. But how do we judge illocutionary force except in terms of its speech act function? In what sense then can there be a different potential? There is only one possible explanation for this suggestion – that different forms are used, in one case *goes,* in the other *will go.* But in that case to argue that with *goes* there is a statement, but with *will go* a prediction, is to define statement and prediction not in terms of speech acts, but of the grammatical form. The fault is like that of the matrix analyses; a limited but rigid framework is provided and the modals have to be fitted in. Yet it is possible to accept a looser interpretation of what Boyd and Thorne are saying. We could argue that English makes a basic distinction between stating and predicting, and that this distinction rests upon formal criteria (the absence and presence of *will*), but that in certain circumstances the semantic difference between them is lost. But to talk of 'illocutionary potential' and of 'illocutionary force' obscures the issues. There is much of value and interest and there is no doubt that illocutionary force must in some way or other be incorporated into an analysis of the modals. It is only the form of the analysis and its formalization that is unhelpful.

Chapter 2

A basic framework

The fact that different scholars have dealt with modals and modality in so many different ways is a clear indication of the complexity of the issues involved and of the difficulty of arriving at any completely simple and completely convincing analysis. This chapter aims, therefore, to give a general idea of the nature of the problem and of an approach to its solution, and to offer some guidelines for the organization of the later chapters.

2.1 The nature of the study

Important characteristics of this study are, first, its theoretical limits – the scope of the work, and secondly, the nature and use of the materials on which it is based.

2.1.1 Theoretical limits

There are two starting-points. By formal criteria we can establish a set of modal verbs; the formal status of six such verbs is hardly in doubt, but others are either marginal or problematic. Semantically we shall assume that the concepts of possibility and necessity are central to modality (1.1.6). A synthesis of the formal and semantic criteria will lead us to go beyond possibility and necessity, since WILL and SHALL are formally modal yet are concerned with notions like will and responsibility, and also to include other verbs, such as BE ABLE TO and HAVE TO, which are not formally modals, yet relate semantically to possibility and necessity.

No clear theoretical limits can be drawn for a study that is defined in terms both of modals and modality. For the modal verbs have some features in common with others, especially, for instance, with SEEM and HAPPEN, and modality might even include the semantics of WANT and INTEND. In practice, however, limits can be drawn. The modal auxiliaries are a clearly defined set, and we can decide to introduce only those other verbs that complete the semantic systems into which the modal auxiliaries fit. But some arbitrary decisions are inevitable.

The scope of this study will, then, be defined as follows:

[i] There is no doubt about the central position of MAY, CAN and MUST. They are both formally modals and clear exponents of possibility and necessity.

[ii] OUGHT TO and SHOULD are also formally modals, and can be shown to be concerned with a facet of necessity (see especially 6.4).

[iii] SHALL and WILL are included because they are formally modals, and although they do not relate to possibility and necessity they have much in common semantically with other modals (see especially 4.4 for SHALL, 3.3 and 7.1 for WILL). Even their use for future time reference has some relation to modality (see 1.1.4, 7.2.5, 7.4.4).

[iv] Briefer consideration will be given to DARE and NEED, which are half in the formal system, to IS TO, and to the more marginal WOULD RATHER and HAD BETTER.

[v] USED TO will not be discussed. It has many of the formal characteristics of a modal, but is outside the semantic system (but see 7.4.3 for a link).

[vi] We shall discuss in some detail BE BOUND TO, BE ABLE TO, HAVE TO, HAVE GOT TO and BE GOING TO. Formally none of these are modals, but they have an important place within the semantic system and either supplement, or contrast with, the modals.

I shall not, however, include WANT in the discussion, although Strang (1962: 147) considers it 'marginal' and it is discussed in some detail by Johannesson (1976: 19–25). For it is clearly not formally a modal and although it has some semantic similarity to WILL and BE WILLING TO, it does not act as a suppletive for, or clearly overlap with, either of these verbs.

Up to now the term 'modal' has been used to refer only to the verbs in the formal system. But in the discussion to follow we shall usually be handling together those modals and the other verbs mentioned in [vi]; we shall often need to contrast these, as a single group, with the other verbs in the sentence – the 'lexical' verbs that do not signal modality. For this reason I propose from now on to use the term 'modal' in a wider sense, to include all these 'modality' verbs, in contrast with the 'main' verbs that refer to the proposition or event (2.4.1). Where a contrast needs to be made we can talk about 'true' modals or verbs that are 'formally' modals, as compared with the others that are 'semi-modals'.

2.1.2 The data

In the preparation of this study extensive use was made of the material in the Survey of English Usage located in the Department of English at University College London. This material has been collected, under the supervision of Randolph Quirk, over a period of years and examples of all the modals have been separately filed. It consists of both written and spoken material.

For the spoken text, the Survey contains a great deal of prosodic and paralinguistic information. I have deliberately excluded this (except emphatic stress occasionally), partly because it is difficult for the reader to follow, and partly because it is, a little surprisingly, almost completely irrelevant to a study of the modals. I have also, as far as possible, converted the spoken texts into a normal orthography, using normal punctuation. I have also ignored interruptions and left out some repetitions. I have used dots (. . .) to indicate that I have deliberately offered an incomplete sentence although there is other material in the context (usually only for reasons of economy, but sometimes because the other material is not grammatically relevant). I have used the long dash (—) to indicate either that the speaker has broken off (and not completed his sentence) or that there is a change of speaker.

Using this material was valuable in three ways:

First, it provided most of the examples given here. Only occasionally are examples invented or taken from other works.

Secondly, it often brought to notice usages that had been completely missed in previous studies.

Thirdly, the immediate linguistic context of a modal often provided evidence of its meaning or its relationship with other modals. There was evidence of at least four kinds.

[i] There are some examples in which the modal seems to be pleonastic or redundant in that its meaning is already signalled by some other form, or perhaps we should say that the modal is 'reinforced' by another form (Halliday 1970: 331). In the following examples the epistemic modality (3.1, 3.2) seems to be signalled by an adverb, so that there would be little difference if there were no modal present:

> You may possibly prefer that one. (S.8.2a.57)
> Here, perhaps, we may see the natural man. (W.4.2a.65)
> Evidently, she must have talked to her mother about them, you see, because . . . . (S.5.10.60)
> It must surely be just a beautiful relic from the past. (W.1.5b.6)

Similarly, the modal seems redundant in its 'sometimes' sense (8.3.1):

> In themselves the effects aren't devastating, but chugging can sometimes trigger off a fit of screaming. (W.1.2b.21)

With dynamic modality there is less likelihood of an adverb, but one is to be found in (cf 6.2):

> This chap doesn't necessarily have to take them away with him, does he? (S.8.1m.2)

Sometimes the redundancy lies not with an adverb, but with the main verb, which has roughly the same meaning as the modal:

The audience can tend to get lost in the action of the play and rather forget that Hamlet is wasting his time. (S.3.5a.41)
May I be permitted to offer you a small gâteau, compliments of the restaurant? (S.7.3i.3)

The meaning of the first is 'the audience sometimes does' and either *can* or *tend* would have been sufficient (8.3.1). In the second *may* is used to ask permission, which is also signalled by *be permitted* (4.2.1).
[ii] In some examples the meaning of the modal is suggested by a rough paraphrase in the immediate environment:

It's an incredibly complicated system – they're obliged to in various ways. They've got to pass our section of it. (S.3.6.15)
I've been telling Peter, as I've been telling several people, 'You know, you must get into permanent jobs' and I've been urging Peter to go back to school teaching or something, where he's very, very good. (S.3.2b.16)

From the first of these we can assume that *They've got to* is synonymous, or nearly synonymous, with *They're obliged to*. In the second *must* seems to have roughly the same meaning as *I urge you*. A comparison of these two shows not only the 'necessity' meanings of HAVE GOT TO and MUST, but also their differences (6.2.2). We may add here examples of modals in subordinate clauses (8.6) where they reflect the meaning of the main verb:

A new insistence from President Nixon that the Hanoi government must negotiate if there's to be any settlement. (W.2.3b.13)
I was going to suggest that we might look through Habitat and see if we can find her anything. (S.7.2b.9)
I intend to see . . ., where firearms are used, that the maximum penalty shall be the maximum penalty available to the law. (W.2.3a.11)

In these the words *insistence, suggest* and *intend to see* reflect the meanings of the relevant modals, laying an obligation (4.3), making a suggestion (8.5) and giving an undertaking (4.4, 4.6.2).
[iii] Just as we found that the context will sometimes provide possible paraphrases, we also find that clear contrasts are made. There is, for instance, a contrast between dynamic possibility and necessity in:

The next time you can take the exam is in April. Otherwise she'll have to wait till – is it September? I'm not sure. (S.7.2l.6)

(There is also some significance in the use of the present *can* and the future *'ll be able to* – see 5.3.4, 6.3.4.) Similarly there is a contrast in terms of 'existential' modality (8.3.1, 8.3.3) in an example in Ehrman (1966: 13):

They speak of the work of Christ as the bestowal of incorruptibility which can mean (though it does not have to mean) deliverance from time and history.

Possibility and necessity are linked, but not specifically contrasted in:

> We can fight, and we must fight, against the world, the flesh and the devil. (S.12.1c–12)

No less significant is the fact that a speaker corrects himself:

> I think it much more likely they'll begin to – going to begin to – look at how many foreign students the country should, in fact, subsidize. (S.11.2.24)

It would seem that he found WILL too conditional, suggesting that the future depends upon events and circumstances, and so corrected to BE GOING TO, which carries no conditionality with it (7.3.3).

[iv] In a few cases we find that different modals seem to be used in identical contexts, and with no obvious difference of meaning. This is so with MUST and HAVE (GOT) TO and suggests that, in some circumstances at least, they do not differ in meaning (6.2.2):

> When this happens you will see the boat's speed fall off and you must pay off just a little. (W.10.2.60-3)
> All you've got to do is to haul in. (W.5.3.41)
> I must have an immigrant's visa. Otherwise they're likely to kick me out, you see. (S.1.5.71)
> I've really got to know when completion date is likely. Otherwise I might find myself on the streets. (S.8.1a.9).

The first pair are instructions about sailing. The second are related in the occurrence of *otherwise,* which shows the penalty for not doing what is necessary, and so why action is necessary.

However, this is not a textual study. I am not concerned with characterizing the uses of the modals in terms of the different styles etc that are found in the Survey, or with giving statistical information about the uses of the modals. The Survey is used for heuristic and exemplificatory purposes only.

2.2 Kinds of modality

Purely as a starting-point let us look at some of the kinds of possibility and necessity that seem to be exemplified in the Survey.

2.2.1 Possibility

[i] They're all very sort of Kentish and they may be in Sussex, actually. (S.7.3f.30)

Here there is the meaning 'It is possible that'. This is clearly epistemic modality, modality concerned with propositions rather than events (3.1).

[ii] If you want to recall the doctor, you may do so. (S.11.1.19)

Here MAY is used to give permission. CAN is also used in this sense, but examples in the Survey are rare (4.2.1).

[iii] It looks as though this chap can take a punch as well as give one. (S.10.3.34).

This is the use of CAN to indicate ability (5.1.2).

[iv] I think partly though that that can be explained by the fact that we're at university in London. (S.3.3.121)

Here we are concerned simply with the possibility of an event; it is 'possible for' the fact to be explained, it is explainable. No permission or ability is involved, but the possibility is 'neutral dynamic' (5.1.1).

[v] We cannot have a coalition government, because they are no use at all, unless you are in terrible straits. (S.5.4.29)

It is not literally true that 'we cannot'. The use of *cannot* here is to indicate what is conceptually impossible, what is completely unreasonable (8.2).

[vi] Yes, I think so, because in the library you can take a book out and keep it out for a whole year unless it is recalled. (S.3.3.10)

This clearly relates to a rule or regulation (8.1).

[vii] You can certainly give me a ring back this afternoon – there might be something. (S.8.1a.23)

This is a suggestion, almost a request. It does not merely say what is possible nor does it give permission. There is a similar use of the interrogative *Can you . . .?* (5.1.3, 5.3.2, *cf* 9.2).

[viii] The squid of the genus Loligo can be as much as two feet long. (W.4.2a.15)

Although we may paraphrase 'It is possible for . . .', the meaning is rather in terms of 'sometimes'; it refers to what sometimes happens (8.3).

I do not claim that this is an exhaustive account of the different kinds of meaning that can be recognized. But they seem to be the most clearly distinct ones, and all will be accounted for in this book.

2.2.2 Necessity

We can similarly provide examples of apparently different kinds of necessity.

[i] This must be one of the finest views of the whole processional route. (S.10.5.49)

This again is clearly an example of epistemic modality, though the paraphrase 'It is necessary that ...' may not seem appropriate. This, however, is more a matter of the sense of *necessary* than of the meaning of MUST which seems to indicate the 'strongest' epistemic modality (3.2.1).

[ii] You must keep everything to yourself, be discreet. (W.5.2.53)

This is the necessity counterpart of permission. The speaker is laying an obligation on the subject; he is insisting, urging him that he should act (4.3).

[iii] I must have an immigrant's visa; otherwise they're likely to kick me out, you see. (S.1.5.71)

We have already noted this example (2.2). It indicates the necessity of an event ('It is necessary for ...'), neutral dynamic necessity, which is indicated by either MUST or HAVE (GOT) TO (6.2.2).

[iv] I've got to be at London Airport at fourish. (S.3.2b.21)

This differs from the last example in that the speaker clearly indicates that the necessity is in no way dependent on him, but that there is 'external necessity' (6.2.2).

[v] The government must act. It must make up its mind about priorities – offices or houses, housing estates or luxury buildings. (W.15.1.48-3)

The speaker is in no position to lay obligations upon the government nor is he saying that there are any external circumstances that force the government. He is, rather, stating what he feels is the most rational course of action; this is comparable to 'reasonable' possibility (8.2).

[vi] All scientific results must depend on a rather specialized form of history. (W.9.3.4-1)

This seems to parallel the 'sometimes' use of CAN; it suggests the meaning 'always' or perhaps 'inevitably' (8.3.3).

I have distinguished two meanings fewer than for possibility. There seems to be no necessity modality that corresponds to ability (but see 6.6). Nor are there any uses of the necessity verbs in suggestions and requests that cannot be fairly simply explained in terms of the other meanings (see 9.2).

2.2.3 Other modals and modalities

Most importantly, we must discuss what may, perhaps, be seen as a third degree of modality signalled by WILL and SHALL:

The real effort is the metaphorical one. It is the memory which shall not grow old. (S.2.5.22)

This refers to Lawrence Binyon's 'They shall grow not old, as we that are left grow old', and the speaker interprets this as an undertaking, a promise that their memory shall not 'grow old'.

> Ian needed somewhere to stay and I said 'Why don't you go and see if Martin will let you stay?' (S.2.7.74)

WILL here indicates the agreement, willingness or 'volition' of the subject (7.1.1).

> Tell him Professor Cressage is involved. He will know Professor Cressage. (S.7.21.8)

This is clearly epistemic (3.3). WILL and SHALL are also used to refer to the future. Since futurity is related to modality (1.1.4), a whole section (7.2) will be devoted to it.

We shall also have to discuss SHOULD and OUGHT TO, though these can both be handled in terms of necessity:

> Well he ought to be more careful about it then. (S.2.5b.14)

Here again there is a kind of obligation, but it is less firm with OUGHT TO than that expressed by MUST (6.4.1).

> You should be meeting those later on this afternoon. (S.3.3.48)

SHOULD is clearly epistemic here; it expresses what it is reasonable to expect (3.4.3).

We must also discuss NEED:

> You needn't take this down. (S.6.4b.8)

NEED is shown here to be a form used for the negation of necessity (4.5.1 but see also 6.5).

Finally we must look at DARE (5.4), HAD BETTER (4.7), IS TO (7.7) and WOULD RATHER (7.8); some problematic forms are discussed in 8.4 and 8.5.

2.3 Grammar and semantics

Let us now look at some basic issues that affect the grammatical and syntactic analysis.

2.3.1 Modality and event

A distinction was made in 2.1.1 between modal and main verb. Since both are verbs, both can in theory be marked for negation and tense. But there are problems. Consider the two sentences:

> John can't come tomorrow.
> John mustn't come tomorrow.

Since *-n't* forms of this kind occur only with auxiliary verbs, we can say that the modal is formally (*ie* morphologically) marked for negation. Semantically, however, the position is less simple. In the first, what is negated is the ability or possibility, the meaning carried by the modal; in the second what is negated is the meaning carried by the main verb, for *mustn't* indicates the necessity for something not to be done.

We might explain this by saying that in the one case it is the modal, and in the other case the main verb, that is negated; indeed, Quirk *et al* (1972: 384) distinguishes between 'auxiliary negation' and 'main verb negation'. But this is misleading, for formally it is the modal that is negated in both.

If we were to consider only epistemic modality, we could say that either the modality or the proposition may be negated. Thus in the following examples what is negated is the modality in the first, but the proposition in the second:

John can't still be reading.
John may not still be reading.

The term 'proposition' is, however, less appropriate where the modal is used to express ability, permission, etc – indeed in all the uses of the modals that are not epistemic. With these I shall, therefore, refer not to 'modality' and 'proposition', but to 'modality' and 'event', (following Joos (1964: 149, 151), who in the index notes that 'event' is a 'key technical term here, signifying the sort of thing that is specified by verb-bases, thus perhaps relations [RESEMBLE, etc], and states [WORRY, BE COLD], as well as deeds [SHOW]'. Moreover, when we are talking about modality in general, including both epistemic and the rest, I shall generally refer simply to the 'event', rather than the more cumbersome 'proposition or event'; 'event' in this sense, will subsume both. We may, of course, ask whether the distinction between modality and event (proposition or event) is a purely semantic one or one of syntax, *ie* of deep structure as opposed to surface structure where the formal markers are to be seen. The answer lies in one's own view of syntax. It is perfectly possible and instructive to write deep structure trees to indicate the relation between modality and proposition/event (and this I shall do in 2.4.3, but without claiming that they have any syntactic status).

We can now proceed to discuss the modality and the event in relation to negation, interrogation, tense and time, voice, etc. But there is a problem of terminology here. 'Negation' has already been used to refer both to the formal negation of the modals and to the semantic negation of the modality or event. Since there is no obvious alternative, I shall continue to use the term 'negation' and related forms in both senses; it is unlikely that there will be ambiguity. But we can distinguish between formal 'tense' and semantic 'time' and this terminological distinction will be made, although 'past' in isolation is ambiguous. Similarly a distinction will be made between formal 'interrogation' and semantic 'question'. But these related grammatical and

semantic issues will normally be treated together in a single section in each
chapter, under the single heading of 'grammar'.

2.3.2 Negation

There are several issues that must be discussed.

[i] As examples in the previous section have shown, we can distinguish
between the negation of the modality and the negation of the event. Thus
while with *can't* it is the modality that is negated, with *mustn't* the negation
belongs to the event. If the negative form negates the event, it follows that
some other form is required to negate the modality. Thus for dynamic
necessity we have *mustn't* to negate the event, but *needn't* to negate the
modality (6.3.1):

> You mustn't take him too seriously. (S.7.2f.10)
> You needn't take this down. (S.6.4b.8)

[ii] If any of the negative forms such as *never, no one, nobody, nothing,
nowhere,* occur with a non-negative form of the modal, the same rules apply
as for the negative forms of the modal. With MUST, for instance, it will be
the event that is negated, and with NEED the modality (but see also 6.3.1 [i]):

> You must never do that.
> You need never do that.
> I must tell no one about it.
> I need tell no one about it.
> Nothing must be altered in the college until this grand plan has developed.
> (S.3.4.82)

[iii] There are some contexts of a negative or quasi-negative kind, which,
following Klima (1964: 313), we might call 'affective'. First, we have the
'semi-negatives' (Palmer 1974: 28) such as *hardly* and *scarcely;* secondly,
there are contexts in which there is some degree of negation semantically,
eg: I doubt if .... Interrogatives are also affective in this sense, but are
sufficiently important to warrant separate discussion in the next section.
There are pairs of forms in English one of which regularly occurs in a purely
positive context, the other in negative or affective contexts. The best known
pair is *some* and *any* as in:

> He has some money.
> He hasn't got any money.
> He has got hardly any money.
> I doubt if he has any money.

Among the modals, epistemic MAY and CAN form a similar pair:

> He may be in his office.

He can't be in his office.
He can hardly be in his office.
I doubt if he can be in his office.

We noted in 1.1.3, and shall discuss in detail in 5.3.1, the fact that *could* will usually not occur in some contexts (*was/were able to* being required instead), yet there is no restriction on *couldn't*. Yet *could* may occur if the context is affective:

He was laughing so much he could hardly get a word out. (S.11.3c.5)
One moment I seem to be everything to him and then all he could think of was this child. (W.5.2.61)

The second of these can be paraphrased either by 'He could think of nothing but . . .', or 'He could only think of . . .'; both suggest that the context is of a semi-negative kind.

There is a similar position with DARE and NEED; these occur as modals only with negation or interrogation (1.2). We find that the negative forms occur freely but the positive forms only in affective contexts:

I needn't read them in full. (S.12.4a.19)
One need hardly ask.
Her field isn't one that I think we need go for. (S.2.6.121)

2.3.3 Interrogation

As we have noted, interrogation provides an affective context. I shall, however, prefer generally to link negation and interrogation together under the heading of 'non-assertion' (Quirk *et al* 1972: 54).

[i] It is only the modality that can be questioned (in contrast, of course, either the modality or the event may be negated).
[ii] In general, if the negative form of the modal negates the modality, this form is used for interrogation. Thus, for the CAN of ability:

John can take a punch.
John can't take a punch.
Can John take a punch?

If, however, the negative form negates the event and a different verb is used for negation, this second verb is usually used for interrogation. Thus, for epistemic possibility we find:

John may be reading.
John can't be reading.
Can John be reading?

But there are complications (see 6.3.1). Similarly, the positive forms *dare* and *need* occur:

> Need I say more? (S.5.6.6)
> Dare I ask?

[iii] Negative interrogatives are often not semantically negative; strictly, they do not negate either the modality or the event. Instead, like Latin *nonne,* they represent a special kind of question – one that 'expects the answer "Yes"'. Thus *Isn't John coming?* is a question about 'John is coming' and not about 'John isn't coming'. Indeed, we can paraphrase the negative interrogative with 'Isn't it the case that...?' (though we are still obliged to use the negative interrogative form even in the paraphrase). *Isn't John coming?* is then to be paraphrased by 'Isn't it the case that John is coming?' and not 'Is it the case that John isn't coming?' (which might be represented by *Is John nót coming?*).

With modals like MUST and OUGHT TO, where the negative form usually negates the event and a different form is used for negating the modality, the form used for negative interrogation is the same as the one used for assertion, *eg:*

> I like to think of those days and how tough it was for the average Englishman, what a hard life they must have had, and mustn't there be endless stories about this mansion. (S.12.6.75)
> Ought it not to be possible for all reasonable men and women in Northern Ireland to accept the reality of today? (W.4.1d.8)

The first example is one of epistemic MUST for which the negative is *can't* (3.5.3). But the question is not about negative epistemic necessity (it does not question 'There can't have been ...'), but about positive epistemic modality (it questions 'There must have been ...'). There is a similar interpretation for the second – the question is about what it ought to be possible for reasonable people to do.

There are, however, some more problems with negative interrogatives and dynamic necessity. A discussion of these is left until 6.3.2.

[iv] English has what are known as 'confirmatory tag questions' in which a negative tag is used with a positive assertion and a positive tag with a negative one:

> John's coming, isn't he?
> John isn't coming, is he?

With modals, if negative tags are regarded as negative interrogatives, they will use the same modal as for assertion; with negative tags it will follow that the two modals must be the same:

> He can come, can't he?

He must come, mustn't he?
not
  *He must come, needn't he?

An example from the Survey is:

> That ought to strengthen your hand, I would have thought, oughtn't it?
> (S.1c.11-22)

The same modal is also used if a positive tag follows a negative assertion:

> He can't come, can he?
> He mustn't come, must he?

The MUST example is a little surprising, for with *mustn't* it is the event that is negated. If *mustn't come* is analysed as 'must' + 'not-come', the modality is positive and we might, therefore, have expected a negative tag, *ie: mustn't he?* How can this be explained? There are two possible solutions.

(*a*) It may be argued that the tags always follow the same rules as negative questions, but that *must he?* here means 'Is it not the case that he mustn't?'. This would imply that the two negatives cancel each other out, *must* being essentially **mustn'tn't*.

(*b*) It may be simply that the absence or presence of negation with the tag is determined wholly by the grammatical form of the preceding modal, irrespective of the semantic question whether it is the modality or the event that is negated. This may seem a simpler solution, but it fails to preserve the relation between tags and the rules for negative questions.

It may be noted that we may have:

> We can't go, can we?
> We can always not go, can't we?

Here, however, it can simply be said that in the first the modal and the modality are negated, whereas in the second it is the main verb and the event that are negated (the separation of *can* from *not* by *always* making it quite clear that this does not equal *can't* or *cannot*). If so, the tags are as expected on both semantic and grammatical grounds.

2.3.4. Past tense and time

There are two problems, one associated with the modal and modality, the other with the main verb and event.

[i] Morphologically WILL, SHALL, CAN and MAY have past tense forms *would, should, could* and *might*. But syntactically and semantically these are related in three different ways.

First, there are very severe restrictions on the past tense forms for past time marking. *Could* and *would* may mark past time, but only under certain conditions (*cf* 5.3.3, 7.4.3). *Might* is rarely used for past time (8.5[v]), and *should* never.

Secondly, all may occur in the sequence of tenses required by reported (or 'indirect') speech. Thus we report as follows:

He will/shall/can/may come tomorrow.
I said he would/should/could/might come tomorrow.

This is the only construction in which there is a regular relationship between the present and past tense forms of the modals WILL, SHALL, CAN and MAY. This is important because it will often account for what would otherwise be impossible or very unlikely forms that do not generally occur with a simple past tense meaning – forms of the epistemic modals (3.5.1), the deontic modals (4.5.3), CAN with actuality (5.3.3 [ix]), MUST (6.3.3) and futurity WILL (7.4.3). For example, *He should have it the following day* is possible as a promise (4.4) in *He said he should have it the following day*. Sometimes there is no verb of reporting in the immediate environment, but the sentence can occur if the context makes it clear that it is still a report of *He shall have it tomorrow*. But because the formation is entirely regular, we need not say much more about it, and it will not be discussed in detail in later chapters.

Thirdly, *would, could* and *might* are used for 'tentativeness' or 'unreality'. If we grant that tentativeness or unreality is one of the meanings of the past tense forms (Palmer 1974: 47), there is no reason to deny that these are equally past tense forms of the modals. But I shall refer to them as the 'unreal' or 'tentative' forms, rather than use the cumbersome expression 'past tense forms used for unreality/tentativeness'. But unreality and its relation to conditionality is a difficult problem, and a whole section is devoted to it in this chapter (2.3.5) with further discussion later (3.4, 4.5.4, 5.3.5, 6.4, 7.4.4).

MUST and OUGHT do not have morphologically past tense forms; neither do the modals DARE and NEED (though the corresponding non-modals do). *Should*, however, is not to be treated as a form of SHALL (see 2.4.1).

The other verbs, the 'semi-modals', which do not belong morphologically to the same class, have normal past tense forms (except WOULD RATHER and HAD BETTER) – *was bound to, was able to, had to*, etc.

[ii] Morphologically only the modal may be marked for tense, for only finite forms mark tense and the main verb is always in a non-finite form. However, it is clear that with epistemic modality the proposition can be marked as past with *have* as in:

John may have been reading.

In its finite forms HAVE is associated not with the past, but with the perfect, yet here there is an indication of past time, and not of the time relation associated with the perfect. For we find:

John may have been reading yesterday.
John was reading yesterday.

But *yesterday,* an adverb of past time, cannot occur with the present perfect:

*John has been reading yesterday.

Yet *have* may also be used with the meaning of the perfect in *eg:*

John may have been reading since lunchtime.
(John has been reading since lunchtime.)

In fact, it could be argued that there is not merely a (double) ambiguity, but as many as four interpretations (see 3.5.1).

2.3.5 Unreality

It was noted in the previous section that the formally past tense forms *would, could* and *might* are often 'tentative' or 'unreal'.

In the simplest case this form simply expresses less assurance. This is true of epistemic *might* versus *may:*

He may/might come tomorrow.

Sometimes, however, the past tense form is not merely 'tentative' but is the mark of an unreal conditional sentence:

If the sun shone, we could go out.

There are also incomplete conditionals, where the protasis (the *if*-clause) is not expressed:

I couldn't do anything like that you see, I mean, I couldn't paint any ordinary sort of portrait. (S.1.8.83)

Here the sense of 'if I tried' or 'if I wanted to' seems to be implied. But it is not always possible to distinguish a tentative and an unreal conditional meaning (5.3.5, 7.5.3, 7.5.4).

I shall argue in some detail in 7.5.4 that forms such as *could* and *could have,* although conditional, sometimes signal the unreality or conditionality not of the modality, but of the event. Compare each of the following pairs:

If I trained, I could run ten miles.
If I wanted to, I could run ten miles.
If I had trained, I could have run ten miles.
If I had wanted to, I could have run ten miles.

In the first and third of these the ability is conditional on the training and the paraphrases 'would be able' and 'would have been able' are appropriate.

In the second and fourth, however, it is not the ability, but the action of running that is conditional on wanting to, and the paraphrases must be more like 'am able and would' and 'was able and would have'. (For a detailed discussion see Palmer 1977.)

This is important for the discussion of the status of SHOULD and OUGHT in 6.4, where I shall argue that they too must be seen as unreal conditionals.

2.3.6 Futurity

It was suggested in 1.1.3 that there is a close link between modality and future time. We find that the modals in many of their uses permit or require future time reference for the proposition or event, though neither the modal itself nor the main verb carries any mark of futurity. Thus, the *may* of permission will refer to the future:

You may come in.

Epistemic *may* and *might* will refer either to the present or the future:

He may/might be in his office.
He may/might come tomorrow.

Yet the *can* of ability usually has present time reference:

He can run a mile with ease.

By contrast the modality itself may be marked for futurity in the case of the dynamic modals by using *will* with the semi-modals – *will have to, will be able to*.

Futurity is not a serious problem, but a separate section will be assigned to it in most chapters.

2.4 General conclusions

We are now in a position to come to some tentative conclusions, to propose a general classification of the modals, and to outline the organization of the book.

2.4.1 Notation and terminology

Although there has been no discussion of notation a convention has already been adopted – to use SMALL CAPITALS to indicate lexical items (lexemes) and *italics* for forms (see Palmer 1974: 10). Thus we refer to the modal WILL but the forms *will* and *would*. But there are problems.

First, it is sometimes difficult to decide whether to indicate the subject of the discussion as a lexeme (in small capitals) or a form (in italics). This results from the procedure adopted in this book, where, for simplicity of exposition, the first section of each chapter will generally consider only the present assertive forms of each modal, and only later deal with the other forms. Most of what is said in the earlier sections will, thus, be valid for the modal as a whole, but largely illustrated by one form of it. It will, for instance, be dealing generally with CAN, but exemplifying with *can*.

Secondly, we sometimes wish to distinguish between all the present tense forms and all the past tense forms, *eg: will* and *won't* from *would* and *wouldn't*. But can we use *will* to include *won't* and *would* to include *wouldn't*? Or should we have yet another set of symbols so that we can distinguish not only the lexeme WILL (which subsumes *will, would, won't* and *wouldn't*) and the form *will*, but also something in between to indicate *will* and *won't* together? The difficulty here is that with the non-modal forms we could, in theory, make yet further distinctions. For should we use *have to* to refer only to the single form *have to* – or to *have to* and *has to* – or to *have to, has to* and also the negatives? If we are to avoid a multiplication of symbols some arbitrariness and inconsistency is inevitable.

Thirdly, there is a problem with the past tense forms that are not used for past time. There is no difficulty about treating present tense *can* and past tense *could* as forms of CAN if they are clearly tense/time markers. We can reasonably extend this principle to include the tentative or unreal forms (2.3.5) so that *may* and *might* are forms of MAY. But *should* is more problematic. It has nothing in common with SHALL, except when it is used with the sequence of tenses rule for reported speech (2.3.4), but belongs rather with OUGHT TO (see *eg* 3.4.3 and 4.6.1). For this reason, I shall treat it as a separate lexeme SHOULD. Yet on theoretical grounds this is not wholly satisfactory, since, as we shall see, the status of both SHOULD and also OUGHT TO is very like that of *could* (4.6, 6.4). Complete consistency of notation is, regrettably, impossible.

As a matter of practice, I shall use small capitals except where it is clear that I am talking about a particular form. Even in the first section of each chapter, where we shall be considering present tense forms, which could be symbolized by *can, may,* etc, I shall usually refer to them as CAN, MAY, etc. There are two reasons. First, as noted above, the present tense forms will very largely be discussed as examples of each modal as a whole. Secondly, we need similarly to refer to present tense forms of BE ABLE TO, etc, where there is not one single form but three (*am/is/are able to*). Unless we devise another type of symbol, these can be indicated only by BE ABLE TO.

2.4.2 Syntactic classification

In 2.3 we considered possible meanings of the modals; but the semantics can be closely associated with the syntactic possibilities. There are three criteria that can be used.

First, we may ask whether the modality, or the event, or both may be marked as past. With the CAN of ability (4.5.3), for instance, we find that only the modality can be so marked:

John can run a mile in four minutes.
John could run a mile in four minutes, when he was younger.

By contrast with the MAY of epistemic possibility (3.5.1) only the event may be so marked:

John may be reading.
John may have been reading yesterday.

With the MAY of permission (4.5.3) neither the modality nor the event can be so marked. One can neither give permission in the past nor give permission for events in the past. No tense distinctions are possible with:

You may (can) come in now.

With none of the kinds of modality does it seem that both modality and event can be marked for past tense.

Secondly, we may similarly ask whether the modality, or the event, or both may be negated. With the CAN of ability (4.5.1) only the modality is normally negated:

John can run a mile in four minutes.
John can't run a mile in four minutes.

Yet theoretically one can have the ability not to do something. With the MAY of epistemic possibility (3.5.3) either the modality or the proposition may be negated (though negating the modality involves a change of verb):

John may be reading.
John can't be reading.
John may not be reading.

It is, perhaps, possible to negate both:

?John can't not be reading.

Thirdly, we may ask whether the modal (the modality) is voice-neutral, ie whether a sentence containing a modal can be passivized without changing the meaning (other than the 'thematic' meaning that may be associated with change of subject). Some modals are voice-neutral, eg the MAY of epistemic modality (3.5.5):

John may be meeting Bill.
Bill may be being met by John.

There is one clear exception – WILL in the sense of willingness (7.4.5). The negative won't makes the point most clearly:

John won't meet Bill.
Bill won't be met by John.

If *won't* is taken here to mean 'is unwilling', then clearly these two sentences differ considerably in their meaning. The status of the CAN of ability is, however, problematic (5.3.6) and there is some question about CAN and MAY for permission (4.4.5).

2.4.3 Kinds of modality

It is fairly clear that epistemic modality is rather different from the other kinds. It is the modality of propositions as opposed to the modality of events, and I earlier made a basic distinction between epistemic and non-epistemic (Palmer 1974: 38). Other scholars have drawn a distinction between epistemic and 'root' modals (*eg* Jenkins 1972: 25, Huddleston 1976a: 69). Halliday (1970) makes a distinction in terms of 'modulation' and modality. However, it would be unwise to overstate the importance and clarity of this distinction for three reasons. First, there is much in common between epistemic and non-epistemic modality, and it is entirely plausible to argue that possibility of propositions and possibility of events can be subsumed under a more general notion of possibility. Secondly, there is not always a completely clear distinction. In particular the status of *could* (8.4) is debatable; most scholars have treated it as epistemic, but there is a clear case for denying this. Thirdly, there are not just two kinds of modality, though the distinction between the other kinds is sometimes even less clear than between epistemic and the rest.

I earlier (Palmer 1974: 100–3) made the threefold distinction between epistemic, subject oriented and discourse oriented modals. I used the distinction between subject oriented and discourse oriented to classify the modals themselves (when they are not epistemic), so that CAN and WILL are subject oriented, and MAY, SHALL and MUST are discourse oriented, the semantic distinction being that the subject oriented modals refer to the ability or willingness of the subject of the sentence and that it is this that indicates the action, while the discourse oriented modals relate to the action of the speaker in giving permission, making a promise or laying an obligation. (I used the term 'discourse oriented' rather than 'speaker oriented' because one may, for instance, not merely give permission, but also ask permission with the modal verb MAY (*May I come in?*). The permission then relates to the hearer and not the speaker.)

I now feel that this is not wholly accurate for two reasons. First, some of the non-epistemic modal uses are neither subject oriented nor discourse oriented, but simply neutral. We can say that an event is possible without relating the possibility either to the subject or the speaker as examples in 2.2 and 2.3 show. Secondly, it seems clear that some of the modal verbs do not fit wholly into one or other of three kinds; for instance, CAN is both subject oriented and neutral and MUST both discourse oriented and neutral.

I now suggest that, if we take the syntax and semantics carefully into account, we can distinguish between three basic kinds of modality which, for convenience, we can label with von Wright's terms 'epistemic', 'deontic' and 'dynamic'. We can subdivide dynamic modality into 'neutral' and, for want of a better term, 'subject oriented' (and deontic might, perhaps, have still been called 'discourse oriented'). This will not entirely exhaust all that has to be said (see Chapter 8). There is one terminological point. Strictly, on this interpretation, only modality is epistemic, deontic or dynamic, but it is convenient, with little risk of confusion, to apply these terms to the modals themselves, when they are used with the appropriate meaning.

Let us then look at each kind of modality in a little detail, considering in particular the verbs involved and their grammatical (or grammatical-semantic) characteristics.

First, there is epistemic modality. This is exemplified by MAY for possibility and MUST for necessity, though other verbs, notably SHOULD and WILL are also used epistemically. The characteristics of epistemic modality in terms of marking for past and negation and of voice-neutrality are:

Past	modality – no	proposition – yes
Negation	modality – yes	proposition – yes
Voice-neutrality		yes

(It is, however, debatable whether there are any negative forms for epistemic necessity – 3.5.3.)

Secondly, we have deontic modality, which is illustrated by MAY for permission and MUST for obligation. However, deontic modality is less clearly defined. The grammar and semantics lead us to distinguish a class of verbs that are essentially performative in the sense of Austin (1962) or discourse oriented (Palmer 1974: 100), or 'relative', *ie* relative to the speaker or, in questions, the hearer (von Wright 1951: 41). By this criterion we can include SHALL (giving an undertaking) among the deontic modals. One quite striking point is that we can contrast, for involvement or non-involvement of the speaker, MAY with CAN and MUST with HAVE TO, though in detail there is considerable difference between the two sets of contrasts (4.2.3, 6.2.2). The characteristics are:

Past tense	modality – no	event – no
Negation	modality – yes	event – yes
Voice-neutrality		yes

(SHALL has no form to negate the modality. The fact, however, that it has forms to negate the event and no form for past tense modality clearly places it with the deontic modals.)

Thirdly, we have dynamic modality. Within that we can distinguish two

subkinds of modality. One is neutral dynamic modality. This is exemplified
by the uses of CAN and MUST to indicate 'possible for' and 'necessary for'.
We shall see that neither of those modals is always neutral, but that HAVE
(GOT) TO always is (and it could be argued that HAVE (GOT) TO represents a
third subkind of dynamic modality, that we might call 'circumstantial' – for
evidence from the Survey see the examples in 2.2.3). The characteristics
are:

Past tense	modality – yes	event – no
Negation	modality – yes	event – yes
Voice-neutrality	yes	

The other subkind of dynamic modality is subject oriented modality
illustrated by the CAN of ability (2.1) and also by the WILL of willingness (see
2.4.3 and 6.1). The characteristics are:

Past tense	modality – yes	event – no
Negation	modality – yes	event – yes/no
Voice-neutrality	yes/no?	

(With CAN it is difficult to imagine an example with the event negated, but
there are examples with WILL – 7.4.2. Voice-neutrality is a problem with
CAN (5.3.6) but WILL is never voice-neutral.)

The semantics or deep structure of these different kinds of modalities
could be shown using phrase structure trees. It was suggested (Ross 1969:
89) that the essential difference between the epistemic and deontic modals
is that the former is intransitive and the latter transitive (with *I* as the
subject of the highest verb). In simplified form the two possible structures
for *John may come tomorrow* would be:

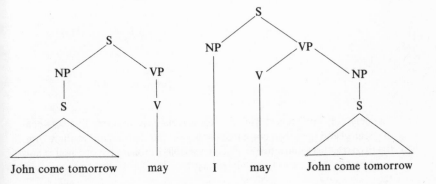

There are, however, a number of difficulties with this. To begin with, it is very debatable whether a structure of this kind should include the 'performer' *I;* to do so confuses syntax with the illocutionary aspects of language (see 1.4). Secondly, as Lyons points out (1977: 792), epistemic modality may be 'subjective' or 'objective'. When it is subjective, there is an equally reasonable case for treating it too as transitive, with the speaker as the higher subject. Our second diagram could, then, be equally appropriate for epistemic modality. It would then be necessary to insert into the structure a verb of judging for epistemic modality and a verb of making or causing for deontic modality, though in both cases we should still need a further verb to express the modality itself ('I judge it to be possible . . . .', 'I make it to be possible . . . .').

For dynamic modality we might, perhaps, more reasonably treat neutral and subject oriented as intransitive and transitive respectively. Thus, for *John can come tomorrow* and *John can run a mile,* the structures would be:

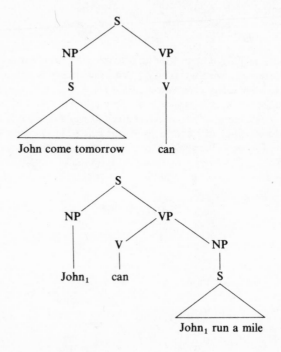

The only difficulty about this is that there is no clear dividing line between the neutral and the subject oriented use of *can,* and that somehow, therefore, the two structures must merge. This is a serious problem, but one that is not restricted to the modals (see Palmer 1973).

We can, perhaps, speculate about the ways in which the different kinds of modality may be related. If we consider the event or proposition as a conceptual 'state of affairs', we begin with epistemic modality which merely states that such a state of affairs is possible or necessary. Dynamic modality suggests, however, that there are circumstances in the real world which make possible or necessary the coming into reality of this conceptual state of affairs. With neutral dynamic modality these are circumstances in general (and perhaps the term 'circumstantial' might be better than 'neutral' to indicate this), while with subject oriented modality they are the characteristics of the subject. Finally, with deontic modality the speaker performatively creates the possibility or necessity for the coming into reality of the conceptual state of affairs. Further modifications are possible but rather less clear or well-structured; these are discussed in Chapter 8.

2.4.4 Organization

In the previous sections we have been talking about 'kinds' of modality, starting first with eight or so possible different kinds and concluding that basically there are three. The term 'kind' of modality will be used as a technical term to refer to this distinction; 'epistemic' and 'deontic' refer thus to different kinds of modality.

We also need, however, to distinguish between possibility and necessity and a third sort of modality that is exemplified by WILL and SHALL. For this distinction I shall use the term 'degree' of modality; possibility and necessity are different degrees of modality. It will sometimes be necessary to refer to kind and degree simultaneously, *eg* to epistemic possibility. For this I shall naturally avoid using the term 'kind', but no technical term is necessary.

If we think of kinds of modality as being in a horizontal plane and degrees of modality in a vertical plane in a two dimensional matrix, it is clear that our exposition can proceed either horizontally or vertically. We can either divide the chapters up into kinds of modality, one on epistemic modality, the next on deontic and so on, or we can divide them into degrees of modality, dealing first with possibility, and then with necessity. In practice neither of these approaches is fully satisfactory. A vertical approach would, ideally, be best; we could deal with each kind of modality in a single chapter, for each kind has roughly the same syntax and semantics. But a vertical division becomes difficult where there is indeterminacy between the kinds of modality; we find that there is indeterminacy between neutral dynamic and subject oriented possibility and also between neutral dynamic and discourse oriented necessity. (By contrast, epistemic modality is fairly clearly distinct from the other kinds.)

However, a vertical division proves the most convenient. I shall therefore deal first with epistemic (Chapter 3) and then with deontic modality (Chapter 4). Only when I come to dynamic modality shall I deal with it horizontally, with possibility first (Chapter 5), then necessity (Chapter 6), and then the degree associated with WILL (Chapter 7). Chapter 8 deals with some kinds that have not been discussed before and the last chapter with theoretical problems.

There is one final, but important point. In 1.3 I was critical of previous studies that attempted to provide an unrealistically highly structured analysis of the modals. There is no doubt that the overall picture of the modals is extremely 'messy' and untidy and that the most the linguist can do is impose some order, point out some regularities, correspondences, parallelisms. But there is no single simple solution and I have some sympathy with Ehrman's (1966: 9) view that we can only arrive at a 'rather loosely structured set of relationships'. Anderson (1971: 113) criticized an earlier work of mine (Palmer 1965) as 'unsystematic' and 'lacking in explanatory power'. There may be a little more system in this book, but the subject is not one that lends itself to any simple explanation.

Chapter 3

Epistemic modality

Our detailed study begins with epistemic modality because it is the simplest to deal with. In both its syntax and its semantics, it is the kind of modality that is most clearly distinct from the others and has the greatest degree of internal regularity and completeness.

The two basic degrees of possibility and necessity are marked by MAY and MUST respectively. Examples are:

> He may be qualified to be recognized as a teacher of French or of German or of something like that. (S.1.2a–7)
> This must be one of the finest views of the whole processional route. (S.10.5.49)

The function of epistemic modals is to make judgments about the possibility, etc, that something is or is not the case. Epistemic modality is, that is to say, the modality of propositions rather than of actions, states, events, etc. Indeed there are examples in which the proposition is separately stated in a subordinate clause introduced by *that*:

> . . . and it may be that the family will disappear as the basis of civilization. (S.6.4a.71)

MAY can be paraphrased by 'It is possible that . . .', but the paraphrase 'It is necessary that . . .' is not an accurate one for MUST. This, however, results not from the meaning of MUST, but from the fact that *necessary* and *necessity* are not words used in ordinary speech to indicate epistemic judgments (unlike *possible* and *possibility*). In fact the most accurate paraphrase is in terms of something like 'The only possible conclusion is that . . .' (3.2.1).

We might expect that there would be a modal to express probability, with the paraphrase 'It is probable that . . .'. In fact, there is a third degree of epistemic modality indicated by WILL, but this is not an accurate paraphrase of it (see 3.3). Further degrees of modality may be expressed by using the tentative forms *might* and *would* (3.4.1, 3.4.2) and *should* (3.4.3). The status of *could* (see 8.5) is more problematic. With the epistemic modals we must also include some that are not true modals – BE BOUND TO and HAVE (GOT) TO.

We noted earlier (1.1.2) that epistemic modals are normally subjective, *ie* that the epistemic judgment rests with the speaker. I have not shown this in the suggested paraphrases, *eg* by paraphrasing MUST as 'The only conclusion that I can draw is that . . .', because in normal circumstances the paraphrases I have given would be given a subjective interpretation. It is, however, possible to invent examples where the epistemic judgment is not specifically that of the speaker, and it is even possible for the speaker to disclaim his own responsibility for the judgment by saying, for instance, *I know this may be true* or *Apparently he must have done it*. But it is significant that this disclaimer has to be clearly signalled. Moreover, the clearest evidence of the subjective ('performative') nature of the epistemic modality is the fact that the relevant modals occur only in the present tense, for the judgment and the act of speaking are simultaneous and so can only be present. But this, too, is not absolute; there are exceptions (3.5.1).

Some linguists, *eg* Huddleston (1971: 311), Leech (1969: 204) and Joos (1964: 195) have used the term 'logical' to refer to epistemic modality. But we are not concerned with logical truth. Unfortunately, what von Wright (1951: 2) defines in terms of 'possible', 'impossible' and 'necessary' is alethic modality, though he recognizes that in ordinary language *possible* and *impossible* are used for epistemic modality (1.1.1).

3.1 Possibility

Epistemic possibility is indicated by MAY, and the paraphrase in terms of 'possible that' is an accurate one. MAY is used to relate to propositions of various kinds. It is used, for instance, to refer to states in either the present or the future:

> They're all very sort of Kentish and they may be in Sussex actually. (S.7.3f.30)
> You may not like the idea of it, but let me explain. (S.8.3b.2)

There are also examples where the reference is to action in progress (again both present and future):

> Who may not have a very strong claim or who may be facing bitterness among their members. (S.6.3.67)
> So we may be seeing some changes in British industry from these students. (S.6.1a.31)

I noted no examples of MAY being used to refer to habitual activity in the Survey, but it would be easy enough to invent some:

> He may go to London every day.
> He may go to London every day when he gets his new job.

MAY is also commonly used where there is reference to a single future action (yet we shall see in 3.2.1 that MUST is not used in a similar way):

I may go up at the end of August. (S.7.3f.49)
On the other hand he may say 'My dear fellow, of course we understand this problem and we would arrange it this way'. (S.3.4.72)

Yet there are no examples of MAY where there is reference to a single non-progressive present action, nor can I invent one. This is to be explained by the fact that we rarely report single actions in the present time, and we therefore are equally unlikely to comment on their possibility. In non-modal forms there are exceptions to this. The football commentator, for instance, uses the simple present to report events in progress – 'and now Jones passes the ball . . .' (see Palmer 1974: 60-2). But in such circumstances the events are immediately observable and epistemic judgments about them are inappropriate.

Under the heading of epistemic possibility we should also, perhaps, handle the 'concessive' (Scheurweghs 1959: 369) use of MAY:

Whatever John may say . . .
However difficult it may be . . .

For the meaning here is that of 'possible that', as in *John may say that . . .* and *It may be difficult. . . .* We are concerned with the consideration of possible propositions (but see also 8.5).

3.2 Necessity

The position with necessity is more difficult and complex. To begin with, as we saw at the beginning of this chapter, a paraphrase in terms of 'It is necessary that . . .' is not really accurate; a better paraphrase would be 'The only possible conclusion is that . . .'. Alternatively, we could paraphrase wholly in terms of possibility with double negation – 'It is not possible that . . . not . . .' (see 3.5.3).

Halliday (1970: 329) makes a contrast between 'possibility' and 'certainty'. Bouma (1975: 318) criticizes this and also rejects, as being too influenced by modal logic, the term 'necessity'. I would agree that 'certainty' is a misleading term, and that 'necessity' does not provide an accurate paraphrase. Bouma is, however, off the point when he says that certainty is expressed by what Joos calls 'factual assertion' (Joos 1964: 81, 169) which requires no modal, equating certainty with 100 per cent probability. For factual assertion is not an expression of certainty or of 100 per cent probability; rather, it makes no epistemic judgment at all. Epistemic necessity, unlike factual assertion, makes such a judgment; making the strongest of all judgments is not the same as making a factual assertion. Indeed, in language, a factual assertion makes a stronger claim than the strongest of all epistemic judgments (Kartunnen 1972: 12).

3.2.1 MUST

Most of the examples of MUST in the Survey relate to states or activity in the present:

> The odds must be slightly with them in these tight, tense situations. (S.10.2.55)
> You must find it quite a change being back in London. (W.5.2.70)
> She is a bridesmaid and she must be all excitement at the moment. (S.10.6a.4)

There seem to be no examples of habitual activity, but it would be easy to invent one – *He must travel to London regularly*.

It is significant, however, that no examples were noted where there is reference to states or activities in the future. MUST seldom occurs with future time reference, because it would usually be open to dynamic interpretation and thus might be misunderstood as in:

> He must come tomorrow.

This would almost certainly be interpreted in terms of obligation. An epistemic sense is, however, possible where the context makes it more likely, *eg:*

> Something must happen next week.
> It must rain tomorrow.

These sentences could, of course refer to what is necessary in a dynamic or even a deontic sense, but they are more likely to indicate what the speaker thinks will happen and so to be interpreted epistemically. But the ambiguity remains.

The appropriateness of a paraphrase in terms of 'conclusion' ('The only possible conclusion is that . . .') is clearly illustrated in many examples in the Survey, where the reasons for the conclusion are either stated or implied (some of the examples below refer to past time – for this see 3.4.1):

> He must have been discouraged because he's been hitting Mitoff with everything in the book and still he cannot keep this man away. (S.10.3.97)
> All the X-rays showed absolutely negative. There was nothing wrong, so it must just be tension, I suppose. (S.5.8.82)
> Evidently she must have talked to her mother about them, you see, because on one occasion I was over at her house and her mother came into the room . . . and she said 'Oh, I thought you were an angry young man'. (S.5.10.60)
> What a sensible Mum she must be. (W.7.5f.3)
> It must surely be just a beautiful relic from the past. (W.1.5b.6)

3.2.2 BE BOUND TO

We must introduce here the form BE BOUND TO. In most of its occurrences it has an epistemic sense:

> It's bound to come out though, I think. . . . It's received such rave notices that somebody's bound to put it on. (S.2.7.18)
> Self exploration and exploration in a small group at that level of complexity and so on is bound, it seems to me, to generate special languages. (S.5.7.19)

It is significant that, in every example that I noted, the main verb is a verb relating to the future and, in most cases, a verb of action. By contrast almost every example of epistemic *must* referred to a present state, very commonly with the verb *be* (see above). Indeed, as we have already noted, if MUST occurs with future time reference, it will almost always be interpreted in a dynamic, not an epistemic, sense. Thus the following can only be interpreted dynamically:

> The government must act. It must make up its mind about priorities – offices or homes, housing estates or luxury buildings. (W.15.1.48–3)
> Now I lunched the day before yesterday with one of the leaders of the Labour Party whose name obviously must be kept quiet – I can't repeat it. (S.5.5.35)

An epistemic interpretation is extremely unlikely here, even if the sentences are taken out of their context. In contrast, MAY in similar contexts might well be interpreted epistemically ('It is possible that the government will act', etc).

Although there is this partial restriction on MUST, that it will not normally be used to refer epistemically to the future, there is no converse restriction on BE BOUND TO. We could say (*cf* the sentence above):

> The odds are bound to be with them in these tight situations.

Usually, then, the occurrence of BE BOUND TO results from the fact that the use of MUST would suggest the wrong interpretation.

Nevertheless BE BOUND TO and MUST are not identical in meaning. There is a difference between:

> John's bound to be in his office.
> John must be in his office.

BE BOUND TO is the more certain, and indeed can almost be paraphrased by 'It is certain that . . .'. Moreover, it has little or no sense of 'conclusion'. The example with BE BOUND TO here is more likely to occur in a context where it has been questioned whether John is in his office and the speaker wishes to assert as positively as he can that this is in fact the only possibility. With

MUST, in contrast, there is a likelihood that the speaker is drawing the most obvious conclusion. It would be more appropriate if, for instance, the remark were made in response to a comment that the lights were on in John's office.

Notice, too, that BE BOUND TO can be modified by, for example, *almost* (whereas MUST cannot):

What's almost bound to happen is, I shall leave Marlborough at about half past one. (S.4.2.58)

When BE BOUND TO is used with future time reference, the meaning is sometimes nearer to 'It is inevitable that . . .' (which may be not wholly epistemic but partly dynamic) *eg*:

The White Paper is bound to affect Colleges of Further Education offering courses leading to the External Degree. (W.13.1.64-1)
If the Government deals with the situation realistically the cost is bound to be great. (W.15.1.49-2)

This, however, may be not so much a matter of the difference in the meanings of MUST and BE BOUND TO as a result of the fact that the concept of conclusivity is more appropriate to the present and that of inevitability to the future.

3.2.3 HAVE (GOT) TO

The forms HAVE TO and HAVE GOT TO are also 'necessity' modals, but I noted only two examples in the Survey of HAVE GOT TO being used in an epistemic sense:

If you've seen all the old Frankensteins you've got to know all the jokes. (S.2.10.94)
Something has got to give in this second half I think. (S.10.2.3)

A possible reaction to the second example is to try to find a non-epistemic sense for it, but it seems clear that it has to be interpreted epistemically.

In American speech, however, HAVE GOT TO is commonly used in an epistemic sense:

You've got to be joking.

The more likely British form has MUST:

You must be joking. (S.4.2.67)

There is, moreover, in British English an interesting contrast between HAVE TO and MUST in:

You must be mad to do that.
You have to be mad to do that.

The first is clearly epistemic – the conclusion from your action is that you are mad. The second is dynamic – it states that being mad is a necessary condition for acting in that way.

3.3 WILL

Examples of epistemic WILL are:

Tell him Professor Cressage is involved – he will know Professor Cressage. (S.7.21.8)
In the 1920s Wilkinson Sword introduced the stroppable razor and then the 'Empire' range which many people will remember. (W.15.4a.5)

These have present time reference. For future time reference see 3.5.2. Epistemic WILL refers to what it is reasonable to expect. It can be roughly paraphrased by 'A reasonable inference is that ...'. Although I earlier suggested (Palmer 1974: 135) that *will* indicates probability, this is not strictly true. One of my examples was:

The French will be on holiday today.

That this does not mean 'probably are' is shown by the fact that the second of the following sentences is much less natural than the first:

The French are probably on holiday today, but I could be wrong about that.
? The French will be on holiday today, but I could be wrong about that.

Will expresses a confident statement. Like *must*, it cannot normally be followed by a suggestion that the proposition may, after all, not be true.
WILL and MUST are both, then, more confident than is suggested by 'probable'. The essential difference between them is that, while *will* indicates a confident statement, *must* suggests a confident conclusion from the evidence available. Compare:

John must be in his office.
John will be in his office.

The first of these would be the more appropriate in response to an observation that the lights were on; the conclusion is that John is in his office. *Will* merely makes a confident statement. It would be used to explain (from previous knowledge) why the lights were on, rather than to draw a conclusion from this observation. The following sequence illustrates this:

John will be in his office now. Yes, the lights are on, so he must be there.

There are no strict rules for the occurrence of *will* and *must*, but merely semantic differences that make one or the other more appropriate.

3.4 Tentative forms

The tentative forms of the epistemic modals are sufficiently important to merit a separate section. *Might* and *would* are obviously the relevant forms of MAY and WILL, but we must also consider the status of what seems to be epistemic SHOULD. *Could* is a more difficult problem, (except where it is used in a negative context – 3.5.3) and is left to 8.4.

3.4.1 *Might*

Might is used exactly as *may* is. It merely indicates a little less certainty about the possibility. There are numerous examples:

> . . . and then you might be back again on that Monday. (S.2.11a.21)
> So he might go and live with his parents for a while. (S.7.3f.62)
> You think someone might be watching us. (W.5.3.106)
> Look, now you might be going in August. (S.6.2.52)

Clearly *might* is the tentative or unreal form of MAY, but in epistemic modality it seems to have no clear implication of conditionality (see 2.3.5 and compare 3.4.3 on *should*).

3.4.2 *Would*

Would is clearly the tentative form of WILL. A rough paraphrase might be 'I should think that . . .' or perhaps, better, 'It would be reasonable to conclude that . . .'. This not only shows how it is related to *will*, but also accounts for the tentativeness as a kind of conditional. A paraphrase in terms of 'probable' is still not quite accurate, but a little more appropriate than for *will*. Examples are:

> Oh, well, how long would that be?—Two years. (S.1.6.69)
> I think it would be Turner as well. (S.2.7.105)

A similar interpretation is, perhaps, to be assigned to:

> I didn't realize that would be your area. It absolutely isn't mine. (W.16.1.20-3)

This is a little more controversial. It is an example of indirect speech; by the sequence of tense rules the 'underlying' direct form could contain either *will* or *would*. What he failed to realize, that is to say, could be either 'that will be your area' or 'that would be your area'. The latter seems to be the more appropriate, since *will* would suggest a conclusion rather than mere probability or 'thinking that'.

3.4.3 SHOULD

There are examples in the Survey of *should* being used in what appears to be an epistemic sense. (There are no similar examples, however, of *ought to*):

Well both of them should be on the Modern Board. (S.8.10.4)
You should be meeting those later on this afternoon. (S.3.3.38)

SHOULD does not express necessity; it expresses rather extreme likelihood, or a reasonable assumption or conclusion. But it implicitly allows for the speaker to be mistaken – compare dynamic SHOULD (6.4) which allows for the event not to take place. This is very clear from the following example (provided it is taken epistemically, for a dynamic interpretation is just possible):

Mitoff comes in, takes a stunning left hand to the chin or what should be a stunning left hand. (S.10.3.85)

The commentator allows for the fact that it might not be what he thinks it is, a stunning left hand.

There is a good case here for arguing that SHOULD is the unreal or tentative marker of epistemic necessity. Indeed like dynamic SHOULD (*cf* 6.4), it is, perhaps, conditional in the sense that it indicates what would be a reasonable conclusion, if circumstances are such as the speaker believes they are. There would then be a close parallelism with dynamic SHOULD; in particular, both have, or often have, a negative implication – that things are not as suggested, that the proposition is not in fact true or that the event does not or will not take place. But, if it marks epistemic necessity, it is related semantically not to SHALL, but to MUST.

There are many examples where it is difficult to be sure whether we have dynamic or epistemic modality. The position is very much the same as with *could* (8.5), except that with SHOULD there are more examples that seem to be undeniably epistemic. Yet it is not at all clear that the following are epistemic:

Should only take three days for the survey report to be in to the building society. (S.8.1a.18)
So he should be around sort of between half past two and half past three. (S.8.1i.3)

There are two examples with the word *reason* in them. It is difficult to decide whether this indicates a reason for conclusion (epistemic) or a reason for being (dynamic). The word *reason* itself can be interpreted either dynamically or epistemically:

There's no reason why it should be so surprising. (S.2.8a.74)
There's no reason why they should be simultaneous. (S.3.2c.17)

In these two, of course, *should* appears in the subordinate clause and it could be argued that this is not strictly comparable with the other examples. (But see 8.6 where *should do* could be replaced by *did*.) There is, then, indeterminacy here between epistemic and dynamic modality. It is possible to understand why this is so: if we consider that it is reasonable for an act to take place, we may equally consider that it is reasonable to expect that it will.

At least these examples provide us with a possible paraphrase for SHOULD, 'It is reasonable . . .', a reasonable 'necessity' in either the epistemic or dynamic sense.

3.5 Grammar

As was clear from 2.4.2, the grammar of epistemic modality distinguishes it from the other kinds of modality.

3.5.1 Past

The functions of the epistemic modal in relation to past tense and time are almost wholly predictable from the nature of epistemic modality.

[i] Generally the modality is in the present only, because the judgments are made in the act of speaking, epistemic modals being in this sense usually 'performative' (see 2.4.2). The modal verbs are not normally used, therefore, in past tense forms to refer to past judgments. Past tense forms are normally tentative with present time reference. It is, of course, possible to report past judgments, but this requires verbs such as THINK, BELIEVE, etc.

[ii] In contrast, the proposition can be in the past, for we can make judgments about past events. This is achieved by the use of *have* before the main verb:

> You may have guessed that it's a dress of pure silk. (S.10.6a.15)
> He might have been there while you were there. (S.2.11b.86)
> Well, he must have been flying too low. (W.5.3.116)
> This would have been about a couple of months ago. (S.1.6.12)

I noted no similar examples with *will*, or with SHOULD, OUGHT TO or BE BOUND TO, but there is nothing odd about:

> He will/should/ought/is bound to have been there.

Notice that these all refer to past time (see 2.3.4). They do not have the time reference of the finite perfect with *have*, which is in clear contrast with the past. The last example is particularly clear because it contains *ago*; the corresponding non-modal form could only be *That was a couple of months ago*. *That has been a couple of months ago* is not a possible English sentence since the present perfect does not occur with adverbs of past time. There is one example in the Survey which might be interpreted as perfect rather than past:

I reckon that must have hurt Cooper. (S.10.3.96)

It is not clear whether this is a judgment on 'That hurt Cooper' or 'That has hurt Cooper'.

There is, however, some difficulty in saying that *have* is ambiguous between a past tense and a perfect interpretation, even if it may have the semantics of both. For, in theory, there is not just a dual, but a quadruple, distinction involving 'past-past' and 'past-perfect' as well as past and perfect. We may compare the following pairs:

He went yesterday. (past)
He must have gone yesterday.
He has gone by now. (present perfect)
He must have gone by now.
He had gone before she arrived. ('past-past')
He must have gone before she arrived.
He had gone by then. ('past-perfect')
He must have gone by then.

These four distinctions (or, more strictly, three, since there is no formal distinction between 'past-past' and 'past-perfect', even in the non-modal forms, though the semantic distinction is clear) are neutralized within epistemic modality (and indeed, in general, wherever non-finite forms of verbs are required). It is, perhaps, sufficient merely to say that with judgments about the past there is formally only one type of past, and not to attempt to distinguish three or four different types.

There is an interesting and important ambiguity in the *might have* form:

I think I might have walked out too, from all accounts. (S.2.5a.32)

This could mean either 'I think it is possible that I walked out' or 'I think it is possible that I would have walked out'. With *I* as the subject, clearly the latter interpretation is the more likely. For an attempt to explain this usage and some other problematic forms see 7.5.6.

There are some potential examples of epistemic modals where the modality is in the past. Consider:

For all I knew he might have done it.

The past tense *knew* suggests that this means 'It was possible that he did it'. However, such interpretations seem possible only in contexts where they are forced by such expressions as *For all I knew*, and this suggests that they might be treated in a different way. One possibility is that there is implied

reported speech ('I thought that'), since reported speech requires the
sequence of tenses rule (2.3.4).

There is also the use of HAVE TO in, for instance:

It had to be there – there wasn't anywhere else it could have been.

Here the epistemic necessity seems to be genuinely in the past, or at least to
overlap into the past with a meaning something like 'It was always
"necessary" that . . .' or 'The only possible conclusion was that . . .'. If this
is correct, it is the modality that is past with *had to*, whereas, of course, it is
the proposition that is past with *must have*.

A similar explanation is probably required for an example from Halliday
(1970: 334):

They wóuld telephone me just as I was going to sleep.

Halliday sees this as an example of 'overtone', signalled by the accent on
wóuld, as contrasted with 'undertone', which is our 'tentative'. But in this
example it is not simply a matter of strongly asserting the modality, and
there is a difference between this example and another that Halliday also
provides:

Predictably, this gazebo would be by Wren.

This second example is the tentative use of *would*, which was discussed in
3.4.2; it suggests what would be a reasonable conclusion. But the first is not
to be paraphrased as 'It would be a reasonable conclusion that . . .', but 'It
was always a reasonable conclusion that . . .'. If so, this too is an example of
epistemic modality in the past (but see 7.4.3 for an alternative explanation).

It was, of course, suggested earlier that epistemic modality is always in
the present and that epistemic modals are always performative. These
examples suggest, however, that although this may be the most common
function of epistemic modals, it is not an absolute requirement of them that
they should always be performative and, therefore, present. But this 'past'
epistemic usage is, obviously, a very odd one. It does not merely refer to the
epistemic judgment but it also suggests that the judgement was, in the event,
proved correct.

There are, finally, two debatable examples. First we have:

How long were the classes? Would they be forty minutes? (S.6.4b.35)

The first question here relates to the past and it would be reasonable to
suppose, therefore, that in the second the proposition is in the past. What is
being questioned is 'that they were forty minutes'. But if so, the verbal form
should have contained *have*, in either *will have* or *would have*. I am not sure
whether the speaker switched from past to present (with the assumption
that the classes still go on) or whether *would* is being used (and can be used)
instead of *will have*, to indicate past time of the proposition, not the modality.

A further possibility, which I find less plausible than the last, is that this is the past habitual form of WILL (7.4.3). Secondly, consider:

> Did you vote at all? I'm surprised actually because I thought you would have been the sort of person that wouldn't have bothered to vote because the whole thing's bunkum and rubbish. (S.2.10.16)

What is the precise analysis of *would have been*? Since this is indirect speech where the sequence of tenses rule applies (after the past tense verb of reporting *thought*), the corresponding direct form would be either *will have been* or *would have been*. (What the speaker thought is 'You will have been . . .' or 'You would have been . . .'.) The former seems the more likely, with an epistemic interpretation to mean 'It is a reasonable assumption that you were . . .'. However, the speaker may well have meant 'It is a reasonable assumption that you are . . .'. In that case, the direct form would be *will be* and in the indirect form *would be* would be expected. If so, it seems that *have* is redundant here, perhaps influenced by *wouldn't have bothered*. For a somewhat similar problem see the discussion of *could have* in 5.3.3 [viii].

3.5.2 Future

MAY (in both of its forms *may* and *might*) is used to make epistemic judgments about propositions relating either to the present or the future. Examples have been given in 3.1 and 3.4.1.

By contrast, epistemic MUST is usually used only to refer to the present. For future time reference BE BOUND TO is preferred (3.2.1, 3.2.2).

The situation with WILL is rather less clear. *Will* may be used epistemically to refer to future events, but if it is so used it is very difficult to distinguish from the use of *will* simply to refer to the future (7.2). Indeed it has been argued that, conversely, the WILL of futurity is, in fact, epistemic WILL. This question is discussed in some detail in 7.2.5. *Would*, similarly, seldom seems to be used in a clearly epistemic use with future time reference.

3.5.3 Negation

With epistemic possibility and necessity we now find that there are some of the logical-type relations discussed in 1.1.5.

[i] For possibility the proposition is negated by *may not* ('It is possible that . . . not . . .'), while the modality is negated by *can't* ('It is not possible that . . .'):

> You may not have met her. (S.2.7.116)
> It sounds as though he can't be at Damion Sampson Hall any more. (S.8.3l.8).
> If he saw a light, it can't have been the light of the motor cycle. (S.12.4a.26)

However, if the main verb is a verb of action and there is reference to the future, *can't* would normally be interpreted as dynamic rather than epistemic, as in:

She can't come on Monday.

This would normally be taken to mean 'It is not possible for her to come on Monday', rather than 'It is not possible that she will come on Monday'. We saw a similar characteristic of MUST, with BE BOUND TO being used to avoid the ambiguity or misunderstanding (3.2.1, 3.2.2). CAN has no similar suppletive to avoid the ambiguity, but an epistemic interpretation can be strongly suggested if the progressive form is used:

She can't be coming on Monday.

[ii] Although *mustn't* and *needn't* occur epistemically (see below), it is not usual to use them simply to negate epistemic necessity. For, in effect, they are not needed, since the logical equivalence of 'Not-possible ≡ Necessary-not' and 'Not-necessary ≡ Possible-not' allow the possibility forms to be used instead. The difference between possibility and necessity is simply that the negation of proposition and modality is reversed. Interpreted in terms of necessity, *may not* negates the modality ('It is not necessary that . . .'), while *can't* negates the proposition ('It is necessary that . . . not . . .'). We can show the pattern in tabular form using round brackets to indicate the logically equivalent forms that appear to fill the 'gaps':

Possible-not	*may not*
Not-possible	*can't*
Necessary-not	(*can't*)
Not-necessary	(*may not*)

However, both *mustn't* and *needn't* may be used where it is important to make the judgment in terms of necessity rather than possibility. Thus *mustn't* would be used instead of *can't* in *eg*:

He mustn't be there after all.

This is to be paraphrased by 'The only possible conclusion is that he is not there' (necessary-not), rather than 'It is not a possible conclusion that he is there' (not-possible). Similarly *needn't* might occur in:

He may be there, but he needn't be.

The paraphrase here is in terms of 'It is not the only possible conclusion that he is there' ('not-necessary'), rather than 'It is a possible conclusion that he is not there' ('possible-not'). Here there is a contrast between possibility that is asserted and necessity that is denied.

It is also possible to use *mustn't* where there is what Halliday (1970: 333) calls 'verbal crossing out', where a previous *must* is specifically denied. In this case it is the modality that is negated, not the proposition:

He must be there.—Oh no, he mustn't.

In a similar way *can* (not *may*) might be used to assert possibility, if it denies a previous *can't*:

It can't be there.—Oh yes, it can.

In view of this it would be wrong to overemphasize the logical equivalences. We often operate with them, and so do not distinguish between 'possible-not' and 'not-necessary' or 'necessary-not' and 'not-possible', but these distinctions can be, and sometimes are, made.

Halliday (1970: 333) concludes from the fact that we usually need only two forms for the four theoretical possibilities that there is 'no negative modality' (*ie* epistemic modality). He has a place, that is to say, only for 'possible-not' and 'necessary-not'. But this is not what the language suggests. If we are to reduce the four possibilities to two, we should reduce them to 'possible-not' (*may not*) and to 'not-possible' (*can't*), since it is the possibility modals that most regularly occur and there is seldom negation of modality or proposition with the necessity modals. It is epistemic possibility that is the more basic (*cf* Lyons 1977: 801).

[iii] There are no clear examples of epistemic *shouldn't*, though the following expressions are, perhaps, epistemic rather than dynamic:

That shouldn't be difficult. What do you want to know? (W.5.3.28)
Well, that shouldn't be hard. (S.8.2a.63)

It is the proposition that is negated – 'It would be reasonable to conclude that . . . not . . .'.

[iv] The past tentative forms *couldn't* and *mightn't* follow the same pattern as *can't* and *may not*, the former negating the modality and the latter the proposition. Examples are found with *have*:

Well, it couldn't have been in April, milord. (S.12.3.24)
It might not have been in April.

(There seems little doubt that here *couldn't have* is epistemic; its paraphrase is in terms of 'possible that' not 'possible for', but see 8.4).

[v] I noted no examples of *won't*, but there is a clear example of *wouldn't* (with *have* for past time of the proposition):

There would have been people living, but they wouldn't have been the same people. (S.5.2.46)

Here again it seems to be the proposition that is negated. The meaning is (roughly) 'It is a reasonable conclusion that they were not the same people'. However, there is not a very clear distinction here between negating the modality and negating the proposition. There is little difference between the paraphrase just suggested and 'It is not a reasonable conclusion that they were the same people'.

3.5.4 **Interrogation**

We seldom question epistemic modality, and there are no obvious examples
in the Survey other than those discussed below.

As we saw in 2.3.3 it is the form used in negation that is generally used in
interrogation. With epistemic possibility, therefore, we should expect to
find, and shall in fact find, that CAN is used:

Can they be on holiday?

There is an example in the Survey with *could have* in an indirect question:

I was wondering if it could have been fear? (S.3.5b.63)

The corresponding direct question is *Can it have been fear?*

With epistemic necessity, however, no obvious form is available because,
as we saw in 3.5.3, instead of using a form that negates the modality, we
normally use only the form that negates the proposition with possibility –
may not. This cannot, therefore, provide an interrogative form. In fact,
however, it seems that MUST, NEED, BE BOUND TO can all be used:

Must they be on holiday?
Need they be on holiday?
Are they bound to be on holiday?

For negative interrogation the modal that is used for the assertion will
occur. This is very obvious with tag questions.

. . . think there must be, mustn't there? (S.7.2l.9)

There is also one excellent example of a negative interrogative clearly
'expecting the answer "Yes"', implying the positive proposition. Although
it has been given already, I will repeat it:

I like to think about those days and how tough it was for the average
Englishman, what a hard life they must have had, and mustn't there be
endless stories about this mansion? (S.12.6.75)

3.5.5 **Voice**

Epistemic modals are voice-neutral. More strictly, sentences with epistemic
modals are voice-neutral, provided that the proposition itself is voice-
neutral. Thus there is voice-neutrality in:

John may have seen Mary.
(Mary may have been seen by John.)

There is none in:

John may want to see Mary.
(Mary may want to be seen by John.)

For in the first the proposition is 'John saw Mary' which is voice-neutral. In the second it is 'John wants to see Mary' which is not.

3.5.6 Adverbs

There are very few adverbs that may occur with epistemic modals (or even modals in general). They are confined mostly to those that themselves express judgments, and so occur largely pleonastically – *possibly, perhaps,* etc for possibility, and *surely, certainly,* etc for necessity, *eg:*

You may possibly prefer that one. (S.8.2a.57)
Here, perhaps, we may see the natural man. (W.4.2a.65)
It must surely be just a beautiful relic from the past. (W.1.5b.6)

Well, however, appears to be used rather differently with MAY:

Well, then, it may well be a back formation. (S.2.5a.62)
He wouldn't know exactly where it came down, but he might well have a rough idea. (W.5.3.107)

The function of *well* seems to be to strengthen the possibility, to say 'this is a perfectly reasonable suggestion'.

There is a similar use of *just* with almost an opposite meaning – to express a bare possibility:

One of the cylinders might just be missing a bit from the sound of it. (S.4.1.28)

Yet, in general, epistemic modals cannot be modified by adverbs, or at least the true modals cannot. Thus we find *almost* modifying BE BOUND TO (3.2.3), but not MUST, or SHOULD.

Chapter 4

Deontic modality

The dividing line between deontic modality and the other kinds is not as clear as that which distinguishes epistemic modality from the rest. Nevertheless, both syntax and semantics can be used to establish modal uses that have much in common and, therefore, justify the decision to recognize deontic modality as a specific kind.

We shall find once again that there are the two degrees of possibility and necessity. It proves quite easy to establish deontic possibility, marked by MAY and CAN; in particular the occurrence or potential occurrence of MAY will usually distinguish this kind of modality from the other non-epistemic kinds. Deontic necessity, however, is more problematic. The verb involved is MUST, but there is no clear line between its uses for deontic and neutral dynamic necessity. For this reason most of the discussion of MUST is left until Chapter 6. A third degree of modality is provided by SHALL.

4.1 Deontic and performative

It was suggested in 2.4.3 that von Wright's term 'deontic' should be used for terminological simplicity, although the earlier term 'discourse oriented', while clumsy, is more accurate and illuminating. For the kind of modality that we call deontic is basically performative. By uttering a modal a speaker may actually give permission (MAY, CAN), and make a promise or threat (SHALL) or lay an obligation (MUST).

If this is so, English does not draw the distinction between deontic and dynamic modality along the lines that von Wright suggests (1.1.2). It is not a matter directly of modes of obligation, but rather of what is discourse oriented or performative, versus the rest. This seems clear enough with regard to possibility and necessity in that:

[i] MAY, if not epistemic, is usually clearly performative; it gives permission. Unlike CAN it is not also used normally for dynamic possibility (5.1, but cf 8.5).

[ii] HAVE (GOT) TO specifically denies any involvement by the speaker, and is, therefore, never performative; MUST, on the other hand, may or may not

suggest his involvement (6.2). Although it is not always possible to distinguish between deontic and dynamic MUST, the fact that MUST may sometimes contrast with HAVE (GOT) TO provides some justification, although of a negative kind, for distinguishing deontic modality from dynamic.

A further argument for recognizing deontic modality is that it accounts for one use of SHALL; this functions both grammatically and syntactically (4.4) with MAY and MUST, and is clearly discourse oriented.

We may take the criterion of being performative as a starting-point for defining the deontic modals. In the assertive forms and in the negative forms, where it is the event that is negated (not the modality), a deontic modal will be performative; it will give permission, lay an obligation, or make a promise. Moreover, there will normally be no past tense forms, for by their nature performatives cannot be in the past; the act takes place at the moment of speaking.

However, we could extend the definition to include some uses that are not strictly performative, but nevertheless relate to the performative uses:

[i] The modals are used in interrogation, to ask permission, etc, (4.5.2). It was for this reason that I preferred the terms 'discourse orientation' and 'subject orientation'.
[ii] We could include SHOULD and OUGHT TO. With these the speaker takes responsibility for the judgment without actually involving himself in a performative action (4.6).
[iii] The modals are used for rules and regulations. These uses could be seen as reports of performative acts by people in authority, but they are also often not clearly distinct from dynamic modality. A discussion will be left until 8.1.

4.2 Possibility

Deontic possibility consists essentially in the giving of permission. But there is one curious 'extended' use of CAN and, to a lesser extent, of MAY, and a theoretical point about the status of CAN that must be considered.

4.2.1 Permission

There are only a few examples in the Survey of MAY and CAN being used in what is clearly the permission use:

If you want to recall the doctor, you may do so. (S.11.1.19)
Can I pinch a ciggie?—Course you can. Would you like a menthol or a plain? (S.2.11b.15)

'Of course you can inspect the nurseries. You have, of course, a Search Warrant from the Home Office.' (W.16.3.207-3)

Evidence from the Survey is insufficient to prove the difference between MAY and CAN (only one example of MAY was noted), but it seems clear that MAY is far more formal than CAN; in the MAY example above, the situation is that of a trial. This is supported by Ehrman (1966: 12) who noted that most of the occurrences of CAN for permission were in dialogue, *eg:*

Even though this is my rock you can use it sometimes.

Examples of MAY are usually from a very formal environment:

I should be obliged if you would make other arrangements for your daughters. You may stay here as long as you wish of course. (Ehrman 1966: 23)
She requested permission to leave at three. . . . He said drily 'You may go at that hour if your work is done.' (Lebrun 1965: 28)

Huddleston (1974: 228 *n* 8) notes that we can say *You may come with pleasure*. Although I do not accept his conclusion that this establishes an underlying subject *I* and a 'higher' verb, it clearly shows that the verb is performative (it is the speaker's pleasure).

4.2.2 Command

Curiously, CAN is often used to convey a command, often of a brusque or somewhat impolite kind:

Oh, you can leave me out, thank you very much. (S.6.2.60)
You needn't take this down and you can scrub that out of this. (S.6.4b.8)
I'm Dr Edgton now, so you can observe my new status. (S.8.3b.2)

Ehrman (1966:13) also has some good examples:

'I don't know what you're up to, but when Brenner—.' 'You can forget Brenner, too,' Curt said.
You can tell Kayabashi-san that the back road is in very good condition and will be quite safe.

Only slightly different is the idiomatic expression:

You can say that again. (S.4.2.40, W.5.2.95)

MAY also is used in such expressions as:

You may take it from me.
You may rest assured.

I noted no such examples of MAY in the Survey (but see Johannesson 1976: 88). This is clearly deontic (not epistemic) MAY, since CAN may also be used here (and is more likely in colloquial speech).

Although a separate section has been devoted to this use of CAN it is not to be seen simply as one of the meanings of that verb, but to be considered as an extended or implied meaning (cf 9.2). To give permission may, in a sarcastic way, be interpreted as requiring something to be done. Yet it is curious that there are some differences here between MAY and CAN.

However, this use of CAN and MAY is different from that of MUST. MUST has some implication of authority on which the speaker relies, or at least the implication that he can impose his authority. By contrast CAN and MAY merely make very confident, and in the case of CAN, sarcastic suggestions.

4.2.3 The status of CAN

We can take the argument about CAN further. It would even be possible to suggest that CAN is, in fact, never deontic in its basic meaning, that the only deontic possibility modal is MAY. On this view, CAN always expresses dynamic possibility, but to say what is possible is often to imply that the speaker will not object, ie that he gives permission.

There is one way of proving this right or wrong. The fact that CAN seems to be used in rules and regulations with, possibly, a different meaning from that of MAY (8.1), might support this view, but it is far from conclusive. In the end the decision has to be somewhat arbitrary and practical. Since it is clear that CAN is often used for permission and in colloquial speech is more likely than MAY, I shall continue to regard it as one of the deontic modals.

4.3 Necessity

There are plenty of occurrences of MUST in the Survey. Not all of them, however, are clearly deontic; many seem to be neutral or indeterminate and are discussed in 6.1. We shall simply note here those in which the speaker (or writer) clearly takes responsibility for the imposing of the necessity. The context makes this clear in:

> I've been telling Peter, as I've been telling several people, you know, 'You must get into permanent jobs', and I've been urging Peter to go back to school teaching or something, where he's very, very good. (S.3.2b.16)

Here the speaker reports what he is doing with URGE. Of course, a speaker may report what someone else deontically requires as in:

> The University is saying 'These people must be expelled if they disrupt lectures'. (S.11.2.59)
> A new insistence from President Nixon that the Hanoi government must negotiate if there's to be any settlement. (W.2.3b.13)

In the second of these MUST occurs in a subordinate clause, but the sense is the same – the speaker reports that Nixon deontically 'insists'. There are similar occurrences of MAY, SHALL and SHOULD (8.6). But there are other examples of deontic MUST, where the context itself is not helpful:

You must keep everything to yourself, be discreet. (W.5.2.53)

This is clearly a very firm piece of advice, almost an imperative.
It might seem odd that MUST is used for invitations:

Well, you must say what you want for a present. (S.2.10.25)
Oh, you must come round and see it. (S.2.7.50)

It is relevant that in both cases the subject is *you*. The important point here, however, is that deontic necessity usually implies that the speaker is in a position to lay the obligation, and is thus in a position of some authority; it would, therefore, not seem to be appropriate in invitations, in which the speaker should not appear to be giving orders or making demands, or in any way implying that he has the authority to ensure compliance. But it is, in fact, polite to be insistent in matters in which the person addressed is the beneficiary from the action; one can thus firmly insist (by using MUST) that he says what he wants for a present, or that he pays a visit (and equally it is polite not to be too keen to accept the proposal). There is nothing, therefore, very odd about the use of MUST here; it merely reflects a social convention (but see 9.2.4).

Must is often used in a rather weaker sense with a limited set of verbs all related to the act of conversation – *I must say* / *admit* / *be honest* / *ask you* / *reiterate* / *confess* / *concede* / *mention* and *you must remember* / *admit* / *realize* / *understand*, etc. With these there is still an element of discourse orientation; the speaker either imposes the obligation on himself and by so doing actually performs the act (*I must admit = I do admit*), or else asks his hearer to behave in a similar fashion. Examples of complete sentences are:

I must say, I've never known that. (S.2.10.16)
I think I must make a confession here. (S.6.4a.33)

There will be no further discussion or exemplification of MUST in this chapter. Most of the relevant issues are dealt with in Chapter 6.

4.4 SHALL

With SHALL the speaker gives an undertaking or guarantees that the event will take place. In a sense, SHALL is stronger than MUST, in that it does not merely lay an obligation, however strong, but actually guarantees that the action will occur. We can thus say:

You shall have it tomorrow.
He shall be there by six.

The only clear examples of SHALL in the Survey are in subordinate clauses (*cf* 8.6, where other examples are to be found):

It is a demand that the Civil Service shall once again return to those traditions of service which have made it so respected. (W.16.6.171-3)
I intend to see that . . ., where firearms are used, the maximum penalty shall be the maximum penalty available to the law. (W.2.3a.11)

Moreover, SHALL is the regular formulaic form in regulations:

The 1947 act shall have effect as if this section were included in Part III thereof. (W.14.1.54)

Jespersen (1909-49, IV: 270) makes a distinction between commands, promises and threats. But, except possibly in regulations, SHALL does not seem today to constitute a command of the kind found with *Thou shalt* . . . in the Ten Commandments, and whether there is a promise or a threat depends not on SHALL, but whether the guaranteed action is pleasant or not.

Deontic modals do not normally occur with *I* and *we* as their subject. With CAN and MAY it would be a little odd to give oneself permission to act. With MUST there seems to be clear discourse orientation only in the examples of 'weak' necessity, as in *I must say*, etc. With SHALL the position is complicated because *I/we shall* is regularly used for futurity (7.2), and it is often difficult, if not impossible, to decide in a given example whether the meaning is simply one of futurity or of an undertaking. There seems, however, to be a fairly clear element of deontic meaning in the following examples:

'I shall certainly apologize to the Chairman, Captain.' (W.16.4.53-3)
. . . and shall take whatever further steps are necessary even if they are unpopular in order to achieve the rate of progress that we need. (W.15.3b.6-1)

However, it could be argued that even here we have the futurity use of SHALL and that making statements about one's future actions can be taken as a promise – and that this is not peculiar to SHALL but would be no less true of BE GOING TO (see 7.3). In the following example the first use of SHALL looks like a promise, but in the second it does not; yet it would seem a little implausible to argue that they are different:

'We shall take care of the Indians. But we shall not let them obstruct the advance of progress.' (W.11.4c.9)

4.5 Grammar

There are some severe restrictions on the deontic modals. Indeed it is the grammar that marks deontic modality as a distinct kind.

4.5.1 Negation

Either the modality or the event may be negated; one can give permission, etc for an action not to take place or one can refuse permission, etc for it to take place.

Curiously, *may not* and *cannot* (*can't*) negate the modality, *ie* they refuse permission, while *must not* (*mustn't*) and *shall not* (*shan't*) negate the event, *ie* they lay an obligation or give an undertaking that the act will not take place. The situation is, then, fairly complex.

[i] To negate the modality with *may* and *can*, *ie* to refuse permission, the same modals are used. No examples were noted in the Survey, but it is perfectly possible to say:

You may not/cannot/can't leave now.

There is no regular way of negating the event, however, *ie* of giving permission not to act. An emphatic *nót* may suggest that permission is being refused in:

You may/can nót come.

But this is ambiguous. It might be taken as a very emphatic refusal, though the context may sometimes resolve the ambiguity as in:

You can come or you can nót come, as you wish.

[ii] To negate the modality for necessity, there is no appropriate form of MUST, but *needn't* may be used as in:

You needn't take this down. (S.6.4b.8)

But there is some doubt about the status of *needn't* (see [iv] later in this section, 6.3.1 and 6.5). *Mustn't* negates the event; it lays an obligation not to act:

Well, you mustn't write tutorial essays with exams in mind. (S.5.8.21)
You mustn't put words into my mouth. (S.5.3.49)
You mustn't take him too seriously, I mean. (S.7.2f.10)

However, *mustn't* may also be used in 'verbal crossing out' (see 3.5.3), *eg He must come—Oh no he mustn't*. Here, of course, the modality seems to be negated (or, better, the whole proposition is denied).
[iii] There is no way of negating modality with SHALL; we cannot, using SHALL, refuse to give an undertaking. Instead we must say something like *I don't promise . . ., I don't guarantee. . . .* The negative form *shan't* negates the event; it gives an undertaking that the event will not take place:

You shan't go there tomorrow.
He shan't come in.

[iv] There is a close semantic relationship between giving permission and laying obligation in relation to negation. We saw with epistemic modality (3.5.3) that 'not-possible' = 'necessary-not' and 'not-necessary' = 'possible-not'. This formula is not wholly applicable to deontic possibility and necessity, for, if we made the identification, the formulation would be:

Not-possible/necessary-not   *may not/can't, mustn't*
Not-necessary/possible-not   *needn't, may not/can't*

But there is an obvious difference between refusing permission (*may not/can't*) and laying an obligation not to (*mustn't*). With the former it is to be assumed that permission is normally required, while with the latter the speaker takes a positive step in preventing the action for which permission may not normally be required. *May not/can't* is not, therefore, the same as *mustn't*; Seuren (1969: 160) is mistaken in treating *mustn't* as the negative of ('universal') permission. It is not so certain, however, whether there is a clear distinction between permission not to act and no obligation; for a speaker would not normally state that there was no obligation or give permission not to, except in areas over which it was known that he had authority, and the meaning difference is far less obvious than with the other pair. It is no accident, therefore, that English has no normal unambiguous form for expressing permission not to act, as we noted in [i], and there is no overriding argument for saying that *needn't* expresses no obligation rather than permission not to act. Formally, it is no more like *not* + *must* than *may* + *not*, and may, it could be argued, serve for both. (I can see no good reason for dealing with *mustn't* in terms of (negative) permission and *needn't* in terms of (negative) necessity, as Seuren (1969: 160) does; if one may be deontic, so may the other. Nor do I understand how he relates the distinction between CAN and MAY to 'present possibility' and 'universal possibility'.)

4.5.2 Interrogation

The deontic modals may be used (non-performatively, of course) in interrogation to ask if the person addressed gives permission, lays an obligation, etc. With MAY, CAN and SHALL the situation is fairly simple. We have:

May/can I leave now?
Shall I receive it tomorrow?

(Either CAN or MAY may be used, as in the assertive form.) There are few really clear examples in the Survey (except in the conventional extended use discussed later). One is:

They're merely saying 'Can we have some kind of assembly in which we decide our own affairs?' (S.2.8a.27)

The negative interrogative forms (expecting the answer 'Yes') are simply:

May I not/can't I go now?
Shan't I have it tomorrow?

To ask a question about the negative proposition emphatic *nót* can be used:

Can/may I nót go now?
Shall I nót have it tomorrow?

With the necessity modals the situation is more complex. Since NEED is used to negate the modality, we might expect it to be used for interrogation:

Need I come tomorrow?

However, when NEED is used, there seems to be little or no discourse orientation. If it is to be understood that the person addressed has the power to impose the obligation, MUST (which normally negates the event, not the modality) is far more likely:

Must I come tomorrow?

The negative interrogatives are still more difficult, and a detailed discussion will be left until 6.3.2.

All of these forms are fairly rare. Much more commonly MAY, and to a lesser extent CAN, are used with what I shall call 'conventionally implied' meanings (for a full discussion see 9.2.2). Examples are:

May I leave my telephone number? (S.8.3e.15)
May I take you back to your broadcast, couple of weekends ago? (S.6.3.16)
Can I get you a drink? (W.5.3.68)
Can I ring you back? (S.8.10.4)

All of these may be interpreted as the asking of permission, but not in the sense that the hearer is in a position to withhold it. It is rather that permission is sought as a matter of courtesy. It would be unusual for permission to be denied, but it is polite to ask for it before acting.

Asking permission in this way may even carry the implication that the person addressed should himself act, in order that the relevant event may take place. A familiar example is:

May/can I have the salt please?

The person addressed is not expected simply to give permission; he is expected, rather, to take action to provide the salt. There is an interesting example in the Survey:

May I finish please? (S.5.6.24)

This is intended to make the person addressed stop interrupting, and so make it possible (not merely permissible) for the speaker to say what he wants to say. In this kind of request both CAN and MAY are common in speech, and MAY does not seem to belong to a more formal style (unless it is the case that we switch to a more formal style in making such requests). An implied request may also be introduced by *if* in:

> This is, if I may say so, begging the question. (S.5.3.42)
> ... if one may be serious again for one moment ... (S.5.4.69)
> I would like to come back again in the afternoon, if I may. (S.1.10.117)

There is a similar use of *shall*:

> Shall we have a cup of coffee? (S.1.8.1)
> Here's our coffee. Shall I pour? (W.5.2.96)
> Are you going to leave him a message or shall I say something? (S.1.8.34)

In all these the speaker asks the hearer if he wishes to act; he gives the hearer the responsibility for deciding that the act shall take place. But he is not interested simply in obtaining this as information; he is offering to act.

4.5.3 Past and future

Deontic modals can have no past tense forms for past time. Neither in the modality nor in the event can there be any indication of past time. One cannot in the act of speaking give permission, lay an obligation or give an undertaking in the past or in relation to past events. (But see 8.1.) Yet a past tense form may occur in reported speech (2.3.4 [i]). Thus we can form the following from examples in 4.2.1 and 4.4:

> He said that, if he wanted to call the doctor, he might do so.
> He said that I should have it the next day.

We shall see in 6.1 that MUST is often used in a neutral sense – and as such parallels CAN. But whereas CAN has the past tense form *could*, MUST has no past tense form. It is sometimes argued that there is a suppletive form *had to*, but this is obviously the past tense form of *have to*, and it is never used in a deontic (discourse oriented) sense (nor could it be!). This absence of a past tense form I take to be evidence that MUST is, or can be, deontic. (But for reported speech, see 6.3.3.)

For similar reasons there can be no future expression of deontic modality, although one can, of course, indicate that permission will be given, obligations will be laid or an undertaking made, by using main verbs, *I shall permit you* ..., *I shall require you* ..., *I promise you* ..., etc. The event is, however, always future; one can only give permission, etc for events to happen after the time of speaking. This too shows the relation between modality and futurity – *cf* 1.1.4 (Lyons 1977: 817).

4.5.4 Unreality

In theory it might be possible to give tentative permission, or to make a
tentative promise, but in practice tentative forms of the modals are not used
for this purpose. It is, however, possible to ask for permission with *might*
and *could* instead of *may* and *can*, the tentative forms being more diffident
or polite:

> Might I come in at the moment, on this, Chairman? (S.3.4.11)
> Well, could we go on to modern novels, then? (S.3.1a.42)

First it might be argued that SHOULD and OUGHT TO are unreal deontic
modals. In fact, I shall suggest that they are not deontic, but neutral dynamic
(4.6, 6.4). Secondly, there is a curious use of *might* that is discussed in 8.5
which could be regarded as an unreal use of deontic MAY.

4.5.5 Voice

In practice it seems that the deontic modals are voice-neutral. If one gives
permission, etc, for someone to perform an action, one equally gives
permission for the action to be performed. There are passive examples in
the Survey which bear this out:

> This, of course, must not be taken as a reason for drawing more cheques.
> (W.7.9.38)
> ... although the sale of these must not be delayed beyond the end of
> November. (W.7.9.37)

In these a bank manager is stating the bank's requirements to a customer.
Although contextually less probable, MAY or SHALL (either positive or
negative) could have appeared in these sentences.

There is, however, a problem. It is not clear whether in fact there is voice-
neutrality in:

> John may/shall/must meet Mary.
> Mary may/shall/must be met by John.

The issue is, of course, whether or not the permission is granted to, the
obligation laid upon, or the undertaking given to, the subject. If I permit
John to meet Mary (using the verb PERMIT), I do not necessarily permit
Mary to meet John. Certainly if I compel John to meet Mary, I do not
compel Mary to be met by John.

The passive examples quoted above are not entirely conclusive, because
the agent is not specified. It is not certain that we could, for instance,
passivize so readily:

> You must not take this. ...
> This must not be taken by you. ...

Passivization, that is to say, is much easier when the agent is not stated, and this we shall see is true of other modals too.

4.6 SHOULD and OUGHT TO

If we were to accept that subject involvement rather than being performative is the essential characteristic of deontic modality (4.1), SHOULD and OUGHT TO would be included.

Lakoff (1972b: 240) argues that speaker involvement, or its absence, is shown in these pairs:

MUST : HAVE TO
MAY : BE ALLOWED TO
WILL : IS TO
SHOULD : BE SUPPOSED TO

Her examples for the first two are:

My girl must/has to be home by midnight.
Bill may/is allowed to have a choice.

The arguments in this book suggest that the distinction between these two pairs is more than subject involvement; the situation is more complicated. Nevertheless the point is, as far as it goes, a fair one. (The distinction between WILL and IS TO, however, seems to be rather different and will, for the moment, be ignored (but see 7.4).) But it seems reasonable to suggest that the distinction that holds between MUST and HAVE TO also holds between SHOULD and BE SUPPOSED TO (although Bouma (1975: 324) questions this).

It would not, then, be entirely unreasonable to treat SHOULD and OUGHT TO as deontic, provided that we extend 'deontic' to include not simply performative uses, but all those where the speaker takes responsibility.

However, this distinction seems to be far less important than the distinction that is so clearly made by MUST and HAVE (GOT) TO, and in comparison with HAVE (GOT) TO, BE SUPPOSED TO is quite rare. For this reason OUGHT TO and SHOULD will be treated with dynamic necessity (6.4), though they sometimes have highly deontic characteristics.

4.7 HAD BETTER

Formally, HAD BETTER is modal – with no third person -s form, no to, and a negative hadn't better or had better not (see 1.2). Semantically it seems to be deontic in the loose sense in which SHOULD and OUGHT TO might be so considered. The speaker advises the hearer of his best course of action, and is fairly firm about his advice with the implication that unpleasant consequences may follow if it is not taken, as in:

You'd better ask him when he comes in. (S.1.8.41)
I'd better take that down again. (S.8.3b.15)

However, it is by no means clear that the speaker is in any way taking responsibility. It would seem rather that he is more concerned with hinting at the consequences. If so, this is not deontic modality, but neutral dynamic, like HAVE (GOT) TO.

Syntactically, however, HAD BETTER is like the deontic modals in that it has no past tense forms. The nearest paraphrase in the past is *It would have been better for* . . ., with the modality indicated by the conditional *would have* rather than a modal. The negative form *hadn't better*, moreover, like *mustn't*, negates the event not the modality; it advises non-action. HAD BETTER also seems to be voice-neutral. For these reasons it seems to be a deontic modal.

It will be seen that, in the assertive form, it normally only occurs with the weak form indicated by *'d*. But the non-assertive forms show that the first part is *had*, not *would*. Yet, curiously, it patterns, in some ways, with *'d rather* (7.8), where *'d* is to be seen as *would*.

Chapter 5

Dynamic possibility

It was suggested in 2.4.3 that there are two subkinds of dynamic modality, neutral (or circumstantial) and subject oriented, and we shall see in Chapter 6 that the distinction is important within dynamic necessity (though in a negative way) to account for the difference between MUST and HAVE (GOT) TO.

There are also two verbs for dynamic possibility, CAN and BE ABLE TO, but the distinction between neutral and subject oriented possibility is not directly related to the difference between the uses of these two. Although many grammars of English refer to 'ability' (which is essentially subject oriented possibility), this does not characterize either CAN or BE ABLE TO as distinct from the other. Indeed, we shall see that they do not differ very markedly at all, although there are a number of factors involved in their relative likelihood of occurrence.

5.1 CAN

We must first see whether we can distinguish a neutral/circumstantial use and a subject oriented use of CAN, but we shall also find that there is an 'extended', 'implicative' use (5.3 cf 9.2) and a special use with 'private' verbs (5.4).

5.1.1 Neutral

There are plenty of examples in the Survey of the use of CAN in a sense of neutral possibility, simply to indicate that an event is possible:

Signs are the only things you can observe. (S.2.9.123)
Who knows? It can go either way. (S10.3.35)

The first says 'Signs alone are observable', while the second refers to future alternative possibility.

This neutral sense is even clearer in examples where the subject is the impersonal *you* or the sentence is in the passive:

You can get quite lost in that, I think, you see. (S1.8.62)

I know the place. You can get all sorts of things here. (S.1.7.91)

You can actually use diagnostic skills. (S.2.9.67)

I've spotted . . . a solecism, but it can easily be rubbed out. (S.8.3h.25)

Well, I'll see what can be done and give you a ring. (S.8.3b.16)

In all these examples the appropriate paraphrase is 'It is possible for . . .', and not '. . . has the ability to . . .'.

There is a very common association of CAN with adjectives and adverbs in comparative or superlative forms or modified by *eg: how:*

. . . buying the most substantial property you can buy. (S.8.2a.18)

I mean, you can travel from Belgium to France with much less palaver than you can travel from the North to the South of Ireland. (S.2.8a.5)

It is really a matter of how quickly can we get the surveyor to move. (S.8.1a.10)

These represent judgments about the degree or extent that an action is possible; clearly this too is dynamic possibility. The description 'circumstantial possibility' is more appropriate if there is a clear indication of the circumstances in which an event is possible:

You can only get the job if you don't want it. (S.2.5a.10)

The only way you can learn it is to think logically. (S.2.9.40)

For Ehrman (1966: 12) the basic meaning of CAN is that 'there is no obstruction to the action of the lexical verb', or 'nil obstat' (1966: 22).

But I am not sure that anything is to be gained by providing this negative definition rather than the positive definition of 'possibility'. She has one very clear example:

'You *can* get *something*' Nadine would snap. 'You *can* get a job working in a grocery store if nothing else.'

In this sense CAN is often modified by *always,* with the meaning 'There is always the possibility that . . .' to suggest that the possibility is timeless, not just present:

You can always say it's just not your style. (S.1.8.31)

Well, if you get the sack, you can always come and work for me. (W.5.1a.36)

5.1.2 Ability

It is often said that CAN may refer to the ability of the subject (Ehrman 1966: 13, Palmer 1974: 115). Yet there are only a few examples in the Survey where ability seems clearly indicated:

I feel that . . . my destiny's very much in my control and that I can make
or break my life and myself. (S.6.4a.68)
They can't speak a word of English, of course, not a word, but, you know,
they can say what they like. (S.4.3.120)
He's one of the senior referees in the league, fairly strict disciplinarian,
can handle games of this nature. (S.10.2.60)

We should not, however, define subject orientation simply and strictly in
terms of ability. Only animate creatures may have ability, but subject
orientation is possible with inanimates, where it indicates that they have the
necessary qualities or 'power' to cause the event to take place. I noted no
clear example of CAN in the Survey, though there is one for BE ABLE TO (5.2).
But there is a good example in Ehrman (1966: 13):

Religion can summate, epitomize, relate, and conserve all highest ideals
and values.

As she says, can here implies positive qualities of religion.
It is by no means always possible to distinguish between mere possibility
and ability, ie between neutral and subject oriented possibility. It is not at
all clear whether, in the following examples, there is or is not an indication
of the ability of the subject to perform the action:

One thing you want to avoid, if you possibly can, is a present from my
mother. (S.2.10.34)
The people who cannot very easily raise their wages. (S.12.2.8)

Does the first refer to the ability of the person to take avoiding action, or
merely to the general possibility? In the second (which is negative – see
5.3.1) the use of the relative might suggest at first that we are talking about
people with the ability to act, but the meaning surely is more like '. . . for
whom it is not possible . . .'.

5.1.3 Implication

CAN is often used not simply to say what one can do or what is possible, but
actually to suggest, by implication, that action will, or should, be taken. We
can distinguish four different types of this use:

[i] It is regularly used with I or with exclusive we ('I and he', 'I and they',
etc) to make an offer by the speaker or speakers:

I can tell you the reference, if that's any help, of the letter. (S.8.3l.4)
Yes, we can send you a map, if you wish. (S.8.3i.2)

[ii] It may also be used with the third person pronouns where the speaker
speaks on behalf of someone else, but leaves it vague whether the initiative
comes from him or not:

I'll send Lewis down tonight to see what he can pick up in the pubs of Port St Mary and then he can call to see you. (W.5.3.66)

[iii] With a second person pronoun it suggests that action be taken by the person addressed:

You can certainly give me a ring back this afternoon – there might be something. (S.8.1a.23)

[iv] If *we* is used inclusively ('you and I', 'you and we') it combines offer and suggestion:

Do come early and we can have a drink. (S.7.3d.3)

5.1.4 Private verbs

CAN regularly occurs with the so-called 'private' verbs (Hill 1958: 207, quoting Joos).

[i] It occurs with SEE and other verbs of sensation where there is little indication of ability, *eg*:

I can see the moon.

This differs little from *I see the moon*. This cannot, I think, be explained in terms of anything that has already been said. For we can distinguish this use of CAN from both its subject oriented and its neutral use even when occurring with SEE, *eg*:

He has marvellous eyes; he can see the tiniest detail.
From the top you can see the whole of the city.

With neither of these examples is it possible to replace *can see* with *see*; the first indicates ability, the second possibility.

Similarly (to anticipate 5.3.3) we can distinguish between:

I couldn't see the moon.
I didn't see the moon.

The sense of possibility or ability is clear in the first, and absent from the second of these.

Johannesson (1976: 46–8) points out that sensation is an involuntary event and suggests that, if the circumstances are such that one can see, then one actually sees. But this does not seem to account for the fact that a distinction can be made between being able to see and actually seeing; nor does it really explain why CAN should be used when there is no intention at all of referring to the ability.

It is worth adding here that this use of CAN cannot be explained in terms of actuality, which we shall be discussing in 5.2[iv] and 5.3.3, *ie* the fact that in some circumstances a possibility verb implies that the event took place.

For as we shall see (see also some comments in 1.1.3 and 2.3.2), the position is that, if there is an implication of actuality, BE ABLE TO is preferred to CAN in the present tense and is almost obligatory in the past. If the question of actuality were involved, we should expect not CAN but BE ABLE TO; indeed it is the case that *I was able to see* implies that I saw. This does not, then, explain why CAN is used. It is an idiomatic use, one that has no further explanation.

[ii] CAN commonly occurs with many other verbs (most of them private verbs) such as UNDERSTAND, REMEMBER, THINK, AFFORD, STAND, BEAR, FACE, BE BOTHERED, etc, *eg:*

> He has the greatest difficulty with drugs because he can never really believe that when somebody takes a drug it's actually going to do anything, anywhere, at all. (S.2.9.83)
> How much competition can I stand from now on? (S.2.9.56)
> What you can remember in two weeks is the thing that matters. (S.2.9.52)

Here, however, there seems to be some sense of ability or possibility. SEE also occurs with the meaning not of 'observe', but of 'imagine' or 'understand':

> Can you see Cynthia stewing in a garret? (W.5.2.109)
> Yes, you must be doing that, I can see that. (S.3.6.21)

Many examples of this type occur in question or negative forms.

5.2 BE ABLE TO

BE ABLE TO also expresses possibility. Our chief task is to see how it differs semantically from CAN.

It might seem reasonable to assume that BE ABLE TO always indicates ability and that, as such, it is always subject oriented. Not only, then, could we say that, if BE ABLE TO occurs, we have subject oriented possibility, but we could also argue that, if CAN occurs, it is subject oriented whenever it can be replaced by BE ABLE TO without any change of meaning. In actual fact, this turns out not to be entirely true.

There are, indeed, examples in the Survey where BE ABLE TO fairly clearly indicates ability:

> Yet at the same time, when it comes to personal things, to family things, you're able to be very detached. (S.6.4a.75)
> And yet you're able to look at the future of it in this very objective way without making a value judgment. (S.6.4a.73)

In both of these examples we are concerned with the ability of the subject to behave in a certain way, not with the mere possibility of such behaviour. There is one example in which *able* is collocated with *willing*, and I take this to be a collocation of BE ABLE TO and BE WILLING TO, which may seem to be related to WILL and is itself always subject oriented (7.6):

> . . . a subtle, complex business needing hard and long thought, which few of us are able or willing to give. (W.11.4b.4)

However, as with CAN, we should not define subject orientation in terms of a strict interpretation of ability. The following example is quite clearly subject oriented (but see 5.3.2 for the past tense):

> In the past, we've had small seminars in our rooms and these were obviously not able to contain them. (S.3.4.5)

BE ABLE TO here is subject oriented in that it relates to the nature of the rooms and the fact that their small size prevented their use. We had a similar example with CAN (5.1.2).

In contrast with this there are examples of BE ABLE TO being used in a neutral sense:

> I feel that the way we operate is one where people who are well read and experienced in modern literature are also able to direct themselves into modern drama. (S.2.6.19)
>
> . . . because they are applying the disciplines already to the illumination of a particular, a practical, problem rather than a purely theoretical one, that they are able to become better communicators on that, on these issues. (S.5.7.50)

In these examples the nearest paraphrases are in terms of '. . . is possible for . . .', rather than '. . . have the ability to . . .'. Moreover, this is essentially 'circumstantial' possibility, for the circumstances under which the event is possible are stated. It would also be possible to replace CAN by BE ABLE TO in every one of the examples in the previous section, with little or no change of meaning. This would suggest that BE ABLE TO is no more subject oriented than CAN.

What, then, are the conditions that favour the use of BE ABLE TO rather than CAN? There are certainly four, and possibly five (and there are further points to be made when we discuss the past (5.3.3) and the future (5.3.4)).

[i] Since CAN has no non-finite forms, only BE ABLE TO is available after other modal verbs or any of the catenatives. There are numerous examples in the Survey of *might be able to, should be able to, has got to be able to, must be able to*, etc.

[ii] BE ABLE TO is not used in any of the 'special' uses of CAN, either in an implicative use (5.1.3), or regularly with private verbs. This is not, of course, to say that BE ABLE TO can never be used with some kind of implication, or that it never occurs with private verbs. It is simply that it does not have the same function as CAN in these circumstances, but can always be accounted for in terms of the more 'normal' uses discussed in 5.1.1 and 5.1.2.

[iii] BE ABLE TO is a little more formal than CAN, as is shown by the fact that the proportion of occurrences of BE ABLE TO to occurrences of CAN is much greater in the written texts than in the spoken. Indeed, in many of the written examples in which BE ABLE TO occurs, CAN would probably have occurred if the text had been a spoken one, *eg:*

> ... is no guarantee that he is able to criticize whatever it is that he himself accepts. (W.9.3.9-1)
> I tell you that this is so, that you may make arrangements elsewhere if you are able to. (W.7.9.37)

But there are not different rules for writing and speech; there is merely a greater tendency to use BE ABLE TO in one and CAN in the other.

[iv] BE ABLE TO is often used in the present tense to indicate 'actuality' (see 9.1). It suggests, that is to say, not merely that the subject can perform the action, but also that he does, *eg:*

> By bulk buying in specific items, Lasky's are able to cut prices on packages by as much as 30 per cent or so. (W.15.4c.13)
> In this way we are able to carry out research and not simply to undertake consulting. (S.6.1c.12)
> Now what we mean by a mathematical symbol is a set of mathematical equations and relationships. We are able, therefore, in mathematical terms, to find the optimum solution. (S.6.1c.26)

CAN would not be impossible in these examples, but BE ABLE TO is preferred because of the implications of actuality.

Rather curiously, if the present positive form *can* is used there may be indication of actuality, but in the future rather than the present (see 5.3.4). That is to say, while *is able to* says 'can and does', *can* says 'can and will do'.

By contrast the negative form is often used to imply that the event does not take place:

> Sorry to keep you waiting. I can't find Mrs Cummings at the moment. (S.8.3h.1)
> ... because he's been hitting him with everything in the book and still he cannot keep this man away. (S.10.3.97)

The use of BE ABLE TO to indicate (simultaneous) actuality is closely related to its use in the past, for there, if there is indication of the actuality of a single event, in most circumstances only BE ABLE TO is permissible and CAN cannot be used; *could* is not used to mean 'could and did' (see 5.3.3). But whereas this is a fairly firm restriction in the past tense, there is merely a tendency for BE ABLE TO to occur in the present.

[v] There is a final point, which may, in part, contradict what was said at the beginning of this section. There is one example in the Survey that I found very odd:

Therefore agricultural planning must be flexible and decentralized in order that the localized condition is able to grow the crops and facilitate the growth of the appropriate economy. (W.6.3c.12)

I, myself, find this example unacceptable and would replace *is able to* by *can*. Why? Part of the reason may be that this is a subordinate clause in which a true modal is more appropriate (*cf* 8.6), but it may also be that there is at least some truth in the view that BE ABLE TO is more subject oriented than CAN. The position is, perhaps, that BE ABLE TO is less acceptable if the subject is such that it really could not have the ability (or qualities) to perform the action. The occurrence of BE ABLE TO does not, that is to say, necessarily indicate subject orientation, *ie* that the ability was exercised, but it is unlikely to occur unless a subject oriented interpretation is, theoretically at least, possible.

Even when BE ABLE TO seems to be needed to provide non-finite forms, as discussed in [i], there is not complete freedom of occurrence. If we find *the localized condition is able to grow* unacceptable, we should equally find *the localized condition should be able to grow* unacceptable, and would prefer *it should be possible for the localized condition to grow*. Similarly, if we dislike *It is able to be cured* and would prefer *It can be cured*, we shall equally dislike *It must be able to be cured,* even though the syntax rules out a form of CAN, and would probably say instead *It must be possible for it to be cured*. Strictly, then, BE ABLE TO does not provide the suppletive forms of CAN – it cannot always be used in environments in which CAN would have occurred but for syntactic restrictions.

5.3 Grammar

The grammar of dynamic possibility is complex.

5.3.1 Negation

Negation is itself no problem, though there are some issues of negation combined with past tense that will be discussed in detail in the next section.

Normally only the modality is negated, by formally negating the modal. CAN has the negative forms *can't* (*cannot*) and *couldn't* (*could not*). With BE ABLE TO, either BE is negated or UNABLE is used in place of ABLE:

You cannot treat of disease unless you know the causes. (S.5.6.46)
National pressure groups cannot exist without full time staffs and a regular income. (W.11.5.45)
I can't judge distance at all. (S.2.5b.40)
She couldn't be left alone. She couldn't do anything. She couldn't sleep, eat – anything. (S.6.2.84)

... a standing order in favour of Bonis Avibus Ltd to which I am unable to give effect at the time of writing. (W.7.9.7)
... the fact that they weren't able to gratify it. (S.12.3.54)

The third is clearly subject oriented. The rest seem to be neutral.
    It is, perhaps, possible to negate the event by using emphatic *nót*:

We can/can't nót go.
We are able/aren't able/are unable nót to go.

Such forms are a little more natural with *always, just, simply*:

We can always/just/simply nót go.

The tag to this is *can't we? (We can always nót go, can't we?)*. This suggests that formally, as well as semantically, the modal is positive (see 2.3.3[iii]).

5.3.2 Interrogation

It is, naturally, perfectly possible to ask questions about dynamic possibility, and both CAN and BE ABLE TO occur in interrogative forms.
    The commonest interrogative use, however, is that of CAN with conventional implication (9.2) to request an action:

Can you just remind me? (S.2.6.109)
Can you push it up to eleven nine fifty? (S.8.1p.11)
Can you tell me what it's in connection with, Doctor Edgton? (S.8.1p.1)
Can you hold on? (S.8.3k.2)
Here, June, can you give me a hand with this harness? (W.5.3.98)

Can't is a normal negative interrogative:

Can't we drop the subject, if you don't mind? (W.5.2.31)

This (expecting the answer 'Yes') implies that we can, and therefore that we should.

5.3.3 Past

Only the modality can be marked for past tense; there is no independent past tense marking of the event. For we can refer either to present or to past possibility or ability, but not to the present possibility or ability to do something in the past or to past possibility or ability to do something in the present. The first is ruled out on the grounds that the past cannot be affected by the present (unless we have a time machine); the second is theoretically possible, but is unlikely. We should not normally say *Yesterday I could do it today,* for if the event takes place the possibility is present, and there is no need of the past time reference, while, if it does not, the past possibility is falsified; yet one can imagine situations in which such a sentence might be appropriate, *eg* where the conditions were right in the past, but changed subsequently – the possibility was there, but then lost.

What is important, however, is that, in general, the positive past tense form of CAN is not used in assertion if there is the implication of actuality, *ie* if it is implied that the event took place. In contrast, however, the negative form *couldn't* will always imply that the event did not take place, and BE ABLE TO may be used in past tense positive forms with the implication of actuality. We may thus compare:

> *I ran fast, and could catch the bus.
> I ran fast, but couldn't catch the bus.
> I ran fast, and was able to catch the bus.

Whether or not this can be explained in any systematic way is discussed in 9.1.

There are numerous examples of BE ABLE TO in past tense forms with the implication of actuality:

> I was able to lead this chap on into directions that I knew about, you know. (S.2.9.12)
> Most people worked harder than me during the University of course, and when it came to the exams, were able to not just draw upon two weeks of knowledge. They were able to draw upon three years of knowledge. (S.2.9.52)
> The only advantages were that I was able to finish reading R. S. Bentley's play 'The Burning Bush' and listen to one or two radio items. (W.8.3a.1)
> He and Professor Andrew Huxley working together were able to establish the actual nature of the excitation process which occurs at each point in a nerve. (W.4.2a.18)

Could would not have been appropriate in any of these examples.

However, the situation is not as simple as the three 'catching the bus' examples would suggest, and we will, therefore, look in some detail at the conditions under which forms of CAN may be used for past time reference (its use for unreality is a different matter, see 5.3.5).

[i] *Could* may be used if there is no implication of actuality, but only a statement of possibility (including ability). Examples are rare, but there is one in Ehrman (1966: 50):

> I was plenty scared. In the state she was in she could actually kill.

Could is possible here because there is no implication of actuality; indeed the implication is rather that there is no actuality, that she could but she did not.

[ii] If there is an indication not of a single action, but of successive or

habitual actions, *could* may be used, even if there is an implication that these actions took place:

> Yet my father could usually lay hands on what he wanted. It all seemed to have a purpose. (W.1.3b.20)
> I could get up and go to the kitchen whenever I wanted to. (S.2.7.57)
> It meant that everybody could learn to play billiards and to make sure that everybody was keen he and his sons used to arrange a competition. (S.12.6.60)
> Until recently, however, it could be dismissed with a simple explanation: long-haired men were, actually or unconsciously, homosexuals. (W.11.2a.2)

None of these refer to single actions; reference is, instead, to repeated or habitual actions. Yet there is an implication that the events took place – I did go to the kitchen, they did learn to play billiards, etc. It may be that *could* is permissible in such circumstances because there was a general possibility over a period of time, not a possibility that resulted in a single definable action.

[iii] There are no restrictions on *couldn't* or on *could* with any of the negative forms (2.3.2[ii]):

> I didn't go in a mask. I couldn't with a child that small. (S.1.8.98)
> Your mother was out and couldn't leave the key. (S.2.13.29)
> When Mr Fortune retired the butler could not live without the boss. (S.12.6.63)
> Why was Chetwynd Road so cheap? Ah, that! There's an answer to that. No one could get a mortgage on it. (S.4.2.21)

[iv] *Could* occurs where there is a meaning of 'nothing but', even though there is formally no negative present:

> One moment I seem to be everything to him, and then all he could think of was this child. (W.5.2.61)
> The crowd of 50,000 could only leave the ground shaking their heads in silent disbelief. (W.12.5f.3)

The semantics is clearly more important here than formal negative marking.
[v] *Could* may also occur in semi-negative or 'affective' contexts (2.3.2), *eg* with *hardly*:

> He was laughing so much, he could hardly get a word out. (S.11.3c.5)
> Fulham's extreme expedience of first flooring Banks could hardly escape Mr Walters. (W.12.5g.3)

Little is also one of the words that provide an affective context:

> There was very little they could think of that you could do with chemistry. (S.1.12.17)

The second example with *hardly* can be accounted for in terms of what has already been said, for the implication is that the event did not take place – Fulham's behaviour did not escape the referee's notice. But in the other examples there is an implication that the event took place – the subject did manage to 'get a word out', they did 'think of something' (but not much). What is relevant is both that there is a negative-type word in the context and that the implication is that, even if the event took place, it almost did not.

[vi] Related to this is the fact that *could* is possible in such sentences as:

> I could almost reach the branch.
> I could nearly reach the branch.
> I could just reach the branch.
> I could reach the branch because it was loaded down.

With *almost* and *nearly* the implication is that the event did not take place, and *could* might then be expected. But *could* also occurs with *just* where the implication is that I succeeded in reaching the branch; but like *hardly, just* suggests that the event almost did not take place. With the last example there is again a clear implication of actuality, but with the reservation that the event took place only because of unusual circumstances.

What all of these have in common is that the possibility is in some way qualified, or that there is a suggestion that the event almost did not take place, or that it took place in a minimal way. There appears thus to be a focus of attention on the modality, whereas in the examples where *could* would not be used the focus of attention is more on the actuality itself. But it must be admitted that the following are rather unlikely to occur (except in a habitual sense):

> ? I ran fast and I could just/almost/nearly catch the bus.
> ? I could catch the bus because I ran fast.

The reason is that catching a bus is a momentary activity and there is no continuing possibility of this action. By contrast, one can be in a position to reach a branch or enter a house for some time. It seems that the occurrence of *could* with *just, nearly, hardly, because* . . . etc depends upon the nature of the event and on the duration of the possibility. It is where *could* is closest to *did* that it becomes most unacceptable.

[vii] Where CAN is used with verbs of sensation or other private verbs (5.1.4) the past tense form *could* is quite normal:

> I could see the moon.
> I could understand all he said.
> As he leaned on the ropes I could hear the ropes and the ring creak. (S.10.3.23)

[viii] More difficult to explain is:

> Jane darling, I'm so glad you could make it. (W.5.2.61)

Here there is a clear implication of actuality; the host, presumably, is saying that he is glad that the guest has arrived. But it is relevant that this does not have past time reference. The reference is rather that of the present perfect, that 'you have made it and are here now'. Subordinate contexts of this kind seem to be appropriate for other modals. *Should,* for instance, may occur in (8.6):

I'm glad he should think so.

The time marking here is not past but present and *should* is, in effect, redundant.

Yet BE ABLE TO may occur in exactly the same kind of context:

Oh, Mr Mayor, we are so glad you and the Mayoress were able to come. (W.1.5a.4)

[ix] It is also possible to say:

I said I could make it and I could.

It would be odd, in contrast, to say:

I said I could make it and I was able to.

The first *could* is accounted for by the sequence of tenses rule. The second seems to echo and so confirm the first, whereas *was able to* would not. This is, perhaps, 'verbal confirmation', the converse of 'verbal crossing-out' (3.5.3, 4.5.1).

[x] There is one further example in the Survey that deserves some comment:

Why couldn't the British have carried out their commitment that the border was a temporary measure, as was said at the time? (S.2.8a.48)

The meaning here is 'Why were the British not able to . . .'. Yet *couldn't . . . have* would seem to mean 'would not have been able to' (see 5.3.5). *Have* is, then, redundant here and actually suggests the wrong meaning. But there is, perhaps, an explanation for it. *Couldn't* alone could be interpreted as a conditional too, but in the present – 'Why would not the British be able to . . .?'. It is possible, then, that *couldn't have* was used to avoid this ambiguity. This, of course, created a new ambiguity, but one that may be less important.

5.3.4 Future

With future time reference the position is less clear, but it seems that neutral and subject oriented modality function slightly differently.

[i] With neutral possibility the present tense form *can* may be used to refer to future events, provided the possibility can be seen as present, *ie* that it is possible for something to occur and that it will or may occur in the future:

What time can you get away? (W.5.3.59)

I'll go to France any time you like as long as I can get a good job there. (S.2.10.3)

Well, who knows? It can go either way. (S.10.3.35)

Of course, the modals are often used in a general 'timeless' present sense, and this extends not only into the present but also into the future. Most of the uses of *can* in 5.1.1 are of this kind.

But the modality itself may be marked as future by WILL/SHALL BE ABLE TO. This is normal if there has already been explicit reference to a specific future time:

When you're in your eighties you'll be able to say 'I had to do Anglo-Saxon for three years'. (S.3.3.71)

WILL/SHALL BE ABLE TO is also likely where there is an implicit reference to the future – where the future scene has been set – and where the future is envisaged (see 7.2.3):

I will describe the scene and you'll be able to hear these recorded descriptions. (S.10.7b.11)

I mean, there'll be his mother and grandad so we won't be able to do anything exciting. (S.4.3.72)

I expect to leave on 3rd October, and whether I shall be able to write en route seems dubious. (W.7.2.13)

They envisage a future when juvenile courts will be able to sentence children to different types of vocational treatment. (W.2.3b.22)

More commonly, WILL/SHALL BE ABLE TO occurs where there is an explicit or implicit future condition (see 7.2.2):

... and he'll be able to save an awful lot of money, I should think, by living there. (S.7.3f.65)

You'll be able to stay living in the same place you're living now. (S.2.5a.25)

Now you'll be able to have them to tea at Number Ten. (S.6.3.73B)

You won't be able to reach me at the office today. (S.8.1a.22)

The presence of a future time indication does not in itself mean that *will be able to* has to be used. Provided the possibility is timeless, *can* may relate to a specifically future event. A very striking example is:

The next time you can take the exam is in April. Otherwise she'll have to wait till – is it September? I'm not sure. (S.7.2l.6)

Can is used because we are concerned with the general possibility of taking exams, but linking it to the occasion in next April; it is thus relevant that the subject is the impersonal *you*. In clear contrast the second sentence has *will have to*, which functions like *will be able to*, except that it refers to necessity rather than possibility (while MUST is like CAN (6.3.4)). The use of this clearly marked future time form is due to the fact that a specific future condition is being indicated, by *otherwise, ie* if the exam is not taken in April. This sentence, moreover, has the specific *she* for a subject, not the impersonal *you*.

Nevertheless, in many cases it would be difficult to decide whether *can* or *will be able to* is the more appropriate. When we are concerned with future events, it is often possible to regard the possibility as either present or future. In some of the examples we have considered, *can* could replace *will be able to* with very little change of meaning.

BE GOING TO may also occur with *be able to,* but much less commonly, with the implication that there is 'current orientation' (7.3.2):

I think, all you people with cars are going to find that you're not going to be able to run them, you know. (S.8.2a.35)
You know, Jeannie, we're not going to be able to live in this place for long. (S.4.2.30)

[ii] With subject oriented possibility, however, the distinction between present ability and future ability is more obvious. It would, therefore, be inappropriate to say:

He can run a mile in four minutes next year.

This cannot refer to ability, though it could refer to neutral possibility, *eg* because next year the stadium will be ready. For ability *will be able to* is required. Of course, with the sense of neutral possibility, *will be able to* is also possible, but it is not obligatory.

Nevertheless, it is possible to use *can* in the present tense to refer to future events, if the meaning is that there is ability now which may be actualized in the future:

John can sink the next putt.
Liverpool can win the cup next year.

John and Liverpool have the ability now, but they will perform the action resulting from that at a later time. For a detailed discussion see Honoré (1964: 463) and Palmer (1977: 3–5).

The conditions on the use of BE ABLE TO that were mentioned for present time reference (5.2) apply equally for future. In particular, it is much more common in written texts and it will not normally occur if a subject oriented interpretation is quite impossible. This latter point accounts for the following example:

In spite of knowing this, I still secretly feel that schools situated in special places cannot be normal for many years. (W.1.5b.3)

There are two reasons why we might, *prima facie,* expect not *cannot*, but *will not be able to,* first, that the possibility is obviously future and, secondly, that this is from a written text. But BE ABLE TO is not used because a subject oriented interpretation would simply not be possible. Nothing (and no one) can have the ability to be normal; rather we are concerned with conditions in which it is possible for them to be normal. CAN is thus preferred, and is used even though it has to be in the present tense, while referring to future events.

5.3.5 Unreality

Could and *couldn't* commonly occur not to indicate past time, but to suggest unreality, usually in what can be seen as an incomplete conditional ('. . . if I wanted to', '. . . if things were otherwise'):

> I couldn't do anything like that you see, I mean, I couldn't paint an ordinary sort of portrait. (S.1.8.83)
> I know I could be average, but I couldn't be very good and I could never do anything new. (S.2.9.81)
> A Gannet could land and take off easily enough in half the runway. (W.5.3.37)

In all these it would be possible to paraphrase with *would/wouldn't be able to.* There are, in fact, plenty of examples of *would/wouldn't be able to,* but with little difference of meaning:

> There are season tickets, but you wouldn't be able to commute. (S.3.2a.28)
> Would Professor Worth be able to sign some cheques this afternoon? (S.8.1m.2)
> We would be able to have a more rational allocation of resources. (S.11.2.68)

Similarly, *could/couldn't have* occurs for past unreality:

> I could not have guessed it was poetry. (S.3.5a.4)
> I could not have done better. (S.2.9.49)
> No one could have foreseen how long father's illness was going to go on. (W.5.2.107)
> I couldn't have agreed more. (S.11.2.55)

In all these there is, perhaps, an implication that things would not have been different whatever the circumstances (if I'd worked harder, if we'd given serious thought, etc). But there are some serious theoretical problems concerning *could* and *could have* and these we will leave until *would* and *would have* have been discussed (7.5.4).

It is by no means certain, however, that all occurrences of *could* are to be treated as conditional. Past tense forms of the modals (especially the epistemic modals) are often no more than tentative ('It is tentatively possible', etc). With CAN this is particularly true of the uses with conventional implication, both assertive (to offer suggestions) and interrogative (to make requests) *eg:*

> If there's any news I could reach you at your office or at your husband's. (S.8.1a.21)
> Alternatively I could ask you to ring the lady concerned direct. (S.8.3e.16)
> Could you tell me the name of the person concerned? (S.8.3k.8)
> Could we go on to modern novels then? (S.3.1a.42)

In none of these are the paraphrases 'would be possible' or 'would be able' really appropriate. Rather *could* functions exactly like *can,* but is more tentative and, in the interrogative, more polite. There is a similar use of *would* (7.4.5).

The difficulty of accounting for *could* is highlighted by the following example:

> Everything they said could be quite true and yet it could still remain a good book. (S.5.9.100)

Are the two instances of *could* the same? They might both refer to what is tentatively possible. But it seems more reasonable to say that the first alone is purely tentative (and might even be epistemic rather than dynamic, see 8.4), whereas the second is conditional *ie,* conditional on the truth of the previous sentence – it could still be a good book even if what was said was true.

5.3.6 Voice

The semantics would suggest that neutral dynamic modals ought to be voice-neutral and that subject oriented ones ought not. If it is possible for Bill to beat John, it is possible for John to be beaten by Bill, but it is not reasonable to suggest that, if Bill has the ability to beat him, John has the ability to be beaten. With WILL, in fact, it is clear that the subject oriented modal is not voice-neutral (7.4.6). But the actual situation is not as simple as this.

[i] Neutral CAN is certainly voice-neutral, as is illustrated by many passive forms such as:

> It can easily be rubbed out. (S.8.3h.25)
> Well, I'll see what can be done. (S.8.3b.16)
> . . . and it can be cured by taking those little tablets of glucose which give you energy. (S.11.3g.2)

[ii] The situation with subject oriented CAN is more debatable. Consider:

> John can't lift that weight.

The passive seems unlikely;

> ? That weight can't be lifted by John.

Yet much more acceptable are:

> That weight can't be lifted by anyone.
> That weight can't be lifted by one man.

This can be explained by the fact that ability is not strictly isolable from the circumstances in which that ability is exercised. To say that someone can do something must include the assumption that there are circumstances in which the act can be done; ability is not something that is totally isolable from circumstances. Indeed, if John can lift a weight, that weight can (in a 'power' sense) be lifted by John. In theory, then, one should not be surprised if a subject oriented possibility modal is voice-neutral. In practice, what happens is that if there is reference to the person who has the ability (as the subject of the active sentence), passivization will not be normal. There is, however, no restriction on the occurrence of a passive sentence where there is no reference to a specific person with the ability, *eg* in an agentless passive or a passive with an indefinite agent (see 5.2[v] and 9.3.1).

[iii] No examples of BE ABLE TO with a passive verb were noted. If we replace CAN by BE ABLE TO in the examples in [i] the results are awkward and barely acceptable:

> ? It's easily able to be rubbed out.
> ?? I'll see what's able to be done.
> ? It's able to be cured by taking those little tablets of glucose.

One reason why these are less acceptable is that a subject oriented interpretation is not theoretically possible or is very unlikely, especially in the second, even if we interpret subject orientation in terms of qualities rather than ability (see 5.2[v]).

5.3.7 BE ABLE TO summary

We are now in a position to summarize the conditions under which BE ABLE TO will be used rather than CAN.

[i] It alone can occur in the non-finite forms, but will still be restricted by other considerations (5.2).
[ii] It will not occur with the implicative function of CAN, or regularly with private verbs (5.2).
[iii] It is much more common in writing than in speech (5.2).
[iv] In present tense forms it will often indicate present actuality (but future actuality is indicated by *can*) (5.2).
[v] In past tense forms it is obligatory if there is an indication of the actuality of a single event (5.3.2).

[vi] It will not normally occur where a subject oriented interpretation would not be possible (this does not mean that it will, in fact, necessarily have a subject oriented interpretation) (5.2).

[vii] A distinction can be drawn between present possibility with reference to the future and future possibility. The latter requires BE ABLE TO with WILL (5.3.4).

[viii] BE ABLE TO rarely occurs with passive forms (5.3.5).

5.4. DARE

There is both a modal verb DARE and a non-modal 'main' verb. They can be distinguished formally in that the latter has non-finite forms, has an -s form, and generally (but not always) occurs with to, while the modal has the 'NICE' properties (1.2) of occurring with negation and interrogation (but not in code or emphatic affirmation). The two verbs can contrast only, then, in the non-assertive contexts of negation and interrogation:

John daren't come./John doesn't dare to come.
Dare John come?/Does John dare to come?
(No one dare come./No one dares to come.)

Examples are:

They're large bits I'm sternly leaving alone, like all the film side – daren't go near it because I shall get all absorbed and interested and I've got a man to do that. (S.1.10.141)
She doesn't dare to tell him that it's really only an insurance policy, if she can't get a decent job in industry. (W.7.1.23)
That is, if you've read it, which I hardly dare to hope. (W16.5.26-2)
They said 'Oh no, no, we wouldn't dare play with you, you know.' (S.11.3d.8)
When I could dare have a little talk. (S.9.1g.1)

The first two are clearly modal and non-modal (negative forms) respectively. The third is an example of the non-modal in a semi-negative context; the modal without to, would have been possible. The last two examples illustrate non-finite forms of non-modal DARE without to.

The meaning of DARE is roughly 'have the courage to', in a rather weak sense since it often relates to actions that do not need much courage.

The modal, however, often has a semi-conditional meaning so that daren't in the first example is closer to wouldn't dare than to doesn't dare. Similarly, the past form daren't have differs from didn't dare in being closer to wouldn't have dared. This is similar to the function of NEED (6.5) and to the 'conditional' uses of SHOULD and OUGHT TO (6.4). It is an indication of the 'modal' nature of the modal as compared with the full verb. It is, however, also possible to use daren't as a past time form:

I wanted to go, but I daren't.

Here there is no suggestion of conditionality – *daren't* is more like *didn't dare* than *daren't have*.

Semantically DARE is obviously subject oriented. We should, therefore, not expect it to be voice-neutral. Yet Ehrman (1966: 71) has:

These two aspects of death cannot be successfully separated, but they dare not be confused or identified.

Pullum and Wilson (1977: 785) similarly note:

Inflation is a problem which dare not be neglected.

In both cases there is no agent – and we have seen similar examples with another modal (5.3.6, *cf* 9.3.1).

Chapter 6

Dynamic necessity

We have already considered MUST as a discourse oriented dynamic modal. But, as we noted, it is often completely neutral, with simply the meaning 'It is necessary for . . .', and there is no clear dividing line between the two meanings. One task, therefore, is to illustrate this indeterminacy. We must also consider HAVE TO and HAVE GOT TO, which I refer to jointly as HAVE (GOT) TO; these never express discourse oriented necessity, but neutral or 'circumstantial' necessity.

6.1 MUST

We saw in 4.3 that MUST is sometimes used where there is deontic (discourse oriented) modality. Yet it often occurs where, in assertion, there is little or no indication of the involvement of the speaker:

> Now I lunched the day before yesterday with one of the leaders of the Labour Party whose name must obviously be kept quiet – I can't repeat it. (S.5.5.35)
> If the ratepayers should be consulted, so too must the council tenants. (W.11.5.32)

There are also examples in which the subject is either *I* or *we*, and it is fairly clear that the meaning is simply 'It is necessary for me/us to . . .'. Generally speaking we do not lay obligations upon ourselves:

> I have no doubt that I must do what I can to protect the wife. (S.12.4b.38)
> Yes, I must ask for that Monday off. (S.7.3f.50)
> We must have it out and use it once or twice. (S.2.10.33)

A more striking example is an interrogative (6.4.2):

> 'Why must I put up with such enraging conditions? Why must the deaf person? Why should our intercourse be baulked like this?' (W.15.2c.98-2)

There is also one negative form (see 6.3.1) introduced by *I think* – the speaker is merely expressing an opinion about what is necessary, not imposing the obligation:

> I think we mustn't worry about this too much. (S.1.1.9)

Further examples of this neutral MUST may be found in 6.2.3, where MUST is compared with HAVE (GOT) TO (with no obvious difference of meaning).

6.2 HAVE (GOT) TO

There are four issues to be considered, first, whether there is any difference between HAVE TO and HAVE GOT TO; secondly, what is the meaning of these verbs; thirdly, how they differ from MUST; and finally, whether in fact the deontic/dynamic distinction is a valid one.

6.2.1 HAVE TO and HAVE GOT TO

There are three points of difference:

[i] HAVE TO is more formal; HAVE GOT TO belongs to a more colloquial style and generally appears only in the spoken texts.
[ii] HAVE GOT TO has no non-finite forms. There is no *will have got to, *to have got to, *having got to. Instead the forms of HAVE TO must be used.
[iii] HAVE GOT TO is much rarer in the past tense, and may differ in meaning from HAVE TO, in that only the latter usually implies actuality (see 6.3.3).

6.2.2 The meaning of HAVE (GOT) TO

Often the meaning simply is that of 'circumstances compel' – external necessity, eg:

> I've got to be at London airport at fourish. (S.3.2b.21)
> There's a whole lot of literature you've got to read. (S.3.3.75)
> 'Oh, well, he's got to go into hospital you know.' (S.1.8.103)
> You have to file a flight plan before you start, give an estimated time of arrival, stick to certain heights, routines and landing drills. (W.5.3.10)
> Will you say to him that I can't come to a meeting next Wednesday because I have to go to a Cambridge examiners' meeting? (S.8.3g.3)

There is one example in which the meaning is clearly shown by a paraphrase:

> They're obliged to pass in various ways; they've got to pass our section of it. (S.3.6.15)

Obliged to suggests that there is some external compulsion and that this is the meaning of the modal.

The sense of external compulsion is sometimes fairly strong. It could be argued that to account for HAVE (GOT) TO we need not only subject oriented and neutral necessity, but also 'external' necessity (but see 6.2.3 and 6.3.6).

6.2.3 HAVE (GOT) TO **and** MUST

In contrasting HAVE (GOT) TO with MUST there are three main points to be made:

[i] There are some contexts in which these verbs are interchangeable and seem not to differ at all in meaning, but it is very difficult to make intuitive decisions about this. In every example in this section MUST could replace HAVE GOT TO (though it would seem a little odder in the context of BE OBLIGED TO), but it is not clear whether the meaning would be really different. One can, of course, insist that with MUST the speaker is in some way involved, even though his involvement may be minimal, but that can hardly be proved. Fortunately, there are two pairs of examples in the Survey where MUST and HAVE GOT TO occur in very similar environments and this justifies the belief that in some circumstances no distinction can be drawn between them, *ie* that there may be some complete overlap in the area of neutral necessity. The first pair both contain *otherwise,* which suggests that the necessity arises from the unpleasant results of not carrying out the action. There is no obvious subject involvement here:

> I must have an immigrant's visa. Otherwise they're likely to kick me out you see. (S.1.5.71)
> I've really got to know when completion date is likely. Otherwise I might find myself on the streets. (S.8.1a.9)

The second pair both refer to instructions about boats. But they are general instructions, and the speaker is in no way personally involved:

> When this happens you will see the boat's speed fall off and you must pay off just a little. (W.10.2.60-3)
> It's on the end of that safety line. All you've got to do is haul in. (W.5.3.111)

These strongly suggest that speaker involvement is not always indicated by MUST in contrast with HAVE (GOT) TO. On the other hand, MUST would not be used where it is clear that there is external necessity. We could, in fact, draw a distinction between three kinds of necessity: deontic (subject oriented), neutral and external, and say that MUST may be either deontic or neutral and HAVE (GOT) TO either neutral or external; negatively, HAVE (GOT) TO is never deontic, MUST never external.

[ii] In the present tense HAVE TO and HAVE GOT TO imply actuality, while MUST does not. This accounts for the use of HAVE GOT TO in the following example where MUST could not be used:

> It's a slow walk down. He's got to fight his way through the crowds. (S.10.3.3)

This refers to a boxer actually in the process of fighting his way through. If

MUST had been used it could only refer to the future, to the necessity in the future to fight his way through; HAVE GOT TO indicates that he is actually doing so. (For actuality in the past see 6.3.3.)

[iii] Since MUST, like the other modals, has no non-finite forms, only HAVE TO can be used where a non-finite form is required, *eg* after another modal or similar form:

> 'It's too late now to put him into an isolation hospital. I would have had to do that a few days ago.' (S.1.8.103).
> Mr Lumsden is going to have to take two mortgages out. (S.8.3h.12)

It is not only MUST that has no finite forms however – neither does HAVE GOT TO (6.2.1). Only HAVE TO can be used in such circumstances.

For rather different accounts of the distinction between MUST and HAVE (GOT) TO see Bouma (1975: 324–6) and Larkin (1969). If, however, Bouma is correct in saying that in his dialect the difference is stylistic and that MUST is rarely used except in writing and formal speech, this is very different from the situation in the Survey (where MUST commonly occurs in colloquial speech) and may represent a difference in British and American usage.

6.3 Grammar

We again have the familiar grammatical issues.

6.3.1 Negation

We have already noted *mustn't* and *needn't* in the relevant section on deontic modality (4.5.1). For neutral dynamic modality their functions are the same:

[i] The negative forms of the relevant modals, with *-n't* or following *not* or in conjunction with any negative word, negate the event and express an obligation not to act:

> I think we mustn't worry too much about this. (S.1.1.9)
> Well, one just mustn't mind. (S.2.5b.14)
> 'Nothing must be altered in the college until this grand plan has developed.' (S.3.4.82)
> There is no argument for saying that in a particular locality nobody must have lived here who earns more than twenty pounds a week. (S.5.1.26)

However, *mustn't* may be used, as in 4.5.1[ii], where there is 'verbal crossing-out'. It is also possible, with negative words and appropriate stress, to deny the whole sentence *eg:*

> No one múst go.
> You never múst do it.

(*Never* must, however, precede the modal for the meaning to be signalled.)

In this it is not the event that is negated, nor strictly the modality, but the whole sentence (in a context where it has already been asserted or implied). [ii] There are no forms of MUST that negate the modality (deny the obligation). Instead forms of NEED are used (but see 6.5 for the status of NEED):

> I don't think we need worry about that any more now. (S.2.6.43)
> The politics of the party machine does not and need not concern them. (W.11.5.28)

(The first example needs some explanation. This is a sentence with 'negative raising', where it is THINK that is formally negated, although the negation clearly belongs semantically to the subordinate clause. *I don't think that . . .* is to be interpreted as *I think that . . . not . . ..*)

It is interesting to contrast the first example above with the first example in [i]. Both are introduced by *I think . . .*, which clearly shows that they are merely expressions of opinion, obligation-performatives, but one negates the event (necessary-not), the other the modality (not-necessary).

[iii] The negative forms of HAVE TO and HAVE GOT TO are also available, but there are two restrictions. First, although HAVE GOT TO has the negative forms *has/have/hadn't got to,* the negatives of HAVE TO are formed with DO – *does/do/didn't have to:*

> They haven't got to juggle about. They've got the total page copy. (S.3.2c.26)
> The chap doesn't necessarily have to take them away with him, does he? (S.8.1m.2)
> She went in the afternoon and . . . she didn't have to queue all that long. (S.2.7.106)

Secondly, the negative form normally negates the modality. The above forms all mean 'not necessary for . . .'. Only very occasionally are the negative forms used to negate the event; *You don't have to do that* can (rarely) mean 'You mustn't do that'.

[iv] The last point raises once again the relation between possibility and necessity in terms of negation. We saw in 4.5.1 that it might be possible for *needn't* to be interpreted in terms of 'possible-not', as well as 'not-necessary' in discourse oriented modality. If we consider neutral modality in the same way we have:

> Not-possible/necessary-not—*can't, mustn't*
> Not-necessary/possible-not—*needn't, don't have to/haven't got to.*

In fact, however, we can make a distinction between *can't* and *mustn't.* There is a difference between:

He can't get a job.
He mustn't get a job.

Even in a purely circumstantial sense, to say that it is not possible for him to get a job is not always the same as saying that it is necessary for him not to. In practice *can't* will normally suggest that the circumstances are unfavourable; *mustn't* will suggest that they are such that if the action took place the results would be undesirable (though emphatic *can't* may also have this meaning).

There is, however, a problem about the means of expressing 'necessary-not' in the past; perhaps the 'not-possible' form has to be used (see 6.4.3).

6.3.2 Interrogation

Problems with interrogation arise only when the negative form does not negate the modality. If it negates the modality, the same modal is used for interrogation. There is thus no difficulty with HAVE (GOT) TO. The necessity is questioned by *eg Have you got to? Do you have to?* We may similarly see NEED as providing the forms that correspond to those of MUST:

> . . . and they both have refused. Need I say more? (S.5.6.6)

It is, however, possible for MUST to be used, but in a context in which it has already been suggested or implied that there is a necessity. It will often, for this reason, be deontic rather than neutral, *eg:*

> Must I go?

This is 'Is it the case that it is necessary . . .?' rather than merely 'Is it necessary . . .?' and is not unlike *mustn't* with 'verbal crossing-out' (4.5.1[ii], 6.3.1).

There is also a distinction with negative interrogation between *mustn't* and *needn't*. In general, negative interrogatives 'expect the answer "Yes"' and this is the obvious interpretation of *Mustn't John come with us?* However, it could also be taken as a positive question about the negative *John mustn't come with us*. We can paraphrase the two possibilities as:

[i] Isn't it the case that John must come with us?
[ii] Is it the case that John mustn't come with us?

Needn't may also be used interrogatively, but only in the second of these senses, *ie* to question the negative *needn't*. Thus *Needn't John come with us?* has the paraphrase:

[iii] Is it the case that John needn't come with us?

With *mustn't* and *needn't* there are, then, three possibilities and we can set these out in a diagrammatic form, if we allow that not only the modality and the event, but also the question itself, may be negative as well as positive:

QUESTION	MODALITY	EVENT	
Neg	Pos	Pos	*mustn't*
Pos	Neg	Pos	*needn't*
Pos	Pos	Neg	*mustn't*

The corresponding forms of HAVE (GOT) TO have the same meanings as those of MUST, *eg:*

Don't I have to come?
Haven't I got to come?

The most likely meaning is that of the normal negative interrogative – 'Is it not the case that I have (got) to come?'. But since the negative forms may, sometimes, negate the modality, it is possible for these interrogatives also to mean (but less commonly) 'Is it the case that I haven't (got) to (=mustn't) come?'.

6.3.3 Past

We have already noted that MUST has no past tense forms (4.5.3). With neutral necessity, however, HAVE TO and HAVE GOT TO are available. In practice the form most commonly used is that of HAVE TO (*ie: had to*). There are numerous examples of this in the Survey, *eg:*

We had to make a special trip down to Epsom to collect the bloody thing. (S.2.13.28)
Colin the shotgun, the one who had to get married. (S.1.13.33)
Oh no! We had to go one better. (S.2.10.172)

With *had to* there is undoubtedly an implication of actuality; the event took place. This is particularly noticeable in the last example, which can almost be paraphrased 'We went one better, as we naturally would'. By contrast if *had got to* had been used there would be simply the meaning 'It was necessary . . .' without the implication that the event took place, *eg:*

We'd got to make a special trip down to Epsom anyway, so it did not matter very much.

But I noted no clear examples of this in the Survey.

Because the negative of HAVE (GOT) TO usually negates the modality and MUST has no past tense forms, there is no obvious, simple way of expressing 'necessary-not' in the past. Only on rare occasions, and only if the context made it clear, would *didn't have to* or (perhaps, more likely) *hadn't got to* have the meaning 'It was necessary for . . . not . . .', *eg:*

He gave the children their presents in early December, but they didn't have/hadn't got to open them until Christmas day.

There is no reason, of course, for suggesting that *had to* and *had got to* are the past tense suppletive forms of MUST, as *went* is of GO. They are simply the past tense forms of HAVE TO and HAVE GOT TO. Moreover, we can see why MUST has no past tense forms. Deontic MUST needs no past tense forms because deontic modals are normally performative, and although MUST may also be used dynamically, it does not differ in that use from HAVE (GOT) TO. The only clear distinction between MUST and HAVE (GOT) TO is, therefore, in the present. There is, then, no need of a past tense form of MUST; whenever such a form might have been used, a form of HAVE (GOT) TO is available.

In reported speech, however, where past tense forms are needed by the sequence of tenses rules, and not to indicate the past time of the event, the difference between MUST and HAVE (GOT) TO needs to be, and is, retained by using *must* as if it were a past tense form:

> You must go. → She said he must go.
> You have to go. → She said he had to go.

But it by no means follows that *must* used for past time relevance is always clearly deontic. Examples of *must* in reported speech are:

> The shock that they had at the end of the war to realize what they'd done and they realized they must never do it again. (S.5.2.13)
> She felt she must apologize to Goodrich for 'our suburban home'. (W.16.5.19-4)

There is an example in the Survey with HAVE GOT TO:

> I think he always desperately thought that he'd got to project himself all the time. (S.2.7.80)

6.3.4 Future

Like other modals, and neutral CAN in particular, the present tense form *must* will often refer to the necessity of future events:

> . . . and we must do something about it. (S.8.1d.7)
> I must have all your news. How long have you been over here, and how's that fabulous husband of yours? (W.5.2.15)

Indeed *must* seems more often to refer to future than to present events as the examples in 6.1 illustrate.

However, MUST seems rather less likely in such conditions than CAN (see 5.3.4); WILL/SHALL HAVE TO (but not *WILL/SHALL HAVE GOT TO – see 6.2.2) will usually occur if there is any suggestion at all that the necessity is future or conditionally future:

> Yes, we'll have to go out, if you're really going to do it, darling. (S.1.11b.48)

Well, I'll have to think about it. (S.8.3g.3)
I shall have to go into total silence for half an hour. (S.2.10.73)
Well, I mean, you'll have to pay more to the likes of me to arrange it, I
think. (S.2.8b.33)
Anyway, I'll have to put it forward to them. (S.8.1d.10)

We noted a striking example in 5.3.4:

The next time you can take the exam is in April. Otherwise she'll have to
wait till – is it September? I'm not sure. (S.7.21.6)

The contrast between *can* and *'ll have to* here reflects the difference between
a general possibility and a conditional necessity.

But it is by no means certain that there will always be a difference of
meaning between forms with and without WILL/SHALL. Compare:

Yes, I've got to be at London airport at fourish. (S.3.2b.21)
Yes, I'll have to be back at the airport at six. (W.5.3.59)

There are a few examples of BE GOING TO plus HAVE TO where there is
some 'current orientation' (7.3.2) or complete lack of any conditionality
(7.3.3):

How long do they reckon we're going to have to wait to find out if the
mortgage advance is forthcoming? (S.8.1a.15)
. . . because they're going to have to do it in their jobs anyway, aren't
they? (S.1.10.83)

What difference of meaning there is between these and the examples with
WILL lies chiefly in the non-conditionality of BE GOING TO (7.3.3).

6.3.5 Voice

Intuitively, all neutral necessity forms seem to be voice-neutral as in:

The men have to/must do it.
It has to/must be done by the men.

Curiously, however, only a few passives were noted with any of the verbs:

A lot of work has got to be done on it. (S.3.4.75)
I believe that if we're going to avoid great climactic experiences and hold-
ups of industry, as such industries fall behind, it's got to be done on the
basis of voluntary collective bargaining. (S.6.3.64)
If they talk about unemployment they say 'The unemployed, they should
be made to do some work and not scrounge off the State'. (S.2.11b.48)
I think that ought to be got under way as soon as possible really. (S.8.3f.3)

6.4 SHOULD and OUGHT TO

It is not at all clear that (except in subordinate clauses – see 8.6) English makes any distinction between SHOULD and OUGHT TO. They seem to be largely interchangeable, even with tag questions, since there is nothing odd about:

He ought to come tomorrow, shouldn't he?

The only point to arise from the Survey is that SHOULD is more common than OUGHT TO.

6.4.1 Status of the forms

In a previous study (Palmer 1974: 120–2) I suggested that MUST is always discourse oriented (*ie* deontic) while SHOULD and OUGHT TO are subject oriented. This was based on two considerations. First, MUST has no past tense forms, while SHOULD and OUGHT TO have the forms *should have* and *ought to have,* and discourse oriented modals, by definition, do not have past tense forms. Secondly, MUST does not allow for the non-event while SHOULD and OUGHT TO do:

*He must come, but he won't.
He should/ought to come, but he won't.

This I now believe to be incorrect. For first, it has been argued here that MUST is not always deontic but may also be neutral dynamic, and the absence of past tense forms with MUST may simply be due to the fact that its deontic function is basic, in the sense that it determines what forms are available (6.3.3). Secondly, there is no clear evidence that SHOULD and OUGHT TO are subject oriented. If they are not deontic, they are neutral dynamic.

Indeed, it seems reasonable to base the distinction between MUST and SHOULD/OUGHT TO on the question whether or not there is an implication that the event took place, *ie* on actuality. Let us look, then, at SHOULD and OUGHT TO in that light.

[i] Often there is actually an implication that the event does not or did not take place, an implication of non-actuality:

If you can't afford to, then you should drop your sights down and buy a flat or maisonette. (S.8.2a.16)
I ought to be ashamed to say so, but I can't. (S.8.3e.5)

It is significant, too, that both occur commonly with a comparative adverb or adjective:

You should read, my dear, more. You don't read enough, my darling. (S.2.10.47)

I think people ought to be better informed about what marriage entails. (S.5.10.24)
You really ought to be buying something a bit more modern and a bit more expensive. (S.8.2a.15)

The implication is, of course, that the subject failed to reach the standards suggested.
[ii] Often, however, OUGHT TO and SHOULD are quite neutral in their implication of actuality (especially where there is reference to future events):

That won't happen again, so I should enjoy it very much. (S.2.10.120)
This should be done before the pollen is ripe. (W.10.3.28)
So perhaps I ought to ask you some further questions. (S.3.6.80)

[iii] In one example there is a suggestion that the event is actualized, but, even so, the speaker does not fully commit himself to that implication, as he would have done with *has to*:

Well it ought to be, at that price. (S.1.7.34)

The forms *should have* and *ought to have* nearly always imply that the event did not take place:

. . . and I should have started on the first of October. (S.1.5.71)
We ought to have done so much this year and we haven't done it, you know. (S.1.5.42)
. . . and the young man who should have been boxing in the arena tonight. (S.10.3.11)

This is in striking contrast with *had to* which generally implies that the event did, in fact, take place.
These forms I earlier (Palmer 1974: 126) treated as the past tense forms of SHOULD and OUGHT TO, with the implication that it is the modality that is referred to as being past. Yet one might imagine, from the form itself, in parallel with similar forms for the epistemic modals, that *have* indicates the pastness of the event. This, however, would make little semantic sense; there can be no obligation, duty, necessity in the present to perform acts in the past.
In fact, the behaviour of *should/ought to* and *should have/ought to have* exactly parallels that of *could* and *could have*. As was noted briefly in 2.3.5, and will be discussed in much more detail in 7.5, the essential characteristics of the latter forms are:

[i] They are the unreal conditional forms of CAN, present and past respectively.
[ii] Semantically unreality often relates not to the modality, but to the event. Thus, *could* often means not 'would be able' but 'is able and would', while *could have* often means 'was able and would have'.

These, then, are the unreal forms of the possibility modal. It is not implausible to argue that *ought/should* and *ought to have/should have* are the parallel forms of the necessity modal. This is in essence the proposal made by Anderson (1971: 79). It explains why SHOULD and OUGHT TO usually imply that the event does not or did not take place (for that is a characteristic of unreality), and why the past time form is formed with *have* (it is not a simple matter of past modality).

The parallelism between the possibility and necessity modals can be expressed by the very rough paraphrases:

could	'is possible and would happen'
could have	'was possible and would have happened'
should/ought to	'is "necessary" and would happen'
should have/ought to have	'was "necessary" and would have happened'

However, although these paraphrases work well for CAN, they are not accurate for SHOULD and OUGHT TO. They have the merit of showing that it is the event, and not the modality, that is unreal, but they suggest wrongly that the modality is real – and that it is or was necessary for the event to take place. Yet, clearly, this cannot be so if the event is unreal, because 'necessity' would usually imply actuality, that the event did, does or will take place, while the unreality of the event would imply that it did, does or will not. (There is, however, no similar problem with possibility.) With SHOULD and OUGHT TO, then, the 'necessity' must be weaker; it must be potential or tentative. But what is important is that the event is unreal.

With CAN, the modality can be unreal, so that *could* and *could have* may mean 'It would be/have been possible'. This is never so with SHOULD and OUGHT TO. They do not ever mean 'would be "necessary"' or 'would have been "necessary"'; these meanings are expressed by *would have to* and *would have had to* (7.5.6).

We cannot say that *should/ought, should have/ought to have* are the unreal forms of any particular modal, although semantically they must be related to MUST in the way that *could* and *could have* are related to CAN.

It is possible to use these modals with an explicit condition as in:

Perhaps if things had been different, this is what I should have done at first because, of course, it would have been so much easier. (S.3.1a.18)

Here the 'necessity' itself is conditional upon the protasis – 'It would have been tentatively "necessary"', and English has no formal way of making this distinction (*I would have should). (The sentence is potentially ambiguous –with *should have* here simply equivalent to *would have,* but I do not think that was what was intended.)

6.4.2 Grammar

The negative forms *oughtn't to* and *shouldn't* negate the event, just as *mustn't* does – there is a necessity not to act. But it is the (negative) event that is unreal, with the implication that it did, in fact, take place:

> They were being very critical on the level on which they were talking, but they shouldn't have been talking on a more general level. (S.5.9.101)
> That chap from Playden should never have spoken at all. (S.2.8b.41)

The rough paraphrases are, then:

shouldn't/oughtn't to	'is "necessary-not" and would not happen'.
shouldn't have/oughtn't to have	'was "necessary-not" and would not have happened.'

To negate the modality, there is no obvious form. NEED may, perhaps, supply the forms but, as we have seen, it seems also to be the verb used to correspond to MUST. (But see 6.5)

Interrogatives can, of course, question only the modality. The negative forms are normally used either in their normal negative interrogative function or as tags:

> Ought it not to be possible, therefore, for all reasonable men and women in Northern Ireland to accept the reality of today? (W.4.1d.9)
> Yes, because that ought to strengthen your hand, I would have thought, oughtn't it? (S.1.1.22)

However, like *mustn't*, *oughtn't to* and *shouldn't* can also be used for questions about the negative. Thus *Shouldn't John come?* may mean 'Is it the case that John shouldn't come?' as well as 'Isn't it the case that John should come?'

There is one problem example where it may be that the negative is semantically redundant:

> This raises very seriously the question of whether this oughtn't to be 128 or 192 pages in extent. (S.3.2c.34)

At first sight this seems to be an indirect question related to the direct question *Oughtn't this to be 128 or 192 pages in extent?* The issue would be whether either of these lengths would be preferable to some other. But it is more likely that what is being asked is which of these two lengths is the better, *ie* the sentence is related to *Ought this to be 128 or 192 pages in extent?* If so, the negative is redundant and misleading. But there are similar redundant (and often misleading) negatives in such expressions as *I shouldn't be surprised if he doesn't come* where the expectation is that he will come.

Like MUST, SHOULD and OUGHT TO often refer to future events:

> Some people are beginning to talk already, that we should abolish the whole conception of a postgraduate on a grant and we should have the whole lot made research assistants. (S.11.2.20)

6.5 NEED

NEED is in most respects formally very like DARE. There is a modal and a non-modal, distinguished formally in that only the latter has non-finite forms, an -s form and occurs with to, while the modal has the 'NICE' properties (1.2) except, once again, that it will not normally occur in code or emphatic affirmation. The two verbs, again, can contrast only in non-assertive contexts (see 5.4). Examples are:

> I may need to stay a couple of nights at Minna before I can find transport for the last 60 miles or so. (W.7.2.33)
> Although she's obviously highly qualified, her field isn't one that I think we need go for. (S.2.6.121)

The first is a clear example of the main verb. In the last the absence of to suggests that this is the modal, and although there is no negation in the clause, there is a negative in a higher clause which might account for the occurrence of a modal.

As we have seen (6.3.1, 6.3.2) NEED often seems to supply the forms for negating necessity modality and for questioning it (in contrast with MUST). However, it could also be argued that NEED is similarly related to the 'conditional' forms SHOULD and OUGHT TO (6.4). Certainly the past form needn't have has much in common with shouldn't have and oughtn't to have. Not only is it formally similar (with have), but it has similar implications of actuality. For both usually imply that the event did take place. A clear example of needn't have is:

> We didn't have a class with Mr Rees after all, so I needn't have gone in. (W.8.2.53)

It is important to note, to begin with, that it does not simply mean 'it was not necessary', which is the natural paraphrase if it is simply the past negative necessity form. This is clear from the contrast between:

> I didn't go – I didn't need to/I didn't have to.
> *I didn't go – I needn't have.

Whereas didn't need to may mean 'wasn't necessary', this is not a paraphrase of needn't have. Like shouldn't have/oughtn't to have, needn't have carries with it the conditional implication 'wouldn't have'.

This is easily accounted for if we see needn't have as the past unreal form of the negated necessity ('not-necessary') as compared with should have/ought to have, where the event is negated ('necessary-not'). But, curiously and unexpectedly, although it is the necessity and not the event that is negated, there is an implication of the unreality of the negative (not the positive) event, with the further implication that the event did, in fact, take place (not that it did not). We can offer the rough paraphrase (in parallel with those of 6.4):

needn't have   'wasn't "necessary" and wouldn't have happened'

We might expect that a similar interpretation would be required for *needn't, ie:*

needn't   'is "not-necessary" and wouldn't happen'

But I can find no clear contrast between a non-conditional *needn't* which is simply the modality-negative corresponding to *must* and a conditional one (not even between *needn't* and *don't need to*). Theoretically, of course, such a distinction is possible; in practice it seems not to be one that English makes.

We have already noted (6.3.2) that *needn't* in interrogatives can only be interpreted as 'Is it true that it is not necessary?' and not as 'Isn't it true that it is necessary?' By contrast, forms of the non-auxiliary NEED carry the latter meaning – we can contrast:

Needn't I come?
Don't I need to come?

This does not, however, directly relate to the 'conditional' status of the modal since *shouldn't* and *oughtn't to* can have both meanings – 'Is it the case that I shouldn't ...?', 'Isn't it the case that I should ...?' (just as *mustn't* does – 6.3.2).

In present positive interrogation there seems to be no difference in meaning between the modal and non-modal, both merely questioning the necessity. This is clear enough in the comparison of:

Need I say more? (S.5.6.6)
'Do I need to say more?' (W.8.1.5)

However, there is a stylistic difference, the non-modal verb being more likely in formal or written texts.

In the positive form, however, the non-modal verb does not simply have the 'necessity' meaning of MUST, but rather indicates what is required for specific purposes or personal reasons as in:

He needs to make a lot of money (if he is to avoid bankruptcy).
He needs to have someone to help him (he cannot manage on his own).

It may seem that NEED is sometimes subject oriented, but it is not always the case that the necessity derives from the subject himself (this is less so with the first example above than the second).

6.6 Further issues

6.6.1 Subject oriented necessity?

Since we had subject oriented possibility, is it possible to distinguish also subject oriented necessity? There is one example of MUST that seems to have such a meaning:

> Protoplasm, the living substance of all plants, contains nitrogen and the rose tree must absorb this nitrogen in the form of nitrates. (W.10.3.3)

Admittedly rose trees are not animate, but MUST here seems to refer to a necessary characteristic, in contrast but parallel with, 'The rose tree can . . .'. Similarly we can say:

> He's a man who must have money.

One other possibility is that the gap is filled with CAN'T HELP as in:

> A kleptomaniac is a person who can't help stealing.

Yet this does not mean that this is an essential characteristic (and equivalent, therefore, to 'is not able not to'), but rather that no blame is to be attached to the action. This is clear enough if we replace *must* above with *can't help:*

> He's a man who can't help having money.

Nevertheless, the meaning is close to that of MUST in:

> He's a man who can't help making money.

6.6.2 Deontic and dynamic

In the light of what has been said it could, perhaps, be argued that MUST and HAVE (GOT) TO are always deontic, provided that a distinction is drawn between 'subjective' and 'objective' deontic modality. This is essentially the point made by Lyons (1977: 833). The difference between MUST and HAVE (GOT) TO would lie essentially, thus, in the deontic 'source'; with MUST it would often be the speaker, with HAVE (GOT) TO it would never be the speaker. While MUST might sometimes be subjective, HAVE (GOT) TO would always be objective, but both would be deontic in that some kind of deontic necessity was involved.

One obvious advantage of such a solution is that it would account for the deontic and dynamic uses of MUST within a single kind of modality; instead of relating these uses to two different kinds, we should account for them in terms of the presence or absence of subjectivity.

On the other hand, such a solution would suggest that a similar analysis should be provided for possibility. Deontic possibility is, however, much more clearly distinct, being marked by actual or potential MAY. Nevertheless, it could be argued that even with possibility we could simply distinguish between subjective and objective deontic modality, the former being marked by MAY or CAN, the latter by CAN or BE ABLE TO. This would, however, leave subject oriented CAN somewhat unexplained; it would be objective (in the sense that it does not derive from the speaker), but the deontic source would be the subject of the sentence. (There is no really similar problem with necessity; see 6.6.1.)

However, we have now arrived at a position where the issue is no more than a terminological one. What I have called deontic modality would now be subjective deontic, and what I have called dynamic would be objective deontic. I shall, therefore, retain my terminology and not pursue the issue further.

There is a lack of symmetry between the formal and semantic relations of possibility and necessity. With possibility there is no form that (like HAVE (GOT) TO) specifically denies speaker involvement, while with necessity there is no form that can be used specifically to indicate that there is such involvement (like MAY). There are also different areas of indeterminacy – between neutral and subject oriented dynamic possibility (CAN), but between deontic and neutral dynamic necessity (MUST). All of this makes it difficult to draw any clear line, but that does not invalidate the distinction, which for methodological purposes, at least, has proved useful in this book.

Chapter 7

WILL, SHALL and futurity

In this chapter I shall discuss the remaining uses of WILL and SHALL (*ie* all except epistemic WILL and deontic SHALL). In particular, we shall be concerned with dynamic, subject oriented, WILL, which has a parallel with CAN, and the use of WILL and SHALL to refer to the future. Other forms that are used to refer to the future, most importantly BE GOING TO, will then be considered.

One of the most obvious problems is the difference between WILL/SHALL when referring to the future and BE GOING TO. This has been discussed in detail by a number of scholars, notably McIntosh (1966), Binnick (1971, 1972) and Wekker (1976: 123–33). I do not basically disagree with their findings, except insofar as they do not entirely demonstrate that the difference lies in part with the modality of WILL and SHALL and the non-modality of BE GOING TO. I shall not begin by discussing this problem, but by setting out the uses of WILL and SHALL; BE GOING TO and its contrast with these two modals, will be discussed subsequently. One other form, which is a potential candidate for modal status, IS TO, will be discussed at the end of the chapter.

7.1 Subject oriented WILL

Under the heading of dynamic subject oriented WILL we can, perhaps, distinguish the three types that Jespersen (1909–49, IV:239) refers to as 'volition, power and habit'. Semantically all three uses are subject oriented, but only the first two clearly parallel the subject oriented uses of CAN in terms of tense, negation and voice (5.3.1, 5.3.3, 5.3.6, 7.4.1, 7.4.3, 7.4.5).

7.1.1 Volition

With the positive form *will* it is not easy to find examples in which there is a clear indication of volition, as contrasted with futurity (or conditional futurity, see 7.2.2) (if we ignore for the moment examples of *I will* . . ., and

Will you . . ., which we shall discuss at the end of this section). But there is, surely, some notion of volition in:

I'm seeing if Methuen will stump up any money to cover the man's time. (S.1.8.23)
I said 'Why don't you go and see if Martin will let you stay?' (S.2.7.74)
I don't think the bibliography should suffer because we can't find a publisher who will do the whole thing. (S.2.1.26)

It is much easier to give examples of the negative forms *won't*, *wouldn't*, where non-volition is almost equivalent to refusal (but see 7.4.2):

'But she loves him and she won't leave him; so she sells herself.' (W.16.2.99-2)
I said I am not competent to do it and I wouldn't have my name on the title page to do it. (S.3.2c.41)

There is, however, one very clear example of *will* where it could be paraphrased by 'are prepared to':

Would he not agree that recent congressional hearings have shown the length to which some American aircraft manufacturers will go to promote and defend the rights of their companies. (S.11.4.82)

With *I* as subject, however, (and, more rarely, with *we*) *will* can express an agreement by the speaker to act. Here it is tantamount to an undertaking by the speaker:

Hang on a minute and I'll try and find it. (S.8.4g.3)
I'll have it lined up for you, dear. (S.1.9.55)
Well, I'll ring you tonight some time. (S.2.12.99)
. . . and I will look into any allegations which might justify the sort of enquiry which he is urging me to take. (S.11.4.80)
Anyway, I will write as soon as I get to Nigeria, and again when I get to Bida itself. (W.7.2.99)

There are two possible ways of accounting for this use. One can say that this is the *will* of volition with the conventional implication that volition associated with the speaker is to be taken as an undertaking to act (9.2). Alternatively, one could argue that this is essentially a deontic use: with *I* and *we*, SHALL is not used deontically (because it is used for futurity), but WILL is used instead (see 4.4). This is roughly the position I took in Palmer 1965. But these two explanations are not mutually exclusive; it is perfectly reasonable to argue that WILL is basically volitional, but that with *I* and *we* it acquires the deontic meaning through conventional implication and so fills a gap left by SHALL. The notion of volition may be very weak. In the following examples WILL simply signals a future action by the speaker that is in some way beneficial to the hearer:

I'll spell that out for you – three words T.E.M.P.L.A – new word – Q.U.A.M – new word – D.I.T.E.C.T.A. (S.9.3.37)
I'll put my glasses on. (S.4.4.19)

WILL is also used in requests, but here there is little doubt that an interpretation in terms of conventional implication is correct; asking if someone is willing is taken as a request for action:

Dick, will you stand by the anchor? (W.5.3.90)
If you stay at home this evening, will you make sure the water's hot? (S.4.1.42)
Will you remind me to ask your mother if she's got an extra button for that cape? (S.4.1.41)
Will the Secretary of State acknowledge the important role that the Development Corporation for Wales has played in developing exports from Wales to E.E.C. countries? (S.11.4.105)

(The last example is a question in Parliament, and is of a stylistically restricted nature.)

An indirect request (with a third person subject) is:

Perhaps he'll let me know. (S.8.3g.4)

With *we* there is agreement – both a request and an offer:

All right, we'll do that, Judith. (S.8.4h.7)
Anyway the best of luck with it all and we'll be in touch. (S.9.11.36)

Although a contrast is being made between volitional WILL and WILL used for futurity, it must be noted that volitional *will* always has the implication of future actuality (compare CAN, in 5.3.4, which often, but not always, has such an implication). It is this, of course, that makes it difficult sometimes to decide whether or not we have an example of the one kind or the other. In contrast, BE WILLING TO has no implication of actuality. We can, therefore, compare the ungrammatical with the grammatical:

*John will come, but he won't/is not going to.
John is willing to come, but he won't/is not going to.

This is to be related to similar facts about CAN (5.2 [ii]) and to the past tense form of WILL (7.4.3).

7.1.2 Power

'Power' is little more than volition applied to inanimate objects, to indicate how such objects will characteristically behave. We noted that there was a similar use of CAN to express inanimate ability (5.1). Examples are:

You know that certain drugs will improve the condition. (S.2.9.104)
Why do you think this ought to be put in a little box, as it were, with

Shakespeare's work?—Because it won't fit into any little box. It's not really a tragedy. (S.3.5a.33)

We should also, perhaps, include here what I called the inference use of WILL (Palmer 1974: 112) as in:

Oil will float on water.
Pigs will eat anything.

The first refers to the 'power' or inanimate ability of oil to float on water. Whether the second is a matter of 'power' or 'volition' depends on whether pigs can genuinely have volition (a philosophical point!). An alternative interpretation could be that these belong with existential WILL (8.2), WILL expressing what sometimes happens, CAN what often, or typically, happens. It can equally be argued that they have something in common with both the subject oriented and the existential use.

7.1.3 Habit

Examples of *will* to refer to habitual (or better, 'typical') activity are:

These are visual things. You don't need words to convey them and countries as far apart as China and Wales will use the dragon to convey basically the same concepts without any words. (S.5.2.38)
So one kid will say to another, one kid will make a suggestion to another, he'll say the moon's further away from the earth than the sun. (S.1.10.52)

Since we are concerned with typical behaviour, typical that is of the subject of the sentence, this is best regarded as a third type of subject oriented WILL.

There is a stronger case for considering WILL to be subject oriented when it is stressed, to suggest persistent and even perverse activity:

You will keep on saying that the hunting of foxes is the merciful way of doing it. (S.5.6.22)

7.2 Future WILL and SHALL

Most older grammars of English have treated WILL and SHALL as markers of the future tense in English. I have argued (Palmer 1965: 62–3, 1974: 36–37) that this is misleading. Part of my argument was simply that WILL and SHALL have the formal characteristics of the modals and that they should, therefore, be treated as modals and not as tense markers. A more cogent argument is that in the spoken language, at least, they are seldom used simply to refer to the future (the 'pure' future), but usually have some other semantic characteristics as well, and that, on semantic grounds, BE GOING TO is more reasonably to be regarded as the form normally used for reference to the future.

7.2.1 WILL and SHALL

The traditional view of WILL and SHALL as markers of the future tense saw *shall* as the form that occurred with the first person forms *I* and *we* and *will* as the form that occurred with second and third person subjects, and similar statements were made for 'conditional' *would* and *should*. The arguments against this view of an English future tense were put most forcibly in the 1920s by Fries (1925, 1927), and it is now generally agreed that *will* occurs regularly with *I* and *we*, even when it indicates futurity. (I assume that the contracted form *'ll* is a form of WILL.)

Yet, disappointingly, I noted no examples of *I/we will* in the Survey that can, without any doubt whatsoever, be regarded as indicating 'pure' futurity, though the following are possible candidates:

I will be perfectly frank with you. (S.2.1.6-12)
He wants to tell Professor Ford that we will meet him at Lime Street Station, Liverpool at ten fifty-three tomorrow, Friday. (S.9.3.75)

There are, however, plenty of examples of the negative *won't* (for the relative frequencies of positive and negative forms see 7.4.1):

I won't be back tonight. (S.7.3k.2)
Well, I probably won't see you. (S.7.3b.7)
I hope I won't be too late, though. (S.9.3.72)
We won't have to get into a rush down there, will we? (S.7.2b.5)
I won't finish my thesis that quick. (S.4.2.37)

It is, however, quite clearly true that SHALL does not occur with second and third person subjects to indicate futurity: with such subjects it is always deontic (4.4). Its occurrence with *I* and *we* (rather than WILL) to refer to the future is undoubtedly determined both by style and dialect. Wekker (1976: 47) has some evidence that it occurs in more formal style, and there are English dialects, notably in the USA and Scotland, in which it does not occur at all. Yet there is one clear example in the Survey where *shall* has the meaning of pure futurity and occurs alongside *will* with a third person subject:

My babe-in-arms will be fifty-nine on my eighty-ninth birthday . . . The year two thousand and fifteen when I shall be ninety. (S.5.5.11)

Less certain is:

No, I shall be back tomorrow. (S.7.3k.10)

This may indicate not simple futurity, but a promise, and so be essentially deontic (4.4). But it is a promise by the speaker that he himself will act, and so *shall* occurs with *I*. However, it could be argued that to make a future statement about oneself can be taken by implication as a promise, and it is difficult, then, to distinguish futurity and promise with first person subjects (but see also 7.4.5). This relation between future and deontic SHALL with first person subjects is thus explained if its function is seen as that of expressing 'a future happening dependent on the will of the speaker' (Christophersen and Sandved 1969: 197).

We are not concerned here with the numerous examples of *Shall I . . . ?* and *Shall we . . . ?* Most of these can nearly always be treated as deontic and in terms of conventional implication (4.4, 9.2). The futurity use is, however, possible as in *eg*:

Shall I be better tomorrow?

Where WILL and SHALL are used in unreal conditionals (in the forms *would* and *should*), there is no doubt at all that *would* is extremely common with *I* (see 7.5.2). Here the evidence of the Survey clearly shows that the traditional insistence on *I should* is not reflected in practice.

7.2.2 Conditionality

In many of the examples of WILL/SHALL being used to refer to the future, there is some element of conditionality. We can distinguish a number of types.

[i] *Will* is the form that is regularly used in the apodosis (the main clause) of a real condition referring to the future (7.5). In the protasis (the *if*-clause) a non-modal present tense form is used. A typical pattern is, then, that of:

If John comes, Bill will leave.

An example from the Survey is:

If he feels like doing it, that'll save me the trouble. (S.8.4e.7)

However, any of the modals can be used in the apodosis; all may have future time reference:

If John comes, Bill may/can/must/ought to/should leave.

Moreover, it is not necessary that the events referred to in the protasis are future. They may be present or even past, as in:

Look, if she didn't grudge you the weekend, she won't grudge you an alibi. (W.3.1c.17)

[ii] There are examples where the condition is expressed by coordination with *and,* and a negative condition by *or else*:

You put it under your pillow, and a fairy will come and give you— (S.4.3.116)

Here pass me my handbag, dear, and I'll get out my old pair of glasses.
(S.2.14.21)
I don't want to stay there for ever, obviously, or else it'll be terribly bad for
me. (S.1.9.81)

[iii] Some conditionality is expressed by other conjunctions:

When the demand for labour exceeds its supply, wages rise. . . . When
there is a surplus of labour, prices will not rise. (S.12.2.8)
Will the minister admit that the trade gap with Europe will not improve,
until the government starts to do something about inflation? (S.11.4.102)

[iv] There is an implicit condition in:

As the orchestra plays, the music from the instruments on the left will be
heard predominantly with your left ear, but also, a fraction later, with
your right. (W.15.4c.16)
I think that will require a considerable change in land use and habitat.
(S.10.8a.53)
This will give us nice time to acclimatize you and have lunch before the
lecture. (S.9.3.73)
Oh dear, Bridget will tell you that she was at the same lecture. (S.1.6.99)

None of these refer to future events that are certain (and in none would BE
GOING TO be appropriate). They suggest what will happen if . . . (the music
is switched on, if 'that' or 'this' is done, if you ask her).
[v] A similar interpretation is, perhaps, to be given to:

Yes, that will be fine. (S.7.1d.13)
That'll be super, yes. (S.9.1g.1)
. . . but I think this will do, you know. (S.7.1d.7)

These are (especially the third) idiomatic expressions, but they seem to
derive from the conditional use of WILL – it will be fine, it will 'do', if it's left
like that.
[vi] There is a whole string of occurrences of *will* in a text dealing with
gardening:

Your nurseryman will probably spare you a few understocks. (W.10.3.20)
Powdered chalk will act as a corrective of too acid soil. (W.10.3.10)
The second and third applications will, of course, be sprinkled over the
surface of the mulch, and need not be hoed in. (W.10.3.7)

These events will, of course, occur only if the reader takes the appropriate
action of asking the nurseryman, putting down powdered chalk, and, in the
last example, simply doing what is required. But it is very clear that there is
no suggestion that these events will take place otherwise.

It should be noted here that it is not always possible (and perhaps not desirable) to draw a clear distinction between conditional WILL and the WILL of volition or 'power'. To say that someone is willing or that something has the power to act is often to say that they will act if the circumstances are right. In particular the example *Oil will float on water* might well be interpreted as 'Oil will float if you place it upon water'. Similarly, it is possible to give either a volitional or a conditional interpretation to:

My secretary will tell you how to find her. (S.3.1b.46)

Jespersen (1909–49, IV: 239) treats the idiomatic *That'll do* as 'closely related' to the power use. I would prefer to handle it under conditional *will* with the examples in [v].

7.2.3 Futurity

There are plenty of examples of WILL that seem to refer to the future where there is no suggestion of conditionality.

In general, however, WILL seems to be used where there is reference to a general envisaged, planned, intended, hoped for, etc state of affairs, as opposed to a statement that a specific event or specific events will in fact take place. It is in this sense that it indicates a 'modal' rather than a real ('tense') future. We can distinguish, at least, five kinds of 'modal' future with WILL.

[i] It is used if events are envisaged. Indeed in the first two of the following examples the word ENVISAGE is used:

Is it ever envisaged that the College will hive itself off from the University? (S.3.4.104)
We can envisage management branch of leading councillors faced by a body of back bench members whose main task will be to question and advise. (S.11.5.6)
Could you perhaps do something about a mortgage, because I suspect the Abbey National will just say 'No' straight out. (S.8.1p.19)

Similarly, the inevitable result of a decision is introduced by MEAN:

It means they will have the utmost difficulty in paying for accommodation which a University College or the University provides ... this means students will have to work. (S.11.2.15)

[ii] Futures that are hoped for, prayed for, decided are indicated by WILL:

May I hope that those interested parties will not only be us here in Parliament, but the passengers who find themselves in Europe having to pay two or three times as much to travel by air as the same passengers would have to pay travelling in identical aircraft in the United States? (S.11.4.35)

What we ask in fact is that God will give us the grace to stand up against the enemies which assail us. (S.12.1c.3)

We pray that God will look upon the hearty desires of his humble servants. (S.12.1c.2)

Who decides what price it'll go on the market?—Whatever people will pay. (S.4.2.21)

(In the last example the second *will* is, of course, an instance of WILL of volition.)

[iii] Most strikingly, the future scene is set by BE GOING TO or IS TO, but the future events within that scene are indicated by WILL (see also 7.3.2 [iv] and 7.7):

Yet here we are going to find that there's going to be a National Enterprise Board which will be expected to do things in Scotland. (S.11.5.71)

The TUC is to launch a publicity campaign against Britain's entry into the Common Market. After the vote against membership at last month's annual congress, posters calling for a general election on the issue will go up all over the country. (W.2.3a.16)

A further example has the future scene introduced by CONFIRM, but subsequently referred to by IS TO:

The postmen's union have confirmed that they will hold a one-day strike on April the sixteenth, and they're to ban all overtime in the last two weeks of April. (W.2.1.1-1)

[iv] In the previous examples WILL occurred either in a subordinate clause or after some other verb had introduced the envisaged, planned, etc future. But equally it is used where there is no subordination or other verb, but where a planned future is being described. It is used throughout, for example, in the Queen's Speech to Parliament:

My government will make it their special duty to protect the freedom of the individual under the law. (W.4.1b.14)

It is also used in a (spoken) commentary on a state occasion:

The fanfare will now sound. (S.10.6b.55)

In a moment the Queen will be alighting from her coach. (S.10.6b.8)

[v] In a similar way it may be used to give instructions:

... and the president with head averted and profile turned to me said 'Mrs Dodgson will walk on my right'. (S.1.3.33)

The president is telling Mrs Dodgson what she should do (in a perfectly polite way) by indicating what has been decided (either by custom or by him). The army uses WILL to give written orders:

Private Jones will report at 08.00 hrs.

Although the verb in all the examples considered so far is WILL, for my speech at least, SHALL would have been equally possible if the subject had been *I* or *we*. The absence of examples with SHALL is, therefore, due only to the fact that the contexts did not require first person subjects.

But WILL and SHALL may occur to refer to the future even where there is no suggestion that the future is envisaged, planned, intended, hoped for, etc:

My babe-in-arms will be fifty-nine on my eighty-ninth birthday.... Occasionally I sit down at home and open my diary for the year two thousand and fifteen when I shall be ninety. (S.5.5.11) They'll be company for you, and whereas other old women might be terribly lonely, you will never be lonely. (S.1.12.93)

More strikingly *will* is used in official weather forecasts:

Most areas will have rain or thundery showers, but it will be mainly dry in Southern Scotland and much of Northern and Eastern England. (W.2.1b.17)

(For a further discussion see 7.3.1 and 7.3.3.)

7.2.4 WILL in protases

We have already seen (7.2.2) that, where the protasis indicates a hypothetical event in the future upon which the apodosis is conditional, the simple present form is used and not a form with *will*. Thus we may compare:

It'll rain tomorrow. If it rains tomorrow ...

But WILL may occur in the protasis, if it is not used to refer to the future. In the following examples it is used for volition (7.1.1), power (7.1.2) and persistent activity (7.1.3):

If only people will vote in sufficient numbers to put the Liberals back! (S.5.5.26) I know that if medicine will save him, he'll be safe. (S.1.8.107) If you will play it this way. (S.1.2.28)

Notice that in the second example the protasis cannot refer to a hypothetical future event, that of the medicine saving him; if it did the statement would be almost tautological, as indeed would be:

I know that if medicine saves him, he'll be safe.

The fact that *will* does not normally occur in protases is, however, not an isolated fact about this modal. There are a number of other constructions in which reference to the future is normally made with the simple present tense form and not with WILL (or any other future time marker). Most comparable with conditionals are the temporal clauses, where it is not normal for WILL to occur:

When/after/before John comes . . .

But there are some other constructions too where the future may be indicated without WILL (see Jenkins 1972: 6, 89):

I hope John comes tomorrow.
Assume John comes tomorrow.
It doesn't matter who comes tomorrow.

I earlier argued (Palmer 1974: 148–9) that *will* could also be used in the protasis if it expressed what Jespersen (1931: 2) calls the 'after future', where the events referred to in the protasis are subsequent in time to those referred to in the apodosis. (The normal pattern is that the events referred to in the apodosis are subsequent to, and often the result of, those in the protasis.) Thus we might say:

If the play will be cancelled, let's not go.
If he'll be left destitute, I'll change my will.

But I noted no examples of this use in the Survey, and it is significant that although Wekker (1976) has a number of similar examples, all are taken from other scholars' works and none from his texts. In fact it would be much more usual to use BE GOING TO in such circumstances, and there are plenty of examples (see 7.3.2 [vi]). (For further discussion see Wekker (1977) and Close (1977).)

7.2.5 Futurity WILL as epistemic

Some scholars have suggested that the WILL of futurity is simply epistemic WILL, and that its contrast with volitional WILL is the familiar contrast between epistemic and 'root' modals. Jenkins (1972:73) contrasts Permission with Possibility (MAY), Necessity with Logical Entailment (MUST), Volition with Future Prediction (WILL) and Ability with Possibility (CAN). This is suspiciously like some of the matrix analyses discussed in 1.3.1.

The meaning assigned to epistemic WILL on this analysis must be Prediction, and not necessarily Future Prediction as Jenkins suggests, since epistemic WILL clearly also refers to the present (3.3.1). Huddleston (1976a: 69), therefore, talks about 'predictions about the present', and he compares present and future time reference using both a non-modal form and three epistemic modals in:

That is the doctor.	The match starts soon.
That will be the doctor.	The match will start soon.
That must be the doctor.	The match must start soon.
That may be the doctor.	The match may start soon.

There is some plausibility in this because it allows us to fill a fairly obvious gap. In the analysis presented in 3.3.1 MAY and MUST may refer to the present or the future, but WILL only to the present. Should we not say, then, that epistemic WILL with future time reference is our futurity WILL? There is also another argument presented by Jenkins (1972: 96): the non-occurrence of futurity WILL in protases is merely a special instance of the more general fact that no epistemic modal may occur in a protasis. (In actual fact all of them can when echoing a previous statement, but that is true of futurity WILL too, and so is not relevant.)

It is perfectly true that WILL is sometimes used in the sense 'It is a reasonable conclusion that . . .' with reference to a future action, *eg*:

John will come tomorrow, I think.

This would, then, be epistemic. It is also almost certainly true that because of the close relation between modality and futurity (*cf* 1.1.4), it will often be difficult to distinguish clearly at all times between an epistemic future and a 'pure' future use. But that does not mean that a distinction cannot be made. There are at least four reasons for not identifying future and epistemic WILL.

[i] There is a device in English for distinguishing the futurity use and the epistemic use with future reference – the progressive form (which is similarly used with *can't*, *cf* 3.5.3). Compare:

John will come tomorrow.
John will be coming tomorrow.

Admittedly, the use of the progressive might also be intended to preclude the volitional use of WILL (see 7.4.2 on WILL in interrogation). But the form with the progressive would normally be given an epistemic interpretation.
[ii] With *I* and *we*, WILL and SHALL are virtually interchangeable, with only stylistic differences, in the futurity use (7.2.1), but SHALL is never epistemic.
[iii] The futurity use has little in common semantically with uses such as that of *They'll be on holiday*, where there is no doubt at all that an epistemic judgment is being made by the speaker. Yet WILL (and SHALL) may be used where no epistemic judgment is being made at all, but a plain statement about the future (*cf* 7.3.3 [iii]) as in:

I will/shall be fifty tomorrow.

[iv] To treat futurity WILL as epistemic in no way explains its 'conditionality'.

There is little value in saying, as Huddleston does, that both uses are 'predictive' (cf Boyd and Thorne 1969); that is merely a matter of labelling, and it is not at all clear to me that there is any prediction in the epistemic uses of 3.3.1.

7.3 BE GOING TO

BE GOING TO is of interest to us because of its contrast with WILL and SHALL, and, in particular, because it lacks some of the characteristics that we have associated with WILL and SHALL. There is some justification in distinguishing between modal and temporal futurity.

7.3.1 Style

There are undoubtedly some stylistic differences; BE GOING TO is rarer in texts that can for various reasons be regarded as formal rather than colloquial. With a few exceptions it does not occur in any of the purely written texts in the Survey (ie excluding conversations in the written texts and those written to be spoken), and Wekker (1976: 124) is undoubtedly correct in suggesting that the low frequency of BE GOING TO in his material resulted from the fact that most of it was of a formal kind. It does not occur in the Queen's Speech to Parliament or a commentary on a State Occasion or in the weather forecast, although in all of these WILL occurs frequently, often in successive sentences.

It is not, however, always possible to be sure whether, in a particular example, the use of WILL rather than BE GOING TO is related to style or other factors. In the Queen's Speech and in the commentary, it may have been used because of the formality of the occasion or because there is reference to a totally planned or envisaged future (7.2.3 [iv]). But in the case of the weather forecast, it seems to be the formality alone, the air of authority, that justifies WILL, for there is no planned or envisaged future here, but only a statement about future events; anyone who hears the forecast and repeats it would normally switch to BE GOING TO (It's going to rain).

Similarly, we may ask why BE GOING TO is used in the following extract from a political pamphlet:

OUR NEW CONSERVATIVE PROGRAMME
This is what we are going to do: (W.15.3c.2-1)

Although this is a purely written text, it seems likely that the intention was to appeal to the electorate by using a colloquial expression. But it may well also be that the intention was to suggest that there was no conditionality and that there was an intention expressed, ie that the Conservatives were certainly going to be elected and that these were their intentions.

Any contrast between BE GOING TO and WILL/SHALL must, then, be found in the spoken texts. It must not, however, be assumed that a meaning difference can always be guaranteed. It is very doubtful whether, for instance, any reason can be given for the choice of form in:

No, I shall be back tomorrow. (S.7.3k.10)
This is Malinda speaking just to say that I'm going to be late in this morning, because I've got to deliver a package for Professor Ford in Piccadilly. (S.9.3.64)

These seem to be simple statements of future events and there is a similar pair of questions about the future in 7.4.3. Of course, one can always insist that there is a difference, but that in the context either will be appropriate. In such circumstances, I would prefer to suggest that there is an overlap of the semantics. Nevertheless, it was clear from the previous section that almost all the occurrences of WILL/SHALL could be accounted for in terms of some notion of modality, and that, in the spoken texts at least, it is BE GOING TO that is used to indicate futurity. But even BE GOING TO has some peculiar characteristics of its own.

7.3.2 Current orientation

Although BE GOING TO is the form most commonly used to refer to futurity in the spoken language, it can be argued that (in its present tense form) it does not simply refer to the future, but rather to the future from the standpoint of the present. It is used to suggest what McIntosh (1966: 105) calls 'Present Orientation'. I prefer the term 'Current Orientation', since where the past tense forms are used the orientation is equally to the past. BE GOING TO is used to suggest, in its present tense forms, that there are features of the present time that will determine future events. It is thus essentially a marker of 'future in the present'. In a similar way its past tense forms will be markers of future in the past – see [v] and 7.4.3. If this is so there is an interesting parallel (cf Joos 1964: 141n with the English perfect formed by *have*, for the chief characteristic of this is what Twaddell (1965: 9) calls 'current relevance': that although the event took place in the past there is some relevance to the present, often a result. Thus *I've broken the window* implies that the window is now broken. It could, therefore, be argued that there is a 'mirror image' of this in the use of BE GOING TO in that, although the event will take place in the future, there is current relevance – not a result, of course, but a cause or an initiation in the present. There are several kinds of evidence for this thesis.

[i] There are some examples in which it is clear that there is current activity leading to a future event:

Free kick given Scullion's way; it's going to be taken by Trevor Hockey. (S.10.2.25)

Fire Raiser fighting his way back. It looks as though Carbon is just going to hold him. (S.10.4a.13)

The choice of BE GOING TO relates to the fact that the commentator can actually see the player moving to take the kick, and the horse in the position where he is almost certain to win.

[ii] Often there is no visible relevant activity, but a present decision or intention is suggested:

What I want to know is if we're going to go away in August some time. (S.2.11a.19)
When are you going to see your parents? (S.2.10.23)
They're not going the whole hog and saying 'Right we're going to be a Republic'. (S.2.8a.27)
At the moment they're decorating their house and they're going to alter odd parts of it. (S.5.8.96)

The last example is particularly illuminating. The adverbial *at the moment* relates both to the present activity of decorating and to the present intention of making alterations.

Similarly, a decision is related to a piece of present information:

They've just said they've now completed the survey at last, and according to the result of that they're not going to give us a mortgage. (S.8.1b.4)

This is very different from the conditional use of WILL:

You see, we have got money with the Abbey National, but they've told us that they won't lend on conversions. (S.8.1p.12)

There is a problem here, however. If BE GOING TO is to be paraphrased by INTEND, it would seem to be subject oriented, relating to the subject's intention, and not, therefore, simply a marker of time relations. But there is often no indication of the subject's intention, even though an intention is indicated, as in:

He had a house in Beckenham and, anyway, now it's going to be pulled down. (S.5.8.116)

For further discussion see 7.4.6.

[iii] Sometimes BE GOING TO seems to refer to the immediate future, but with no present activity as in [i]:

I'm going to play that same chord as loudly as possible but immediately release those keys. (S.10.8b.4)
All right, I know, I'm just going to send his contract out today just to keep him happier, you know. (S.8.3h.30)
What are you going to play us? (S.2.8b.2)

This is particularly interesting because there is a similar use of the present perfect. In British English at least, *just* is used (in a temporal sense) only with the perfect and not with a simple past tense form (*I've just seen him, *I just saw him*); the perfect is also used without *just* to refer to the immediate past, what McCawley (1971: 104) calls 'hot news'. We find in these examples that BE GOING TO is used with *just* to refer to the immediate future. It seems that both the immediate past and the immediate future are sufficiently close to the present to justify marking current relevance or current orientation.

[iv] Often there is a sense of inevitability – the train of events is already in motion:

> Will my Honourable friend accept that many people in the House think that Concorde is going to be a gigantic financial disaster? (S.11.4.88)
> Now the first six are the only people who are going to get a look in, and the first four are the only people who are actually going to make it. (S.2.9.63)

One of Wekker's examples actually has the word *inevitably*, though he treats it in terms of immediate futurity, which, I think, is not the relevant point:

> Inevitably, however, the Government is going to look silly. (Wekker 1976: 133)

[v] Very often GOING TO occurs first in a sentence to be followed by WILL:

> Is the Government going to say that we are going to have a National Enterprise Board which on the one hand will have powers . . . ? (S.11.5.68)
> The National Enterprise Board is going to be in this difficult situation because it is the servant but it will have two masters. (S.11.5.77)

We saw similar examples in 7.2.3 [v]. Wekker even quotes one example of BE GOING TO occurring as the first future marker in a weather forecast, to be followed by a series of instances of WILL. (But this seems not to have been the forecast by the weatherman, but the forecast being relayed by the reader in a topical programme.) It seems that BE GOING TO sets the scene by relating the future to the present, but that, once the scene is set, WILL is used.

[vi] BE GOING TO often occurs in the protasis of a conditional sentence:

> Yes, we'll have to go out, if you're really going to do it, darling. (S.1.11b.48)
> Well, perhaps I should choose a London map, if I'm going to look at Clapham. (S.1.11b.28)
> I think Sheffield have got to keep a very close eye on him, if he's not going to sneak one before the end. (S.10.2.74)
> If you're going to do honours, you've got to have done it well, you know. (S.2.9.34)

It will be remembered that WILL/SHALL are not used in the protasis to refer to the future, the simple present being used instead (7.2.2, 7.2.3, cf 7.5). But BE GOING TO is used here for a quite different purpose. If the simple present is used, the events of the apodosis are usually subsequent in time to those of the protasis. In our sample sentence *If John comes, Bill will leave* (7.2.2), Bill's leaving follows John's coming. With BE GOING TO, however, the events in the protasis are subsequent in time to those of the apodosis; the present events depend conditionally on the future ones, not vice versa. It is significant that in all these examples the main clause contains a dynamic necessity modal, indicating what is needed now if the right future events are to ensue.

This use of BE GOING TO requires no special grammatical explanation if it is treated as a present tense form (which it is formally), just as the present perfect is a present and not a past tense form. For then we have a perfectly regular pattern with a present tense form in the protasis and a modal (with future time reference) in the apodosis. Our first sentence would then be grammatically like:

Yes we'll have to go, if John comes.

[vii] BE GOING TO is regularly used in the past tense (7.4.3). This is easily explained if it is seen as referring to events (past or present) with current orientation. By contrast *would* does not occur for future-in-the-past except in literary texts (7.4.3).

[viii] BE GOING TO is rare in the negative, whereas WILL is common. For the significance of this see 7.4.4.

7.3.3 Contrasts with WILL and SHALL

One way of establishing the meaning of BE GOING TO and the modals is to look at some clear contrasts, and also to consider some examples in which both are used.

[i] In the following examples the use of BE GOING TO suggests that the futurity is in no way conditional:

I'm buying an awful lot of books here. It's going to cost me a fortune to get them home. (S.1.10.99)
It's not going to be feasible, well I don't think it's going to be practical. (S.8.2a.76)

In the first example the speaker clearly intends to take the books home, and so it will, for certain, cost him a fortune; he is not saying that it will, if he takes them home. In the second example the proposal referred to by *it* is clearly going ahead, feasible or not. In a similar way we can explain the difference between (Palmer 1974: 164):

> The paint'll be dry in an hour.
> The paint's going to be dry in an hour.

In the first there is the implied condition 'if you leave it', 'if you are patient'. In the second there is inevitability; nothing will change the future event. While, then, the first might merely counsel patience, the second might be a warning 'Do something quickly'. There is one example where the speaker corrects WILL with BE GOING TO:

> They'll begin to, going to begin to, look at how many foreign students the country should, in fact, subsidize. (S.11.2.24)

[ii] Similarly BE GOING TO suggests that there is no volition and the following sentence is not, therefore, a request, as it would have been if WILL had been used:

> So, are you going to leave a message or shall I say something? (S.1.8.34)

[iii] In contrast WILL and SHALL are used where it is clear that there is little or no present activity involved, as in:

> She'll be in soon. (S.8.4j.3)
> I'll think of his name in a moment – it's there, in print. (S.1.14b.15)
> My babe-in-arms will be fifty-nine on my eighty-ninth birthday. . . . The year two thousand and fifteen when I shall be ninety. (S.5.5.11)

[iv] If there is any suggestion of a condition, WILL and SHALL will be used. This probably explains the choice of form in:

> I shall be back tomorrow, and then I'm going to do some work this evening. (S.7.3k.10)

SHALL suggests 'if you want to find me'. Compare, similarly:

> I'll be at home all day today except for about a half an hour just after lunch. (S.9.3.91)

[v] WILL and SHALL are more common than BE GOING TO with BE ABLE TO and HAVE TO (see 5.3.4 and 6.3.4 for examples). This is probably related to the fact that with possibility and necessity (*a*) future conditionality is often suggested, so that WILL and SHALL would be more appropriate, (*b*) an indication of current orientation is less likely, in that if there is possibility or necessity in the present *can* and *must* may be used.

[vi] We must not be too dogmatic. In all of the following BE GOING TO might seem to be out of place; and some special explanation is needed:

> But I said 'Don't have any doubt about this, dear friends, that if you are going ahead with doing that, you are going to be dealing with me!' (S.3.2c.42)
> I get the impression that some of them seem to think that all they need to

do is say a social compact three times a day before meals and keep their
fingers crossed, and everything's going to be all right. (S.6.3.39)
The things that are poisonous we don't eat, so we don't know if they taste
nice or not— . . . —Like the kingfisher.—Except a kingfisher is probably
not going to taste very good. (S.2.10.185)
But are we not approaching the time when a totally different way of
looking at things is going to come, about refectories, when refectories are
going to be places where food, prefrozen, is brought into the establishment
and then warmed up and served? (S.11.2.28)

In all of these, the choice of BE GOING TO makes the event more immediate
or more certain. The first shows that WILL is not absolutely essential in the
main clause of a conditional; BE GOING TO is chosen because it is assumed
that the events will, in fact, take place – the future is 'extra-real'. In the
second the suggestion is that they believe that they are doing what is right
and that everything will therefore turn out right, in spite of the fact that this
is in the form of an implicit condition with *and* (*cf* the example in 7.2.2 [ii]).
In the third there is a fairly firm statement that the kingfisher has a nasty
taste and not simply that it will (or would) taste awful if eaten. In the final
example it is the immediacy of the event that dictates the choice of BE GOING
TO. For what is being described is an envisaged future which would normally
require WILL. But the scene is set by *approaching the time;* which suggests
that the events are already in progress towards coming about.

7.4 Grammar

As in other chapters I shall deal first with negation. But there are some
problems with the negative past tense (past time) forms of WILL, similar to
those of CAN (5.3.2) that will be left until the section on past time.

7.4.1 Negation

Let us first consider whether it is the modality or the event that is negated.
With subject oriented WILL, it is usually the modality that is negated:

Even in the Sixth Form there are one or two who will not talk about sex.
(S.5.10.56)
They won't give me a key to get into the building, so I can't work.
(S.2.4a.31)
They won't touch anything under three months, you see. (S.2.1.29)
The key won't go in the lock. (S.1.2.52)
It seems to Nabarro that you people just won't do your homework.
(S.5.3.12)

Less frequently, however, in the volition use, it is the event, not the modality,
that is negated as in:

'I won't ask for details.' (W.16.1.29-2)

This does not mean that I am unwilling or I refuse to ask for details, but that I am willing not to ask.

With the WILL of futurity and with GOING TO it is the event that is negated or, rather, there is no distinction between negating the futurity and negating the event:

I won't be back tonight. (S.7.3k.2)
Yes, but you won't be going back till next October. (S.4.1.37)
That one, I thought, I'm definitely not going to have, because I would find the colours depressing. (S.1.8.47)

Notice that if BE GOING TO were interpreted as 'intend', the intention would not be denied but an intention not to act would be asserted. This is equally true of the verb INTEND, since *I don't intend to* is the assertion of an intention not to act. With INTEND we need to postulate 'negative raising', the raising of the negative from the subordinate to the main clause. But there is no need for a similar explanation for BE GOING TO, it is sufficient to say that, as with WILL, the future event is denied.

7.4.2 Interrogation

With subject oriented WILL it is possible to question the modality, *eg :*

Will John come?

In the vast majority of examples, however, interrogation is used with a second person subject to make a request with conventional implication (9.2 and *cf* 4.5.2 for a similar use of CAN):

Will you pass that on to him? (S.7.3a.2)
Will you remind me to ask your mother if she's got an extra button for that cape? (S.4.1.41)

However, even in this use WILL may have a third person subject, if the third person is used for the addressee:

Will the Secretary of State acknowledge the important role that the Development Corporation for Wales has played in developing exports from Wales? (S.11.4.105)

The WILL of futurity is comparatively rare in interrogation. One example is:

Will you be at your college at lunch-time? (S.1.10.120)

With a second person subject, however, WILL will usually be interpreted as subject oriented, and so suggesting a request, if that is a possible interpretation. Thus, the following would almost always be treated as an invitation and not as a request for information:

Will you come to the party tonight?

To avoid this interpretation either *Are you coming. . . ?* (where the progressive suggests that the subject already has an intention to come) or *Will you be coming . . . ?* (see 7.4.5) must be used.

There is no problem with BE GOING TO; there is a simple question about the future in:

Are you going to be around this evening at your home? (S.7.3d.2)

There are some examples of negative interrogation with BE GOING TO:

Aren't you going to sit down? (S.1.8.14)
Aren't you going to tell me what it is? (S.7.2b.4)

In general, negative interrogatives suggest that the positive proposition is true; *Isn't it going to rain* would suggest that it is. But in these two examples there is also a conventional implication. They are invitations to act, with the suggestion that it would be unreasonable not to do so – it would be silly to stay standing, it would be unfair or unkind not to tell me.

7.4.3 Past

With subject oriented WILL there is a situation, in relation to actuality, exactly like that of CAN (5.3.3). In the past tense the form *would* is not used where there is an implication of actuality, although *wouldn't* is perfectly normal. We can thus compare the ungrammatical and the grammatical:

*I asked him, and he would come.
I asked him, but he wouldn't come.

There are therefore no examples at all of past tense *would* with the implication 'did', but plenty of examples of *wouldn't* with the implication 'didn't':

Melissa was very noisy at night, and wouldn't go to sleep. (W.8.2.2)
Married to a woman who wouldn't sleep with him after the birth of her second son. (W.7.5c.6)

Scheurweghs (1959: 385) has an example of *would* with a negative word:

This man would have nothing to do with mere barbaric slaughter.

He also has one in a semantically negative environment introduced by *all* (cf 5.3.3 [iv]):

This he refused and all he would accept from them was the gift of two cows.

There is, however, no form in common use that will imply actuality (as BE

ABLE TO does instead of CAN). BE WILLING TO might seem the most likely candidate:

I asked him, and he was willing to come.

But this verb is comparatively rare, and, in striking contrast with BE ABLE TO, there are few examples in the Survey. One is:

So it appears that the skipper was willing to sacrifice a win over a team we had never beaten before for a 'moral' victory. Golly, I was mad! (W.7.3.46)

In its 'power' use, however, WILL may be used with adverbs such as *just* and *hardly* to imply that the event did, in fact, take place (compare the examples with CAN in 5.3.3):

The books just/hardly fitted on to the shelf.

Subject oriented WILL also has a 'habit' sense, and this also occurs in the past. As with the habitual use of CAN actuality is implied even in positive forms. Ehrman (1966: 46) has:

. . . and whenever she gardened, she would eat with dirt on her calves.

Similarly Scheurweghs (1959: 385) has, along with other examples:

Morning after morning I would hear the rattle in the post-box.

Here *would* is fairly close in meaning to USED TO which, it was decided, would be excluded from the list of modals (1.2), though clearly it could be argued that there is some connection between *would* and USED TO. But there are two differences. First *would* is subject oriented in a way that USED TO is not. The example above is describing an unpleasant characteristic of the subject, and this would not have been indicated by USED TO. Secondly *would* normally suggests that the action is iterative, whereas USED TO does not. Anderson (1971: 84–5) compares:

He would live in that house $\left\{ \begin{array}{l} (a) \text{ whenever he came.} \\ (b) \text{ (in those days).} \end{array} \right.$

He used to live in that house (in those days).

An example of subject oriented *would* from the Survey is:

He would always talk, he wouldn't stop talking—the thing was—he would concoct anecdotes and had to tell them to me over and over again. (S.2.7.81)

If there had been stress on *would* the meaning would not have implied that this was a habitual or characteristic action, but that the subject insisted or persisted, to the disapproval of the speaker (see 7.1.3 on WILL).

Would, often accented, may also be used to refer to a single action that is typical of the subject. This is more easily accounted for if we think of this third type of subject oriented WILL (7.1.3) as 'typical' rather than 'habitual'. Thus Leech has:

Of course, he would put his foot in it. (Leech 1969: 236)

This is a possible alternative explanation of the example from Halliday (3.5.1):

They would telephone me just as I was going to sleep. (Halliday 1970: 334)

Let us now turn to the forms used for future time reference. For future in the past BE GOING TO is regularly used (as we noted in 7.3.2 [vii]). Examples are:

I was going to say that it looked a bit like a pheasant in flight. (S.10.8a.46)
It was a matter of complete unimportance unless you were going to be a school master, which I never was. (S.6.4a.54)
. . . and the North just wasn't going to have it at any price. (S.2.8a.33)

Although I noted no examples in the Survey, would is similarly used in a literary style. Leech (1971: 48) has:

Twenty years later, Dick Whittington would be the richest man in London.

However, there is a difference between would and was going to. Would can only be used to refer with hindsight to events that were in fact to take place at a time later than the past time being referred to. By contrast, was going to usually simply indicates current orientation in the past, ie that there were features of the relevant time in the past that in some way determined a later event. Most commonly, there was an intention which may or may not have been carried out; this is to be seen in all three of the examples above. But was going to can also be used in the sense of would, where it is known that the event actually took place. It could replace would in the Leech example, but in spoken English a more likely form is was to (7.7).

In reported speech both would and was going to may be used with the sequence of tenses rule:

There was news from Aintree this morning that Fleetwood, a fifty-to-one outsider, was lame and wouldn't run in the Grand National on Saturday. (W.2.1a.17)
I knew really from the moment I started doing medicine I wouldn't do surgery. (S.2.9.77)
I think it was decided that they couldn't hope to keep up the zoo and they liberated those animals which they thought would survive in this climate. (S.10.8a.81)

Professor Clark asked if you were going to collect some scripts tonight. (S.9.1k.2)

Until well after the battle of the Coral Sea Australians were perfectly convinced they were going to be invaded by Japan. (S.1.10.19)

There is nothing here that cannot be explained in terms of the uses of the present tense forms.

So far in this section we have been concerned only with past tense forms of the modals, forms, that is to say, in which it is the modality that is past. Both WILL and SHALL, however, occur with HAVE to produce forms that are usually referred to as 'the future perfect':

By the end of the present century a number of other coins will have followed the farthing, and the two-shilling-piece, the florin will be the basic unit. (S.12.2.2)

These are closely parallel to the forms of the epistemic modal in which *have* indicates the past time of the event (3.5.1). There is one difference, however. We noted (*cf* also 2.3.4) that *have* may have a past or a 'perfect' interpretation. With the epistemic modals the past meaning is by far the more common. With WILL and SHALL it is the perfect meaning that is more normal (as the examples show). A past meaning is possible but less likely; we may contrast:

I shall have seen him by then.
I shall have seen him the day before.

But as we suggested in 3.5.1, it may not be useful to regard these as examples of a grammatical ambiguity.

It should be noted that this use of HAVE with WILL would be evidence for the view that futurity WILL is epistemic WILL (7.2.5) were it not for the fact that SHALL occurs in exactly the same circumstances.

It is theoretically possible for GOING TO to occur with HAVE with similar 'future perfect' sense:

I'm going to have seen him by then.

But I noted no examples. In all possible examples I would prefer WILL or SHALL and cannot clearly envisage any possible contrast of meaning.

7.4.4 Negation again

There are some examples in the Survey in which there is a contrast of negative *won't* not with *will*, but with some other forms (in one case a form with no modal at all, and in two others with a positive form of BE GOING TO). This seems to have something in common with the fact that *wouldn't*, but not *would*, is permissible in certain circumstances (7.4.3). The examples are (the third is an extended version of an example in 7.3.1):

They know that there are certain arguments which work and certain arguments which won't work. (S.11.2.54)

You don't seriously suppose that children are going to start saying 'trash can' and indeed they won't of course. (S.1.10.50)

This is Malinda speaking to say that I'm going to be late in this morning, because I've got to deliver a package for Professor Ford in Piccadilly; but I hope I won't be too late. (S.9.3.64)

In the first example we have 'power' (7.1.2), *ie* 'inanimate volition' and the suggestion not merely that certain arguments 'will', but that they also 'do' work. It seems clear that *won't* is chosen to indicate that the event does not take place, but that *will* would not be sufficiently positive, and so the simple form is used instead. Of course, it would be perfectly possible to say either '. . . will work . . . won't work' or '. . . work . . . don't work'. But there is clearly a reason for the preference of the positive *work* and the negative *won't work*. It is fair to add that the text continues later with:

There are certain arguments which will work and they work in times of prosperity; in, of course, the times we're in now they don't work at all. (S.11.2.55)

Here the choice seems to be reversed, with *will work* and *don't work*. But now there is a contrast between a hypothetical future and a very real present, and it is this contrast that determines the forms. It is significant too that, in general, it is far easier in the Survey to identify examples of *won't* for negative volition than examples of *will* for positive volition, except in the forms with conventional implication (7.1.1). (Jenkins (1972: 80) notes that whereas *I will eat my supper* would not usually be interpreted volitionally, *I won't eat my supper* will almost certainly be given a volitional interpretation.)

In the second and third examples we have not the volitional use of WILL, but its futurity use, as is clearly shown by the contrast with BE GOING TO. But again while *won't* is used for the negative, a form of BE GOING TO is used for the positive. Even with reference to the future, *won't* indicates a firm denial, while *will* does not indicate a firm assertion, and for this reason BE GOING TO is preferred. The argument is supported by the fact that, while the positive forms of BE GOING TO are very common, negative forms are far rarer, and *won't* is also common.

What all these examples suggest is that WILL is essentially modal, but that BE GOING TO is not. For, as with CAN, positive modality does not imply actuality, but negative modality denies it.

7.4.5 Future

Although the futurity uses of WILL and BE GOING TO have been discussed in detail (7.2, 7.3), there are still several points to be noted about the future.

[i] We have noted (7.1.1) that volitional WILL has the implication of (future) actuality. The power use of WILL (7.1.2) relates rather to a conditional future. Yet it may be argued that often there is no clear distinction between a volitional and a conditional WILL (see 7.2.2).

[ii] WILL and BE GOING TO may in theory combine to form what is essentially a future-in-the-future, but I noted no examples. For WILL plus BE WILLING TO however see 7.6.

[iii] WILL and SHALL may combine with BE to produce 'future progressive' forms:

In a moment the Queen will be alighting from her coach. (S.10.6b.8)
But we won't all be running around buying books if we can't print the stuff off. (S.1.10.112)
Because I tell you now, I won't be seminaring tomorrow. (S.1.7.64)

There is nothing new to be said about many examples of this kind; reference is to a 'progressive' or continuous action in the future. But often these future progressive forms are used where there is little or no indication of progressivity:

I don't know if I'll be coming in on Thursday; presumably you'll be going to the seminar. (S.9.1h.11)
Yes, but you won't be going back till next October. (S.4.1.37)
I assure the Honourable gentlemen we shall be be giving it very, very careful thought, indeed. (S.11.4.40)

The lack of progressivity here can best be illustrated if we consider what would be the comparable forms in the past tense. They would, surely, be *came, went, went back* and *gave* whereas for the previous examples *was alighting (at that moment)*, *were running* and *were seminaring* are appropriate.

The progressive form seems to be used to indicate unambiguously that a futurity meaning is indicated, often with an implication that the future event has been planned or arranged. If WILL is used with a simple infinitive there is always the possibility of a volitional interpretation; we have already noted (7.4.3) that in interrogation WILL will often be taken to suggest a request. In a similar way *I'll see John tomorrow* might suggest agreement; to indicate 'pure' futurity *I'll be seeing John tomorrow* would be preferred. There is, clearly, volition in:

O.K. I'll see you at twelve then. (S.9.1g.2)

In contrast, consider:

What I shall be trying to do in this short demonstration is to give you some idea of the different ways in which a string can vibrate. We'll be concentrating on just one particular string. (S.10.8b.1)

There is no volition here. The speaker does not want the agreement of his audience; he is telling them what has been planned. Similarly the speaker asks about future plans in:

> Yes, could you let me know when you'll be coming in first, so we, you know, make sure there's somebody here? (S.9.2j.6)

With SHALL, it is, perhaps, the case that without the progressive there is still some element of promise (the deontic use); if the progressive is used, this meaning is excluded and a 'pure' future is indicated.

GOING TO also occurs with progressive BE plus -ing:

> For the second time, they want to know whether the MA in Old English is going to be running in seventy-six. (S.9.1m.3)
> But I said 'Don't have any doubts about this, dear friends, that if you're going ahead with doing that, you're going to be dealing with me!' (S.3.2c.42)

These need no special explanation; they refer to 'progressive' events in the future (with current orientation). (For the second example see 7.3.3 [vi].)

7.4.6 Unreality

I shall discuss here only the WILL of volition. The other forms will be dealt with in 7.5. There are few examples in which there is a clear indication of the unreality of the volition, but one is:

> Certainly doesn't want to do Reigate. He would do Cuckfield, and, of course, Horsham, and up to Guildford that way. (S.1.11b.48)

Here would is clearly 'would be willing to', present and unreal. It could not have the meaning 'was willing', even if the context allowed. For with the implication of actuality would cannot be used to refer to past time, as we have just seen (7.4.2). (It is theoretically possible, however, to require the meaning 'was willing, but did not act', but for this the form would have is required – see 7.5.5.)

Would appears very commonly in requests, simply as a weaker form than will:

> Would you ring me? Might that be best? (S.9.1b.7)
> Would you please let me know if you have sold the balance of your securities yet? (W.7.9.49)
> Would the members of the panel please explain why should old age pensioners wait for their promised increase, when Civil Servants receive increases backdated? (S.5.5-53)

It is worth noting, from the last example, that the subject of the modal does not have to be a second person pronoun. There can be a third person subject, if such a subject is being indirectly addressed as here. As with *could* (5.3.5), however, it is by no means certain that all of these are to be regarded as conditional. They are often no more than 'tentative', a little more polite than forms with *will*.

As with the present tense *will*, this 'tentative' *would* of volition may also occur in protases of conditional sentences:

> I'd be very grateful if you would get in touch with the Classics Department at Caroline College and give the message to either the secretary or its real recipient, Mr Howard. (S.9.3.32)

It may also, of course, occur in the apodosis (in a purely tentative sense):

> If Professor Ford is in the office, would he please ring me at this telephone number? Thank you. (S.9.3.103)

In neither of these examples is *would* to be explained as a conditional form (see 7.5.2).

7.4.7 Voice

It is fairly clear that volitional WILL, being subject oriented, is not voice-neutral; the volition is that of the subject. In contrast, futurity WILL is always voice-neutral, since it in no way relates semantically to the subject.

Examples of volitional *will* in which passivization would produce a different or unnatural sentence are:

> It seems to Nabarro that you people just won't do your homework properly. (S.5.3.12)
> I don't think the bibliography should suffer because we can't find a publisher who will do the whole thing. (S.2.1.26)

In fact, voice-neutrality may be used to distinguish between futurity and volitional WILL. In the following example whether WILL expresses futurity or volition can be decided by a judgment on voice-neutrality:

> He wants to tell Professor Ford that we will meet him at Lime Street Station, Liverpool at ten fifty-three tomorrow, Friday. (S.9.3.75)

Would the meaning be changed if this read . . . *he'll be met* . . . ? The passive would exclude the volitional meaning (another test would be to replace *will* by *shall*, since the subject is *we*). This is a difficult judgment. Marginally I feel that there would be a change, that there is an element of volition – 'we have agreed' or 'we have decided'.

This might seem a useful test to decide whether to treat the examples discussed in 7.2.2 [vii] in terms of power or of conditionality. Consider:

> You know that certain drugs will improve the condition. (S.2.9.104)
> You know that the condition will be improved by certain drugs.

Now it seems that these have the same meaning, and in that case they ought not to be treated with subject oriented WILL but with conditional future WILL, *ie* what will happen if the drugs are given. But the argument is not conclusive because it could be said that the characteristics of the drugs and the characteristics of the condition are mutually related, and it is for that reason that there is no change of meaning with passivization. We might still, then, be concerned with subject oriented power. It will be remembered that there was a very similar problem with the voice-neutrality of *can* (5.3.6).

BE GOING TO is also normally voice-neutral as can be seen from:

Free kick given Scullion's way; it's going to be taken by Trevor Hockey. (S.10.2.25)
Free kick given Scullion's way; Trevor Hockey's going to take it.

But it might be argued that there is no voice-neutrality where BE GOING TO indicates an intention on the part of the speaker (*cf* 7.3.1 [ii]) as in:

We're going to call our next child Malaprop. (S.2.10.138)
Where are you going to put it all? (S.2.10.27)
When are you going to see your parents? (S.2.10.23)

My own feeling is that apart from the loss of indication of the agent, there is no significant difference in:

Our next child is going to be called Malaprop.
Where is it all going to be put?

Moreover, as we saw in 7.3.1 [ii] the intention is not always that of the subject.

There is, however, a difference between the active form above and the passive:

When are your parents going to be seen?

But this relates not to BE GOING TO but to the semantics of SEE, which is more likely to be interpreted as 'visit' in the active, but as 'be inspected' in the passive.

7.5 Conditionals

In 7.2.2 we discussed the use of the present tense forms of WILL and SHALL in conditional sentences such as:

If John comes, Bill will leave.

But an equally, or perhaps more, important part is played in conditionals by *would, should, would have* and *should have*:

If John came, Bill would leave.
If John had come, Bill would have left.

These are 'unreal' conditionals, present and past respectively, as compared with the first which is a real (present) conditional.

7.5.1 WILL and SHALL

We noted in 7.2.1 that *shall* occurs, but only rarely, with *I* and *we* for futurity. In the unreal conditional the position is very much the same. There are dozens of examples of *I would* and comparatively few of *I should*. However, in my own speech I would use *should* in all the examples, except where there is a suggestion of volition.

7.5.2 Kinds of conditional

In Palmer 1974: 142–3 I distinguished between predictive conditionals and three other types. The predictive conditionals were of the type illustrated at the beginning of this section with *will, would,* and *would have* in the apodosis. The three other kinds were:

'whenever'   If it rains, I go by car.
implication   If he's here, he's in the garden.
relevance   If you're going out, it's raining.

I now feel that this was a mistake, and that there is no essential difference between these and predictive conditionals. The 'whenever' type is no more than a habitual form of the conditional, while the relevance type simply involves some ellipsis in the semantic link ('It's relevant to say that . . .'). The implication type is no more than a conditional in which the time relations are not of the most common kind: events referred to in the apodosis are not subsequent to those of the protasis, but are previous or (as here) contemporary. There is no obvious distinction between prediction and implication beyond the fact that the former involves futurity. Indeed, I now feel that I was perhaps more correct in saying (Palmer 1965: 132) that in a real conditional any one sentence can be made conditional on any other irrespective of the tense of either.

It is tempting, however, to see a correlation between (Palmer 1974: 143):

If it rains, the match will be cancelled.
If it rained, the match would be cancelled.
If it had rained, the match would have been cancelled.

Starting with the real present conditional, one can transform it into the unreal present by a simple change of tense (*rain → rained, will → would*); past unreal is generated by adding a further past tense marker with the help of HAVE (though in a different way in each of the two clauses: *rained → had rained, would → would have*).

This is a very neat solution. It permits us to handle unreal conditionals simply in terms of the occurrence of past tense (unreal) forms, with an extra past marker (HAVE) where the condition is past and unreal. But there are some objections to this which make it implausible simply to see *would* as the unreal form of WILL, and which suggest that we must rather, with the traditional grammarians, treat *would* as a marker of conditionality in a way that *will* is not.

[i] In a real conditional referring to the future WILL is not essential; BE GOING TO can also be used (7.3.3 [iv]). Yet there is no possibility of using BE GOING TO alone for the unreal conditional. Contrast:

If John comes, Bill is going to leave.
If John came, Bill was going to leave.

The second sentence could not be an example of an unreal present, but only of a real past. The use of the past tense form for unreality is strictly confined to WILL in such sentences.

[ii] *Would* and *would have* may be used where the corresponding real forms contain no modal:

If he acts like that, he is a fool.
If he acted like that, he would be a fool.
If he had acted like that, he would have been a fool.

Now it might be argued that these three sentences are not comparable because the first one is an implicative, not a predictive, conditional (which would require *will*). But this argument would rest upon the fact that the events in the apodosis are contemporary with, and not subsequent to, those of the protasis. Yet, in fact, we find that this is precisely the more common type of time relation when *would* and *would have* occur. Only in a minority of cases of the examples in the next section (which deals with unreality) are the events in the apodosis subsequent to those in the protasis; generally they are contemporary. Therefore the time relation associated with *will* fails to apply to the majority of the examples that contain *would* and *would have*, for these do not reflect the futurity of *will*.

[iii] There are problems with *could* and *could have* which make it difficult to see them as the unreal forms of CAN; they often do not mean 'would be able' and 'would have been able' (7.5.4). This suggests that the issue is not a simple one of unreal WILL and SHALL (and CAN).

Scholars who regard futurity WILL as epistemic (7.2.5) handle *would* and *would have* in a similar way, ie as unreal forms of the epistemic modal (*cf* Huddleston 1977: 46). But I have already argued against this treatment of futurity WILL (and even if this view were accepted, it would not justify a similar treatment of the unreal forms, because, as has been shown in this section, they are not always related to the present tense form *will*).

7.5.3 Unreal WILL and SHALL

The forms *would, should, would have* and *should have* are, then, essentially the grammatical forms required for unreal present and past conditionals in English. They are morphologically forms of WILL and SHALL, of course, but are not directly related to any of the uses of the present tense forms of WILL. In particular it is a mistake to suggest that it is the modality that is unreal. On the contrary, it is the event that is unreal (if indeed we can contrast modality and event); in *John would come* it is the coming that is unreal or hypothetical.

Would come, would have come are, then, best seen as the conditional forms of COME, just as in Latin *veniret, venisset* are the corresponding forms of VENIRE, and there is little to be gained in further explaining their function in relation to WILL in any other of its uses. Examples from the Survey are:

I wouldn't offer, if I didn't want to do it. (W.5.2.106)
Ah, yes, but, if you worked Sunday mornings, you would have Monday morning off. (S.1.5.20)
If one went up there, one would go up to Streatham and turn left. (S.1.11b.36)
I suspect if we'd been on a slightly different course it would have just sat there and we'd have gone past it. (S.10.8a.31)
Wouldn't it have been awful if I'd won? (W.7.5g.3)
It wouldn't have made any difference, then, if it had been in the next scene or the previous scene. (S.3.5a.43)

Notice that in all of these the events in the apodosis are not subsequent to those of the protasis.

As with *will* there are plenty of examples of implicit conditionals. We can recognize a number of slightly different types:

[i] The condition, while not introduced by *if*, is referred to in the linguistic context:

I do not think that it would be helpful to engage in a sort of name-calling against the opponents of the Concorde project. (S.11.4.86)
In fact, I would have said that it looks as though London would be worth going through. (S.1.11b.43)
... and nobody would publish it anyway because there wouldn't be a big enough print run. (S.1.10.160)
And unless I said something I wouldn't want recorded for posterity, I would certainly say 'Yes'. (S.2.5b.21)

[ii] The condition is implicit in a pronoun (*it, that*) or in a noun ('if this were done/attempted', 'if this/these had existed', etc):

That wouldn't be impossible. (S.8.2a.84)
That would be very nice. Yes. (S.9.1i.14)

Well, I am willing to consider any measure which would be of assistance to exporters in any part of the United Kingdom in relation to the E.E.C. market. (S.11.4.106)

You see, women dentists, in the days when you had to pay, would never have made a living because nobody would have gone to a woman dentist. (S.1.13.10)

It really would have been much more disastrous because it gets much more populated towards that end. (S.1.11b.5)

[iii] 'If I were you' is implicit in some conditionals with *I* (especially with negatives):

I wouldn't be in too much of a hurry. There can't be more than about eight feet of water under your keel. (W.5.3.2)

I wouldn't take the slightest risk getting trapped.—No, don't worry, I won't. (W.5.3.99)

[iv] The implicit condition is often much vaguer ('if the opportunity arose', 'if things were different'):

. . . and I would certainly encourage firms to do that. (S.11.4.7)

That punch would normally put a man down, but it didn't seem to have hurt this fellow at all. (S.10.3.82)

Would you make Ireland into one? (S.2.8a.52)

It tends to deteriorate to sheep pasture. 'Deteriorate''s, perhaps, the wrong word. The farmers wouldn't agree with me. (S.10.8a.54)

. . . and the questions that the other chap who got it was asked, I wouldn't have known. (S.2.9.43)

Under this heading we should include expressions such as *I would say* . . ., *I wouldn't dream* . . ., *I wouldn't know* . . ., *I wouldn't mind* . . ., though the implied condition is very vague. It is virtually impossible to suggest an implied condition for *I would like*. Indeed it is enough simply to account for such forms in terms of tentativeness or unreality without the implication of conditionality. Some, however, will be more obviously conditional than others (see also volitional *would* (7.4.4) and *could* (5.3.5 and 7.5.4)).

In all the examples of an unreal present conditional that have been given, the mark of unreality in the protasis has been the past tense form of the verb. But there are two other ways of expressing improbability. First, the protasis may contain *were to* to express a rather more remote possibility. Secondly, the protasis may contain *should,* which may occur in initial position without *if;* in this case, however, the apodosis will normally be in the present and not the past tense. Although the use of *should* indicates the unlikelihood of the event, the form used is strictly not that of an unreal condition, but of a real one:

If it rained
If it were to rain } the match would be cancelled.
If it should rain
Should it rain } the match will be cancelled.

(For *were to* see 7.6.2 and for *should* 8.6.)

7.5.4 CAN and volitional WILL

With CAN and with volitional WILL the forms, *could, could have, would* and *would have* can be used to refer to the conditional unreality of the ability or volition. They are, so to speak, equivalent to **would can, *would will, *would have can, *would have will* or, of course, *would be able to, would be willing to, would have been able to, would have been willing to*. Examples are:

We could stay in bed later in the morning, couldn't we? You wouldn't have to rush to get up and cook the dinner. (S.4.3.86)
And then you could ask for the most monumental presents. (S.2.10.122)
I wouldn't have been without them. (S.5.9.63)

The first of these is particularly illuminating; it shows the parallelism of *could* and *wouldn't have to*.

In all of these examples it is clear, then, that it is the modality that is conditionally unreal. Yet sometimes *could* and *could have* (and to a lesser extent volitional *would* and *would have*) indicate conditionality, not of the modality, but of the event (see Palmer 1977 for a detailed discussion). Compare the first pair with the second:

If he worked hard, he could pass the exam.
If he had worked hard, he could have passed the exam.

If he wanted to, he could pass the exam.
If he had wanted to, he could have passed the exam.

In the first two, ability to pass the exam is conditional on working hard. In the second pair, however, the ability is not conditional on wanting to. What is conditional is the passing of the exam; it is the event, not the modality, that is conditional. Whereas for the first pair a paraphrase is 'would be able' and 'would have been able', for the second pair we need something nearer to 'is able and would' and 'was able and would have'. Examples are:

But I would add one point which I think has got to be, or deserves to be, stated. (S.11.4.60)
No one could have foreseen how long father's illness was going to go on. (W.5.2.107)

In the first, the meaning (unless it is merely tentative as in 7.4.4) is 'I wish to add and I would add, if allowed . . .'. In the second the meaning is 'It was not possible for anyone to foresee, and they would not have foreseen'. We have already discussed the relevance of this for the status of SHOULD, OUGHT TO and NEED (6.4, 6.5).

However, the distinction between conditionality of modality and event is not always clear, because modality itself is in some ways conditional. Consider:

A Gannet could land and take off easily enough in half the runway. (W.5.3.37)

Are we to paraphrase this by 'A Gannet is able to . . . and would . . .' or 'A Gannet would be able to . . .'? The problem is that ability itself is conditional (as is willingness) in the sense that to say that one can includes the notion that, in the appropriate circumstances, one will.

This type of problem goes beyond the modals. Consider:

First of all, a message for Professor Ford that I would be interested to offer a course of lectures next session on Heidegger Ethics. (S.9.3.53)

This means 'I am interested and I would offer a course if I were asked or allowed to'. It is the offering, not the being interested, that is conditional.

7.5.5 Unreal epistemic modals

In the last section we discussed the possibility that with the subject oriented modals it may be that it is the event, not the modality, that is semantically unreal. If we consider epistemic modals, it is even more clear that it may well be that the unreality (and even the past time) relates not to the modals at all, but to the proposition.

The most striking example of this are those that contain *might have, eg:*

I think I might have walked out too, from all accounts. (S.2.5a.32)
This might not have mattered much had the November declaration been seen as having put sterling wholly out of danger. (W.12.6c.7)
Well, it wasn't important and you might have gone out of your way to give it to him, so I didn't really like to. (S.5.9.1)
Probably a good thing that it did hit him on the jaw; it might not have cleared it otherwise. (S.10.1.17)

An example discussed in 3.5.1 was:

He might have been there while you were there. (S.2.11b.86)

But there is a very clear difference. This last example can be paraphrased 'It is tentatively possible that he was there . . .' with *have* clearly indicating the past time of the proposition, and *might* the tentativeness of the modality. But, in the examples now offered, the required interpretation is quite different. The first does not have the meaning 'It is tentatively possible that

I walked out', but 'It is possible that I would have walked out'. The second similarly means 'It is possible that it would not have mattered much', the third 'It is possible that you would have gone out of your way' and the fourth 'It is possible that it would not have cleared it' (though out of context the third could well have had the other meaning 'It is tentatively possible that you went out of your way').

Clearly in all of these the epistemic modality is not past, and may not even be tentative. It is the proposition that is past and tentative. *Might have,* that is to say, expresses *may + would have* (or, possibly, *might + would have,* since here there is no way of distinguishing between the tentative and non-tentative meanings of *might* and *may*).

Similar considerations hold for *might* alone. We may, perhaps, contrast:

It might not be very important all the same. (S.3.5a.1)
That might be nice. (S.2.10.83)

The most likely interpretations for these are, on the one hand, 'It is tentatively possible that it is not very important' and, on the other, 'It is possible that it would be nice'. The second, that is to say, is probably a judgment about a hypothetical event. Two different interpretations are available, and *might* has the same type of ambiguity as *might have.*

An obvious question now is whether there can be a similar interpretation for the other epistemic modals. Huddleston (1977*a*: 46) has:

[If he had stayed in the army] he $\left\{ \begin{array}{l} \text{[i] must} \\ \text{[ii] might} \\ \text{[iii] would} \end{array} \right\}$ have become a colonel.

[ii] illustrates the use of *might have* that we have been discussing. It is important to note, however, that where, as here, a condition is stated, the condition is essentially part of the proposition. The epistemic judgment, that is to say, is about what is in the apodosis as well as the protasis and the sentence is to be paraphrased as 'It is possible that, if he had stayed in the army, he would have become a colonel', and not 'If he had stayed in the army, it is possible that he would have become a colonel' (and still less as 'If he had stayed in the army, it is tentatively possible that he became a colonel' – the interpretation with the unreality assigned to the modality, not the proposition). [i], however, illustrates the corresponding 'necessity' form and is to be paraphrased 'It is "necessary" that if he had stayed in the army he would have become a colonel'. The only difference here is the fact that, whereas in [ii], the modal has the past tense form *could,* in [i] it has the present tense form *must;* but the reason is obvious – *must* has no past tense form available. In these circumstances, therefore, *must have* functions like *might have* to make judgments about what would have happened.

It was briefly noted above that *might have* could theoretically be interpreted either as *may + would have* or as *might + would have, ie* even if it marks past unreality of the proposition, there is still, in theory, a distinction between the tentative and non-tentative epistemic possibility that is expressed by *might* and *may*. With possibility this distinction is not one that can be made in the language, but with necessity it is clearly correct to say that *must have* expresses a non-tentative epistemic judgment, that associated with *must*. If a tentative epistemic judgment is required, we have available *should have* (3.4.3).

Huddleston's [iii] has *would* and, in theory, this too could be an epistemic judgment of the type expressed by *will*, relating to a proposition of the 'would have' type. But just as there seems to be no very clear way of making this kind of epistemic judgment about the future, so there seems to be no way of making a similar judgment about what would have been. This could be used as evidence for the argument that futurity WILL is essentially epistemic WILL (7.2.5) (and to suggest that this conditional use is also epistemic). But the arguments against such a view have been presented in 7.2.5 and 7.5.2 and will not be repeated. I would prefer to use this evidence to show the close relationship between modality and both futurity and conditionality, rather than to attempt to reduce different uses of WILL to a single type. (For detailed discussion see Huddleston 1977*a* and Palmer 1978.)

Although the examples in this section can be explained without postulating unreal conditional epistemic modality, there are some problem examples still to be discussed in 8.5 [iii].

7.5.6 Other forms

There is no problem at all with such forms as HAVE TO, and BE ABLE TO. The forms *would have to, would have had to, would be able to, would have been able to* etc are available and with these it is normally the modality that is conditional (though *would have been able* may sometimes be used, like *could have,* to refer to the conditionality of the event). Examples are:

I would have to order it at the single unit price. (S.8.1e.5)
I wouldn't be able to have that one for some reason, you see. (S.1.8.91)

I noted no examples of *would be going to*, although this is a possible form. Its rarity is, presumably, due to the fact that part of the distinction between WILL and BE GOING TO lies in the conditionality of WILL. If a conditional form is required, this distinction is largely lost or obscured.

There is no need of any unreal conditional form for the deontic modals. Since they are essentially performative, they need no conditional forms. This means that we are not concerned here with deontic MAY, SHALL or MUST. MUST is, of course, also dynamic, but as a purely dynamic modal it is equivalent to HAVE TO, and so, as with the past, forms of HAVE TO are available and can be used instead (6.3.3). Equally, there are no unreal conditional forms of epistemic modals in which the modality (not the proposition) is conditional (see 3.4 and 7.5.5).

7.6 BE WILLING TO

It is tempting to see BE WILLING TO as related to WILL in the same way as BE ABLE TO is related to CAN. We have already noted (5.2) one collocation of ABLE with WILLING:

> . . . a subtle, complex business needing hard and long thought which few of us are able or willing to give. (W.11.4b.4)

We also saw (7.4.3) that there is one example in which BE WILLING TO is used in the past tense where, because there is the implication of actuality, *would* cannot be used:

> So it appears that the skipper was willing to sacrifice a win over a team we had never beaten before for a 'moral' victory. Golly, I was mad! (W.7.3.46)

It would equally be possible to invent examples of BE WILLING TO with WILL for future time reference, where the futurity of willingness has to be clearly indicated (*cf* 5.3.4):

> He's very reluctant at the moment but when he realizes what it's for, he'll be willing to take part.

There are examples, moreover, of the conditional *would be willing*:

> . . . and that yes, of course, I would be willing to come into the common room. (S.1.3.52)

Notice, however, that in both of these examples it would be possible to use WILL (*will* in the first and *would* in the second). The choice of BE WILLING TO is, then, deliberate, to express much more clearly the notion of willingness, rather than simply the 'volition' of WILL. This meaning is clear too in two present tense forms, one of which collocates *willing* with *anxious*:

> The University is both anxious and willing to discharge its responsibility in this sphere. (W.13.1.58-3)
> Yes, I'm willing to consider any measure which would be of assistance to exporters in any part of the United Kingdom in relation to the E.E.C. market. (S.11.4.106)

Even for the past, BE WILLING TO is not essential as a replacement of WILL, since there are other ways of expressing willingness with actuality:

> I asked him and he agreed to come.
> I asked him and he said he would come.

Finally, it is relevant that BE WILLING TO is very much rarer than BE ABLE TO. Although in some respects it may seem to be related to WILL as BE ABLE TO is to CAN, it is obviously far less important in the modality system.

7.7 IS TO

As we saw in 1.2, IS TO belongs formally with the modals. In particular it has no non-finite forms; we cannot say *he seems to be to ...*, *he may be to ...*, *being to ...*, etc; it cannot, therefore, be represented as the verb *BE TO*.

There are at least four different uses, two of them essentially temporal, the other two more modal in character.

7.7.1 Temporal

The past tense forms are commonly used to refer to events that are known, in retrospect, to have been subsequent to other events (a 'pure' future in the past):

> He was asked to prove that he was the son of God by coming down from the cross but this was not to be. (S.12.1c.6)
> Fortunately for Vernon he was to make amends in great style just before the interval. (W.12.5g.3)
> Worse was to follow. (W.12.5b.5)

There is a similar use of the present tense forms, but only, it would appear, where the future is immediate:

> McKenzie's figures now two for twenty-three – he's to bowl to Parfitt. (S.10.1.76-34)

More commonly, present tense forms refer to future events that are planned:

> Certain colleges are to be designated for special development as Polytechnics including five in the area of the Inner London Education Authority. (W.13.1.64-1)
> The old group is still going strong but there's to be a new girl from Norwich. (W.7.1.24)

With past tense forms the distinction between a planned and a 'pure' future is not always clear, as in the first of the following examples; but the notion of plan may be indicated, as in the second:

> True, the cocktail party which was to precede the dinner party on Saturday night nearly came to grief. (W.16.5.22-1)
> She dreaded today because it was to be a 'time test' – goodness knows what of. (W.7.1-8)

It should also be noted that the infinitive form of a verb may be used above to indicate futurity as in:

> The batsmen still to come . . . Parfitt next and then Sharpe . . . (S.10.1.1)
> . . . and it went bouncing back on the off side of the wicket, to be picked up by mid-off. (S.10.1.38)

There is no problem with negation; the future event is denied.

7.7.2 Modal

IS TO is also used to refer to what can be, or what can reasonably be, in both present and past:

> I cannot see how this kind of overlapping is to be avoided. (W.11.1.19-1)
> After a day of torrential rain, however, conditions were inclined to be treacherous and mistakes were to be expected, if not condoned. (W.12.5h.2)

It is also used to report a command:

> You are to come tomorrow.
> He is to work all day.

In the first of these senses only the infinitive may occur alone:

> . . . the quaint aspects of working class life to be found in many major novelists . . . (W.11.1.15-1)

With negation, where IS TO is used to refer to what cannot, or cannot reasonably, be, it is the modality that is negated:

> We realize that true civilization, general genuine progress is not to be found in all those marvellous twentieth-century inventions and marvellous achievements. (S.12.1b.11)

The meaning here is that it is not reasonably possible to find progress in this way. By contrast, where IS TO reports a command, it is normally the event that is negated:

> You are not to come tomorrow.
> He is not to work all day.

However, it is possible to negate the modality (the reported command) in appropriate contexts:

> He is to be ready by four.
> He is not to be ready by four.

It is worth noting that, although the two modal uses seem so different, if one is paraphrased by 'possible' and the other by 'necessary', the negatives are 'not-possible' and 'necessary-not' which are, in some circumstances, equivalent (1.1.5, 3.5.3, 4.5.1).

Another modal use, perhaps, is that of *were to* (or *was to*) in the protasis of a conditional sentence. But this is a quite unrelated use (7.5.6).

7.8 WOULD RATHER

Formally WOULD RATHER is simply a form of WILL plus *rather*. Examples are:

I'd rather do the second half of the autumn term if that's all—(S.9.3.84)
I would rather cook – sort of – four flans when I'm doing a flan. (S.4.3.28)
She had been living with them, but it wasn't working out and she decided she'd rather be independent. (S.5.8.100)

Semantically, WOULD RATHER expresses a preference. It could simply be treated as the unreal form of WILL plus *rather*, but in view of this specialized meaning and the constant association with *rather*, it deserves to be treated independently as a semi-modal.

It is clearly subject oriented and is to be compared with the discourse oriented HAD BETTER (4.7). Here the speaker expresses what he thinks is preferable, and to some degree there is a parallelism between the two, comparable to that of, say, MAY of permission and CAN of ability.

Semantically WOULD RATHER is always present, referring to a preference for present or future action. But, as the last example shows, it may be used in reported speech where the sequence of tenses rule would normally require a past tense form (*cf must* – 6.3.3).

Either the modality or the event may be negated, the former with *wouldn't rather*, the latter with *would rather not*:

Who wouldn't rather die in a ditch than a pool? (W.5.1b.8)
I would rather not comment beyond making perhaps the obvious point that his view on this doesn't seem to accord with the view of many people associated with the second force airline. (S.11.4.33)

Chapter 8

Further issues

This chapter will be largely devoted to a discussion of some uses of CAN and MAY that do not unambiguously belong to any of the kinds of possibility that we have been discussing. Some seem to belong equally to two kinds of modality; rules and regulations, for instance (8.1), may be seen either as reported deontic possibility or as dynamic neutral possibility. Others, *eg* the uses of MAY discussed in 8.5, are simply problematic. In a few cases there are parallel uses involving necessity. These will be discussed within the same sections.

8.1 Rules and regulations

Both CAN and MAY are used to refer to rules and regulations:

In the library you can take a book out and keep it out for a whole year unless it is recalled. (S.3.3.10)
A local health authority may, with the approval of the Minister, recover from persons to whom advice is given under this section . . . such charges, (if any) as the authority consider reasonable. (W.14.1.53)
. . . and it is subject to the final prerogative of mercy of the Home Secretary who may recommend a reprieve. (S.5.3.58)

The first reports a library rule, and the second and third the powers granted by some higher authority. In both cases there would, it is assumed, have been an original document giving such permission. (The library rules themselves, however, would almost certainly have used *may* rather than *can*.)

MUST similarly occurs in the reporting of a rule:

A spokesman for Devon County Council's Weights and Measures Department said 'Where a landlady says her place is "two minutes from the sea" it must not mean by jet aircraft'. (W.12.4.57)

It is fairly obvious that rules can be seen either as reports of deontic modality or as saying what is dynamically possible or necessary (and we have already noted that deontic CAN might be regarded as derived by implication from dynamic CAN – 4.2.3). Let us see if there are any reasons for preferring one solution or the other.

[i] The occurrence of *may* suggests that we should treat some of the examples as deontic; where *can* occurs either interpretation is possible.

[ii] There is a potential difference in the use of *can* and *may* in, for instance:

You may smoke in here.
You can smoke in here.

Both give permission, the first in a more formal style, but with *may* there is a greater possibility that the speaker himself not merely reports a rule, but himself imposes it (he may be a member of the institution that has made the rule). In this sense it is still to some degree deontic, performative.

[iii] With CAN the past tense form is available for reporting rules of the past:

You could smoke on the upper deck.

The only clear example in the Survey is in reported speech (with sequence of tenses), and in the negative:

I was angry at the School of Applied Linguistics when I found that as a student I couldn't get a key. (S. 2.4a.45)

But it would be perfectly possible to say simply *As a student I could get a key*, with the permission sense of CAN.

The past tense form of MAY, *might*, is used only in a very formal literary style. Scheurweghs (1959: 365) notes:

No one but the Duke might build castles.

The fact that *might* does not occur, except in very formal styles, supports the deontic interpretation, for a deontic modal normally has no past tense form.

We have here a gradation between:

[i] Giving permission, laying obligation.
[ii] Reporting rules and agreeing with them.
[iii] Reporting rules.
[iv] Saying what is possible or necessary.

[i] is clearly deontic and [iv] clearly dynamic. The other two are in between, and there is no non-arbitrary way of drawing a clear distinction.

8.2 Rational modality

There are some examples of the present tense negative form of CAN, or of a positive form with a semi-negative such as *hardly* in which the speaker refers to states of affairs that he finds quite unacceptable, and that are, in that sense, not possible:

> We cannot go on fining and levying our people for the benefit of farmers, whether rich farmers or poor, inefficient, farmers in the Market. (S.6.3.82)
> These are terms we cannot accept. No British government should, no Labour government would. These terms are unacceptable. (S.12.5.56)
> What are you going to do with a woman on her own? You can't even ask her to a dinner party. (W.5.2.64)
> Come off it! You can hardly call Cynthia inscrutable. (W.5.2.35)
> Britain of all nations cannot stand by as an inactive observer of this tragic situation. (W.15.3a.22-1)

It is noticeable that in all of these examples the subject is either (*a*) in the first person, (*b*) the impersonal *you* or (*c*) something with which the speaker identifies himself (*eg Britain*).

There is often not merely the sense of 'unreasonable', but also the suggestion that the speaker is unwilling to accept the situation. Indeed, *can't* with *I* is often used simply to refuse to act:

> No, I can't be rude – he's seen me. (W.5.2.88)
> Oh, can't have that. (W.5.2.69)

In none of these examples is there reference to what is strictly impossible, but only to what is unreasonable and unacceptable.

There are fewer examples of positive forms, but two (one with the tentative *could*) are:

> The reason it was quiet before 1968 was because, you can argue—is because the British didn't stand up to the Northern, the Ulster Protestants. (S.2.8a.53)
> So in some degree you could say it would be taking him rather too literally. (S.3.6.75)

Ehrman (1966: 14) has a very clear example:

> The societies can expect to face difficult times.

In all of these examples MAY (*may* or *might*) could equally occur with little change of meaning, and there are examples of it in the Survey:

> I'd go further. There are things outside what may be called normal sexual intercourse. (S.12.3.49)
> We operate what might be described as a gigantic tutorial system. (S.6.1c.8)

If we can take the CAN and MAY forms together, it would follow that rational possibility is not to be treated as a sort of dynamic possibility, because MAY is not a dynamic modal. However, it is not possible to replace CAN by MAY in the negative forms. Nor could we have MAY in the following example, which refers to reasonable possibility, not actual possibility, in the past:

> Now it had to be a well because you could not build a house in those days without digging the well. (S.12.6.8)

One possible explanation of these forms is similar to that proposed for 'rules and regulations' (8.1), that they are partly deontic (what is reasonably permissible) and partly dynamic (what is reasonably possible). But *might* in the example above raises a problem, for this form does not normally occur either as a deontic or a dynamic modal. Perhaps, then, we should treat the CAN forms as essentially dynamic but with the meaning of reasonable rather than actual possibility, and look for the explanation of the MAY forms elsewhere (8.5).

MUST is used in a similar way, and does not seem to be either deontic or strictly dynamic:

> The government must act. It must make up its mind about priorities – offices or houses, housing estates or luxury buildings. (W.15.1.48-3)

The speaker is not, one would assume, in a position to give the government orders or to lay any obligation on it to act. Nor is he saying that there are circumstances which force it to act. He is merely stating what he thinks is rational in the extreme – 'It is utterly unreasonable for the government not to act'.

Notice that HAVE TO and HAVE GOT TO would be less likely in this sense. The usual meaning of *The government has got to act* would be that there are circumstances which now force it to do so.

8.3 Existential modality

Leech (1969: 223) offers the sentence:

> Lions can be dangerous.

This is clearly different from the epistemic *Lions may be dangerous*. It does not mean 'It is possible that lions are dangerous', but 'It is possible for lions to be dangerous', in the sense 'Some lions are dangerous'.

The paraphrase 'possible for' makes this use look as if it is another variety of dynamic modality, but it is of particular theoretical interest because of von Wright's (1951: 1–2) suggestion that there is a close parallelism between the existential mode involving 'some' and 'all', and the dynamic mode involving 'possible' and 'necessary'. We could well argue, then, that this is yet another kind of modality, distinct from dynamic modality, but dealing with quantification, rather than with modality in any of the senses we have been discussing.

8.3.1 'Some' and 'sometimes'

Often CAN does not have the meaning of 'some', but of 'sometimes', and our first example might well mean 'Lions are sometimes dangerous' or even 'Some lions are sometimes dangerous'. In individual examples, of course, it may be possible to draw a 'some'/'sometimes' distinction as in:

Roses can be mauve ('some').
The weather can be awful ('sometimes').

(Curiously *sometimes* may have the 'some' interpretation – *Roses are sometimes mauve,* but not vice versa.)

Surprisingly, perhaps, the 'some' interpretation does not require a plural subject, as is clear from:

The squid of the genus Loligo can be as much as two feet long. (W.4.2a.15)

This does not mean that a squid may vary in length from time to time, but that some squids are two feet long. The same kind of interpretation seems likely for:

It's a great mistake to think that nothing of a school's inner spirit is disclosed on such formal occasions. On the contrary, the speech day can be remarkably revealing. (W.1.5a.18)

Yet the 'sometimes' interpretation is the more common. It is clearly signalled in both of the following examples:

... and this can mean, it doesn't always mean, it can mean, that the students are restructuring their learning, one's teaching, by asking questions. (S.5.7.51)
In themselves the effects aren't devastating, but chugging can sometimes trigger off a fit of screaming. (W.1.2b.21)

In the second example there is clearly some redundancy (see 2.2) with both *sometimes* and *can* occurring. Similarly, we find:

... because the audience can tend to get lost in the action of the play and rather forget that Hamlet is wasting his time. (S.3.5a.41)

Either *can* or *tends to* alone would be sufficient here.

MAY as well as CAN is used:

The process may be carried out indiscriminately by the wind or by insects which fly from flower to flower. (W.10.3.27)
Or the pollen may be taken from the stamens of one rose and transferred to the stigma of another. (W.10.3.27)

It is, however, significant that these are both from a semi-technical book. Huddleston (1971: 297–8) has a number of similar examples, all taken from scientific texts,including some with a 'some' interpretation, *eg:*

> One of us has evidence which agrees with the earlier hypothesis of Chapman and Salton (1962) that the lamellae may arise de novo from the middle of the cell and migrate to the periphery.

8.3.2 CAN and MAY

In general there is a contrast between CAN and MAY. Leech (1969: 220) has, for instance:

> The monsoon can be dangerous.
> The monsoon may be dangerous.

The latter is likely to have an epistemic interpretation. Nevertheless, the example quoted above and numerous others offered by Huddleston show that MAY is also used in an existential sense.

Moreover, there is, in the negative, a clear difference between:

> Lions cannot be dangerous.
> Lions may not be dangerous.

The first has the meaning 'No lions are dangerous' or 'Lions are never dangerous', while the second may mean 'Some lions are not dangerous' or 'Lions are sometimes not dangerous'. This is exemplified by one sentence from the text and one from Huddleston (1974a: 298):

> This makes quite a dent in the theory, for the short back-and-sides man believes tenaciously that proletarians cannot be homosexuals. (W.11.2a.4)
> The hairs are there all the time although they may not grow noticeably before puberty.

In this respect existential modality is like epistemic rather than dynamic, since epistemic *cannot* means 'It is not possible that . . .' and *may not,* 'It is possible that . . . not . . .'. *Cannot,* that is to say, negates the modality, while *may not* negates the proposition.

Reference may be made to past time with *could* (and possibly *might*). An example from the Survey is:

> Yes, but she could be nasty. (S.5.9.16)

For the 'some' interpretation we can invent:

> Dinosaurs could be dangerous.

8.3.3 Necessity

There are several examples in the Survey in which MUST carries with it the suggestion that what is said is true of all the things being referred to; but at the same time it has an implication that this results from an essential characteristic, *eg*:

> All scientific results must depend on a rather specialized form of history. (W.9.3.4-1)
> ... because the farmer saw ... that any trampling about the field must severely damage the basic crop. (S.12.1a.5)

It is significant that these contain either *all* or *any*. This is pleonastic; virtually the same meaning would be indicated with the omission of either the quantifier or the modal (*Scientific results must depend* ... or *All scientific results depend* ...).

However, MUST is also used to indicate what is an inevitable result of the nature of some other event being considered, as in:

> I think both these are extremely dangerous, because I think they will and must strike, in fact, at the roots of the independence of universities. (S.11.2.69)

Similar, but perhaps less obvious, are:

> The resulting impression must be complex, since two sentences are implied. (W.9.4.57-2)
> 'For the English historian it must have a peculiar importance because of the possible light it throws on Melpham.' (W.16.6.168-7)

These two could be interpreted epistemically, to suggest that the speakers are drawing conclusions from the circumstances indicated by *since* ... and *because* ..., but, in fact, they seem rather to be giving reasons why things must be so, not why they believe they are so. But the dividing line between an epistemic and a 'characteristic' interpretation is not very clear.

For negation, *mustn't* would normally negate the modality ('not always', 'not all'), and the negative forms of HAVE TO the proposition. There is, possibly, one example of the latter in Ehrman (1966: 13), where there is a contrast with CAN:

> They speak of the work of Christ as the bestowal of incorruptibility, which can mean (though it does not have to mean) deliverance from time and history.

8.4 Epistemic CAN?

As we have seen in previous sections, CAN is used for epistemic modality only in non-assertion, *ie* negation (3.5.3) and interrogation (3.5.4). The modal for assertion is MAY. There are, however, some assertive uses of CAN in the Survey that look at first sight as if they are epistemic. These are all in the tentative forms *could* and *could have*, *eg*:

This could be the all important round. (S.10.3.99)

The banging on the ceiling could have been water in the pipes or the central heating or something. (S.5.8.39)

Clearly both of these refer to what is possible in a conceptual sense.

However, there is a case for arguing that these are not examples of epistemic CAN, but of a use closer to that of dynamic CAN. It might be thought that in all examples *could* may be replaced with *might* with very little change of meaning, if any. But there is a difference. Although both may refer to what is conceptually possible, *might* commits the speaker to a judgment about the possibility of the truth of the proposition, whereas *could* merely says that it is theoretically possible, *ie* that such a judgment would be a reasonable one, without in any way committing the speaker. This is very clear from an example in Johannesson (1976: 58):

This picture could be a Chagall, but is in fact a Braque.

Boyd and Thorne (1969: 73) similarly suggest:

We could be in Africa.

This 'can be meaningfully used, say, on a fine night in Scotland'. *Might* would be less appropriate here, for it would seem to involve a contradiction in which the speaker denies a proposition which, he allows, may be true (but see the discussion in 8.5 [iii]). But *could* merely suggests that such a judgment would be a possible (reasonable) one, even though it is in fact wrong. There is an example in the Survey too:

Well, now we're coming to this big fight of the evening described in the programme right here in front of me as 'Eliminating World Heavyweight Contest'. Well, it could well be that, and it probably is. (S.10.3.1)

Could, here, introduces what is theoretically possible, and is followed by a judgment not denying it, as in the previous example, but asserting the probability that it is true. Similarly, in examples like those given at the beginning of this section, it would be possible to deny the possibility that the proposition is, was, or will be, true.

Now it could be argued that the difference between *might* and *could* is essentially one of subjective vs objective epistemic judgment (Lyons 1977: 792, *cf* 1.1.2, 1.1.3), *ie* that with *might* the speaker indicates what is epistemically possible from the evidence, even if he does not himself wish to draw that conclusion. But that does not really explain why *could* is used for this 'objective' epistemic possibility.

It is relevant to note that with CAN the paraphrase 'possible for' is appropriate, *eg* 'It is possible for this to be the important round . . .'. With the other examples we need 'would be possible', as in 'It would be possible for this to be a Braque'. An interpretation in terms of 'possible that' is less appropriate in both cases. Since 'possible for' is the paraphrase of dynamic necessity, there is a case for arguing that these examples are best explained in terms of dynamic rather than epistemic modality.

In non-assertive contexts, of course, CAN is used quite regularly as an epistemic modal. An epistemic interpretation is, thus, correct for (*cf* 5.3, 3.5.4):

Yes, well, it couldn't have been in April, my lord. (S.12.3.24)
I was wondering if it could have been fear. (S.3.5b.63)

We should not also confuse the use of *could* discussed here with:

It isn't raining in Chicago, but it could be. (Kartunnen 1972: 4)

This is a simple example of what would be dynamically possible (if some circumstances were different).

Our examples have all been of *could* and *could have*, but Johannesson (1976: 56) provides some of *cán have* (with *cán* stressed). These he invents by taking genuine examples with *may*, replacing *may* with *cán*, and then adding a denial or reservation beginning with *but*:

This important step in man's cultural advance cán have occurred 1.5 million years ago, but it need not have happened until considerably later. The fossil people cán have been related to each other but this can, of course, not be proved.

Johannesson also offers:

This picture can be a Chagall.

But he stars:

*This picture can be a Chagall, but is, in fact, a Braque.

In theory he may be right in suggesting that *can* may be used to introduce what is theoretically possible. In practice, I would prefer *could,* especially where the proposition is later held in doubt, and, as he himself notes with the last example, *can* would not be used to refer to a proposition in the present which is known to be untrue.

8.5 Dynamic MAY?

There are a number of examples of *may* and *might* being used in what seems, at first, to be a dynamic sense. In all such cases it is possible to substitute *can* and *could* with very little change of meaning, if any. There are clearly two ways of accounting for these forms, either to say that MAY is in some circumstances used in a dynamic sense, or to explain it in terms of epistemic or deontic MAY.

[i] A purely stylistic explanation seems to be the correct one for:

> Cader Idris, however, may be climbed from other points on this tour. (W.11.3.86-3)
> Where, in a secluded valley in the west, you may find the neat little Norman church of Pennant Melangell. (W.11.3.80-4)

In both of these, MAY is to be paraphrased by 'possible for' and clearly has a dynamic sense. The first could be read in a deontic ('rules and regulations') sense, and the second in an epistemic sense ('perhaps you will'), but neither is the correct reading here. It seems clear that MAY is used in this kind of written text in a dynamic sense; it would, however, be much more normal, especially in colloquial English, to use CAN.

[ii] We noted in 8.2:

> I'd go further. There are things outside what may be called normal sexual intercourse. (S.12.3.49)
> We operate what might be described as a gigantic tutorial system. (S.6.1c.8)

Although one has *may* and the other *might,* the uses here seem to be the same; in particular both are concerned with what is a proper description ('may be called', 'might be described'). If these are simply dynamic there is no problem, except to account for the use of MAY rather than of CAN. They are almost certainly not examples of deontic MAY, for, although the first might seem to be accountable for in terms of 'what one may be permitted to call' (*ie* a use very similar to that of 'rules and regulations'), the deontic modals have no tentative (past tense) forms and we thus have no explanation at all for *might.* An epistemic interpretation is, perhaps, possible – 'It may be that it is called', 'It might be that it is described'. Alternatively, there may be blending between 'can be called' and epistemic 'may be that it is', *ie* MAY is preferred to CAN because of the general epistemic quality of the expression. (MAY is also used in subordinate 'purpose' clauses, where the meaning could be interpreted in terms of dynamic possibility (8.6).)

[iii] There is one example in the Survey of *might have* that seems difficult to explain:

> They did their best, but it soon became clear that they were in a foreign country. I might have been talking to them in Coptic. (W.15.1.6-3)

This is not an example of the kind discussed in 7.5.5, for it does not mean 'It is possible that I would have been talking to them in Coptic'. It means, rather, that it would have been possible, *ie* conceivable, that I was talking to them in Coptic. If so, this is an example of epistemic possibility, but with the past unreality relating not to the proposition, as in the examples of 7.5.5, but to the modality.

Notice that we could equally say:

For all the notice they are taking I might be talking in Coptic.

This, again, can be interpreted epistemically if the epistemic modal is treated as an unreal present condition – 'It would be possible that . . .'.

However, the suggestion that epistemic modals can occur as unreal conditionals is a new one. In 3.4.1 (cf 7.5.5) it was argued that *might*, in particular, is merely tentative (not an unreal conditional). But a tentative interpretation would be wrong in our example here. The speaker is not saying 'It is tentatively possible that I am . . .', which leaves open the possibility that the proposition is true, but 'It would be possible that I am . . .', with the implication that the proposition is false.

[iv] *Might* is often used to put forward a suggestion:

> You might try nagging the Abbey National again. (S.8.3h.5)
> You might even pay a visit. (S.7.2b.9)
> No, I was going to suggest we might look through Habitat and see if we can find her anything. (S.7.2b.9)

There is what I take to be a similar use of *might have* in:

> You might have told me.

Might expresses what is possible, and so suggests action; *might have* says what would have been possible but did not in fact take place, and so implies a reproach. This also accounts for the use of *might* in interrogation, since *could* would be used if it were epistemic (3.5.4):

> Would you ring me? Might that be best? (S.9.1b.7)

But is this dynamic possibility? That is one solution. Yet *might* here seems to be almost deontic; yet, as we noted before, the deontic modals do not normally have tentative (past tense) forms. The forms could also be explained epistemically, like those in the previous paragraph – 'It would be conceivable that you will . . .', 'It would have been conceivable that you would . . .'.

[v] English also has the expressions *might (just) as well* and *might (just) as well have* with the meaning 'It would be/would have been (just) as good if . . .':

> I might as well stay at home.
> I might as well have stayed at home.

But since this meaning is carried only if *(just) as well* occurs, it should be treated as idiomatic.

[vi] *Might* is also used to refer to habitual activity in the past:

> In those days we might go for a walk through the woods.

This is, perhaps, an existential use (8.3.2), but with a habitual meaning like that of *would* (7.4.3).

We ought not to be too dogmatic about any of these solutions. The truth is rather that, in some circumstances, the semantic distinction between different kinds of modality is very clear, and the choice of CAN or MAY determined. In others, the distinctions are far less clear and the choice between CAN and MAY is no longer determined.

There is, however, another possible explanation – that MAY is the most neutral modal, used in a variety of cases in which there is simply non-factivity and in which a modal with a more specific meaning is not appropriate (though its own epistemic and deontic uses are quite specific). This would account not only for the uses of MAY in this section, but for others that do not entirely fit into other chapters, *eg* the 'concessive' use (3.1), the subordinate use (8.6) and the use for wishes (8.6). If this is so, it may, after all, be the closest form in English to the subjunctive of other languages.

8.6 Modals in subordinate clauses

Modals can, of course, occur like any other forms in English in subordinate clauses and generally there is little more to be said, though we have already noted their very special use in conditionals. There are, however, several uses in subordinate clauses that require specific notice.

[i] Deontic modals may occur after verbs of insisting, deciding, intending, etc, where the verb itself is an indication of the performative. Thus we have seen with MUST (4.3):

A new insistence from President Nixon that the Hanoi government must negotiate if there's to be any settlement. (W.2.3b.13)

Similarly we find with SHALL:

Nevertheless, it is agreed that the School of Yiddish shall comprise the Department of Yiddish literature, the Department of Yiddish language and mediaeval literature and the division of contemporary Yiddish. (S.1.2.3)
Our political correspondent points out that the government hasn't decided yet where the new cities and expanded towns shall be. (W.2.1.6)

[ii] SHOULD may also occur in similar circumstances but, rather strikingly, not OUGHT TO; this seems to be a fairly formal use. Scheurweghs has examples with the verbs REQUIRE, DESIRE, INSIST and FAVOUR. One of his examples and one from the Survey are:

It is also proposed that an economic commission should be appointed. (Scheurweghs 1959: 376)
Robert Ibbs is very keen that we should talk about the Australian television. (S.9.1l.2)

Here, perhaps, we can treat *should* as a tentative form of SHALL referring to a desire, proposal, or recommendation, rather than a decision or agreement. If so, it is the only use of *should* that can be so treated, since elsewhere it seems to belong, with OUGHT TO, to the necessity modality and not to the third degree that is represented by SHALL (and WILL). But the semantics and the fact that OUGHT TO cannot be used here strongly supports this interpretation.

[iii] *May* occurs where what is intended or envisaged is possible, but especially where there is a purpose clause introduced by *in order that* or *so that*:

> How can you keep bees? You have to have lots of land in order they may eat. A bee like yours can feed in London. (S.11.3a.13)
> ... and will examine ways in which this may be more efficiently safeguarded. (W.4.1b.15)

Can could also occur here, and would be more usual in colloquial speech, especially if the clause-introducing element is *so that*:

> ... so that they can eat.

Slightly different, but still interpretable in terms of purpose, is the use of *shall* in:

> Medical science is keeping people going a very long time now, and we've got to find some way that they shall enjoy it. (S.5.2.25)

[iv] In all the examples we have considered so far the modals have much in common with their uses in non-subordinate clauses (except for the SHALL-type use of *should,* which is, on formal grounds, not very surprising). But it is far more difficult to see why *should* is used in:

> Well, it surprises me that Eileen should be surprised. (S.1.13.9)
> ... but it's ridiculous that I should be allowed to work in another college and not allowed to work in my own. (S.2.4a.47)
> Sort of tries to find an excuse to get me away and apologizes profusely that I should have been lumbered with him. (S.4.3.79)

In all of these the modal seems to be redundant; the meaning could have been expressed without it – ... *Eileen was surprised, ... I was allowed to ..., ... I was lumbered....* For many other examples see Scheurweghs (1959: 375, 379) and Kruisinga and Erades (1911: 623).

There are some examples, however, where *should* has a more modal meaning. It occurs, as we saw in 3.4.3, with *reason:*

> It wouldn't be so. There's no reason why it should be surprising. (S.2.8a.74)

Not very different are examples with *why:*

We can see why Hamlet should have a father like that. (S.3.5a.45)
You see, I find it difficult to understand why he should have given all that
up and come back to all our grubby lot of so-and-so's. (W.5.2.22)

These could, perhaps, be handled in terms of 'reasonable necessity' (8.2),
but it is surely significant, that with both these and the examples of
'redundant' *should*, OUGHT TO would be impossible.

In both cases there is an expression of our attitude towards an event, and
even though it is implied that the event took place, this actuality is itself not
particularly important. The speaker in the third example of the first set is
not apologizing that the event happened, but for its happening. These are
contexts similar to those in which some languages would use a subjunctive;
perhaps, in English too, they are treated as modal rather than factual.

[v] Here, perhaps, is the most convenient place to mention the use of MAY
in wishes, *eg* (Scheurweghs 1959: 369):

May God bless you all through the coming year.

This is very formal indeed. However, MAY is more likely in a subordinate
clause after verbs such as PRAY:

I pray that God may bless you.

This subordinate use is not very different from the other subordinate uses of
MAY that we have been considering (in [iii]). It is not difficult, therefore, to
explain. Can we, perhaps, regard the non-subordinate use as synchronically,
at least, implying an understood 'I pray that . . .'? If not, it must simply be
seen as a wholly idiosyncratic and archaic form.

[vi] For conditional *should* see 7.5.6.

Chapter 9

General and theoretical issues

In this chapter we will discuss four issues that relate in a general way to the problems of modals and modality.

9.1 Actuality

We have discussed, in a number of places, the question of the implication of actuality, *ie* the implication that the event did, does or will take place. We found that in certain circumstances a true modal will have no implication of actuality and so may not be used if actuality is implied, whereas a closely associated semi-modal has no such restriction or, at least, that if there is an implication of actuality the semi-modal is preferred. A number of different instances were noted.

[i] Most importantly, past tense *could* and *would* do not normally have the implication of actuality if there is reference to a single action in the past, whereas the negative forms *couldn't* and *wouldn't* quite clearly deny the actuality of the event. By contrast the past tense forms of BE ABLE TO (and to a lesser extent of BE WILLING TO) carry with them the implication of actuality (5.3.3, 7.4.3). Invented forms to illustrate this were:

*I ran fast, and could catch the bus.
I ran fast, but couldn't catch the bus.
I ran fast, and was able to catch the bus.

*I asked him, and he would come.
I asked him, but he wouldn't come.
I asked him, and he was willing to come.

However, it was also noted that where there is either syntactically or semantically any kind of negation, or even the suggestion that the event almost did not take place, the positive forms may still be used.

[ii] Even in the present tense form BE ABLE TO is more likely to be used than

CAN if there is the implication of present actuality (5.2.[ii]). An example was:

In this way we are able to carry out research. (S.6.1C.12)

For necessity, moreover, HAVE TO must be used rather than MUST, if actuality is implied (6.2.3[ii]):

He's got to fight his way through the crowds. (S.10.3.3)

[iii] In contrast with [i] and [ii] CAN often, and volitional WILL always, imply future actuality (5.3.4, 7.1.1):

Liverpool can win the cup next year.
Anyway I will write as soon as I get to Nigeria and again when I get to Bida itself. (W.7.2.29)

We may now ask whether any explanation for this apparently complex state of affairs can be given. In fact, the explanation may be quite simple. The future is the period of time that has the least factual status; there is a sense in which we can never know the future (cf Lyons 1977: 815 for a discussion of the philosophical-linguistic implication of this). By contrast, the past is the most factual; we can, and often do, know whether events took place. If, then, modality is concerned with events and propositions whose factual status is in doubt (cf 1.1.3 and Lyons 1968: 307), it is not surprising that a modal verb may be inappropriate to refer to past events whose factual status is established, but perfectly appropriate to refer to future events whose factual status cannot be established. Future actuality is, in this sense, not actuality at all but another kind of modality. But this applies only to true modals, and not the semi-modals – to CAN and WILL but not to BE ABLE TO and BE WILLING TO. This shows that, as one might suspect, they are not only formally but also semantically distinct.

In terms of factual status, the present is between the past and future. Present tense forms usually refer to events both before and after the immediate present, and so include both events whose factual status is known and events whose factual status is not known. Not surprisingly, then, BE ABLE TO is preferred to CAN if there is present actuality, while HAVE TO seems to be required instead of MUST. (There is no issue with volitional WILL, since it implies only future actuality.)

With the negative forms the position is different. It follows, quite logically, that what is, was, or will not be possible, does not, did not, or will not take place. Negative possibility must, therefore, always imply negative actuality, and this is as true of *couldn't* as of *was/were not able to*.

There is, however, not quite such a simple solution for *wouldn't*. For negative volition does not logically imply negative actuality and, unlike *was not able, was not willing* does not imply negative actuality; yet *wouldn't* does:

He was not willing to come, but he came.
*He wouldn't come, but he came.

Why, then, does *wouldn't* imply actuality? It might seem to be relevant that in the present tense WILL always implies actuality, both positive and negative (unlike BE WILLING TO):

*He'll come, but he's not going to.
*He won't come, but he's going to.
He's willing to come, but he's not going to.
He's not willing to come, but he's going to.

(The first two are possible if the first part is taken as a report of what was said.) But although this would explain why *wouldn't* implies negative actuality, it would fail to account for the fact that *would* may not be used where positive actuality is implied. The only possible explanation is that it functions like *could,* for CAN and WILL have much in common; the restriction is thus determined by analogy.

9.2 Conventional implication

We have discussed in a number of places the use of modals with, what I have called, 'conventional implication'. With this, it would seem, the modal is 'not to be taken literally', or, to put it another way, the speaker does not 'say what he means'. (For the general issue see Grice 1968.)

9.2.1 Four types

We may distinguish at least four types.

[i] Both dynamic CAN and WILL are used in interrogation with *you,* not merely to ask whether the person addressed is able or willing to carry out the action, but as a request that he does so (5.3.2, 5.3.5, 7.4.2, 7.4.5):

Here, June, can you give me a hand with this harness? (W.5.3.98)
Could you tell me the name of the person concerned? (S.8.3k.8)
Will you pass that on to him? (S.7.3a.2)
Would you ring me? (S.9.1b.7)

These cannot be taken simply as questions about the ability or willingness of the person. It would be perverse, especially with the CAN example, for someone simply to reply *Yes* and then take no action at all on the grounds that he was certainly able to and that that was all that was asked.
[ii] Deontic MAY and CAN may be used with a first person subject in interrogation, not merely to ask permission from the person addressed, but actually to request him to take action (4.5.2). The classic example is:

May/can I have the salt?

Although this, as an interrogative, has the form normally associated with a question, its conventional use as a request is so well established that it will often, even usually, occur with *please*:

May I have the salt, please?

[iii] Deontic CAN in assertion may be used more as a command than simply to give permission. In some circumstances, that is to say, the granting of permission has the conventional implication that the person addressed should or must act (4.2.2):

You can leave me out, thank you very much. (S.6.2.60)

[iv] With first person subjects, and less commonly with third person ones, the WILL'of volition expresses not merely willingness, but also constitutes an offer or agreement to act (7.1.1):

Anyway, I will write as soon as I get to Nigeria and again when I get to Bida itself. (W.7.2.29)

The implication is an obvious one, for there is little point in saying that one is willing if one does not intend to act.

In recent years there have been a number of articles that have discussed problems of this kind. In the next two sections we shall consider two solutions that have been proposed. Following those, in 9.2.4, we shall consider a further proposal, only to suggest that it is not in fact relevant to our problem. 9.2.5 will return to a more general discussion and conclusion.

9.2.2 Conversational postulates

Gordon and Lakoff (1971 : 63–6) argue that a sincere request 'conversationally' implies:

(*a*) that the speaker wants the action performed;
(*b*) that the hearer can do it;
(*c*) that the hearer is willing to do it;
(*d*) that the hearer will not do it unless requested.

The principles are stated in the form:

(*a*) SINCERE (a, REQUEST (a, b, Q)) → WANT (a, Q)
(*b*)   „   → ASSUME (a, CAN (b, Q))
(*c*)   „   → ASSUME (a, WILLING (b, Q))
(*d*)   „   → ASSUME (a, −Q)
   where Q is of the form FUT (DO (b, R)) [b will do act R].

They consider the sentences:

(*a*) I want you to take out the garbage.

(b) Can you take out the garbage?
(c) Are you willing to take out the garbage?
(d) Will you take out the garbage?

They then point out the relationship between these sentences and the right-hand side of the set of principles (the 'sincerity conditions' of the requests), where (a) is a 'speaker-based sincerity condition' and the remainder are 'hearer-based sincerity conditions'. They then proceed to the conclusion:

One can convey a request by (i) asserting a speaker-based sincerity condition or (ii) questioning a hearer-based sincerity condition.

There is, unfortunately, a problem for them with (d) since this is a negative condition, yet like the rest is still questioned by a positive question, and, moreover, should really include 'otherwise' (the hearer will not do it unless requested) which cannot occur in the question sentence. The first point is dismissed on the grounds that we can only question a negative with a positive question, but the second is left unanswered with a grudging confession in the footnotes that the omission of *otherwise* is 'fudging'. Yet there is an obvious solution. *Will* here cannot simply mean FUT (DO), for if it did there would be no explanation at all for the fact that we cannot also use *Are you going to take out the garbage?* in a similar way. That is a reminder rather than a request, which seems intuitively to make sense; to ask whether something is going to take place is appropriate when it normally would happen, but the hearer seems to have forgotten. *Will*, therefore, must be taken in a volitional rather than a future sense; we need neither the negative nor *otherwise* and (d) may read:

(d) SINCERE (a, REQUEST (a, b, Q)) → ASSUME (a, WILL (b, Q))

Gordon and Lakoff are concerned with formalizing the conversational principles and incorporating them in a theory of generative semantics and believe that their strategy is based on notions of natural logic. But, although they may explain why a form may be used, they cannot predict that it will so be used. There are conventions of a fairly arbitrary kind that regulate the use of particular forms of expression. For instance, it is not the case that a request is usually made with BE WILLING TO as suggested by (c); yet if BE WILLING TO were used, a native speaker of English would be able to infer that a request was being made. By contrast CAN and WILL are the forms that are conventionally used.

But Gordon and Lakoff's account will not always work. For consider the use of the expression *Do you want to pass the salt?* as a request. This is not used in England, but occurs in some parts of the United States. Yet the Englishman who hears this immediately recognizes it as a request; and would not take it as a question and so reply *Yes, I do* or *No, I don't*. This is evidence against Gordon and Lakoff's claim, for a request does not assume that the speaker wants to act; wanting to act is not one of the sincerity conditions. This sentence cannot, therefore, be explained by their schema. Moreover, the fact that the Englishman does not use the form, but can still understand it, suggests that it is convention not logic that is involved, though the precise form of the convention has to be guessed in this case. This is possible because it fits a fairly general pattern (polite requests are made by asking about ability, willingness, etc). (For a detailed discussion of Gordon and Lakoff, see Sadock 1974: 74–95.)

9.2.3 Deep structures

Fraser (1973) argues for the recognition of different illocutionary forces, a request being different in that respect from a question. But he suggests that in the case of sentences like *Can you pass the salt?* (with *can, could, will, would, couldn't, can't, won't*) there are two different deep structures, one interrogative and the other imperative. The arguments in favour of this rest upon eleven formal differences between the sentence with its question force and the sentence with its request force:

[i] *Please* may occur in a request but not a question (see 8.3.2).

[ii] *Can you*, etc may be postposed to final position in requests only (*Give me some milk, could you?*).

[iii] With requests the main verb must denote a voluntary action.

[iv] The subject NP in requests must be *you* or the indefinite *somebody/someone*.

[v] Adverbs such as *willingly, easily, voluntarily* cannot occur in requests.

[vi] BE ABLE TO is not a paraphrase of CAN in requests.

[vii] *Can*, etc cannot be emphatically stressed in requests.

[viii] The contracted negative forms *can't*, etc are not synonymous with the uncontracted forms *cannot*, etc in requests.

[ix] *Some* and *any* both occur in questions, but only *some* in requests.

[x] A request is not well formed unless an indefinite object actually exists – *Will you send me a unicorn in the morning mail?* has the force of a request only if unicorns are assumed to be available.

[xi] The various modals can be arranged in an order of decreasing politeness – this has to be accounted for in the grammar.

Of these, [i], [vi], [ix] and [xi] seem to be entirely valid. [ii] is a misleading interpretation. It would normally be said that we have here an imperative with a tag question and not something derived from *Could you give me some milk?* But it is to be noted that such tags are used for requests although they have the form of a question, and so are relevant to Fraser's argument. [iv] is not strictly true; the subject can be in the third person (*Can the panel explain why...? cf* 7.4.5 for a similar example with *would*). [iii] and [v] make a single point – that the verb must be one over which the subject has voluntary control, but in themselves they are not arguments for making the distinction, because it follows naturally that one can only reasonably request an action if it is one that the person addressed can choose to do or not to do; there is, then, some circularity of argument here. [vii] and [viii] do not seem to me to be wholly true. [x] is nonsense. Questions no less than requests are in some sense 'not well formed' if they are concerned with unicorns.

We must accept with Fraser that there are grammatical differences; whether this is a matter of deep structure is by no means proved. Unfortunately for his argument, he next considers *May I have the salt?* Here again, there are potentially two different illocutionary forces, one merely asking for permission, the other requesting action by the hearer. But with these Fraser cannot find differences like those noted for *Can you pass the salt?* In particular, *please* may be used either to ask permission (for the speaker to act) or to request an action by the hearer. He is forced, therefore, to conclude that requests and questions have the same deep structure, but different forces. The permission force, however, is 'directly a function of the meaning of the sentence', while the request force follows from this together with some 'rules of conversation'.

This is unsatisfactory for several reasons. First, if there are deep structure differences in the one, there surely ought to be similar differences in the other, irrespective of the presence of specific formal marks. (After all *sheep* can be plural with no *-s*.) Secondly, the rules of conversation explain the dual function of CAN as easily as that of MAY. It is reasonable to argue that both asking someone whether he can act and asking for permission for oneself to act may equally be taken, in appropriate circumstances, as requests for the hearer to do something. But the deep structure analysis would make such explanations superfluous.

9.2.4 Honorifics

R. Lakoff (1972*b*) considers the sentences:

You must have some of this cake.
You should have some of this cake.
You may have some of this cake.

The occasion is one in which the hostess is offering her guests a cake that she herself has baked. Lakoff points out that these sentences are arranged in order of politeness and suggests that the first, the most polite, is very like a sentence in other languages in which honorifics are used. In such languages there is 'linguistic abasement' and the hostess would say 'Honourable Mrs Snarf have some of my humble apple pie', though in translation, of course, this sounds quite ludicrous. She argues that the sentence with *must* would be a much closer translation of a sentence from a language that uses honorifics than the more literal translation 'Have some of this revolting cake'.

The puzzle is, however, that it would appear at first sight to be more polite to use MAY than MUST rather than vice versa. Why is it more polite to impose an obligation than to advise or to give permission? Lakoff argues that we impose obligation when the person would not otherwise do what he is instructed to do, *ie* when there is an assumption that the act is distasteful to him.

MUST, she suggests contains an amalgam of three meanings:

[i] That the speaker is higher in rank than the hearer.
[ii] That the thing is distasteful to the hearer.
[iii] That something untoward will happen to him if he does not carry out the instruction.

Theoretically, the sentence is triply ambiguous, but the context disambiguates and we decide on meaning [ii]. It is the humbling force that makes the use of MUST the most polite of the three.

This is, surely, mistaken. The correct explanation does not lie in the use of modals at all but in the general, and not specifically linguistic, convention that it is the duty of a hostess to persuade her guests to take as much food as possible (just as it is the guests' duty not to be too greedy). For generosity is a virtue in almost all societies. The hostess can achieve her end in various ways, by offering large helpings, by keeping the guests' plates (and glasses) full, or by using linguistic means which include not only the obligation modals but even imperatives. The guest accepts this behaviour even though in different circumstances he would object to being given orders. But the essential point is that we do not need a linguistic explanation here at all.

This is not to say that there is no relation between the meaning of a sentence and its context or that the meaning cannot be inferred from the context. Certainly we can recognize here the use of MUST as a polite way of offering food to one's guests. But we do not need a linguistic explanation for this; the linguistic behaviour is of a pattern with non-linguistic behaviour and the problem is more a matter for sociology than linguistics.

9.2.5 Convention and implication

The sentences that we have been considering, apart from those in 9.2.4, have two characteristics. First, they are conventionally determined; secondly, their meaning can be seen as derived from, or implied by, a more basic meaning.

There are other sentences that may have only one of these characteristics. For instance, *How do you do?* is a purely conventional form, but it would be difficult, if not impossible, to derive its meaning from the more literal meaning of the words. It is more important to contrast sentences that seem to have an implied meaning, yet are not determined conventionally. One can, for instance, say *It's hot in here* in order to get someone to open a window. Similarly, identical effects may be achieved by either of the following:

Here, June, can you give me a hand with this harness? (W.5.3.98)
This harness is too heavy for me to move.

The differences between these two types of sentences are quite clear:

[i] With conventional implication the precise form of words is important. In particular, for instance, BE ABLE TO is not used instead of CAN in sentences like those above (5.3.2, 9.2.3).

[ii] The form of the sentences that may be used with conventional implication is limited (*Can you . . . ? Will you . . . ? Could you . . . ? Would you . . . ?*). There is no limit on the other type; to get a window open one might say *It's stuffy in here, I'm hot, There's not much air,* etc.

[iii] The conventions differ from language to language, but in any language comments of the kind mentioned in [ii] may serve to get the window open (though, of course, there may be some conventions that forbid or encourage certain types of remarks).

There is a neat analogy in the highly conventionalized rituals such as bidding in the game of bridge. *Four no trumps* has as its 'basic' or 'literal' meaning that the speaker contracts to make ten tricks (he will be penalized if he does not and rewarded if he does). But for some players there is the convention that this is a request for the partner to say how many aces he holds in his hand. This is like conventional derived meaning. Yet it is also possible that the speaker may say *Four no trumps* simply to give his opponents a false impression of the cards he holds in his own hand. This is not a matter of convention, but a matter of using the rules and conventions to one's best advantage, just as one can get a window open by saying *It's hot in here*.

We can, then, see at least three levels of meaning. They are, however, not entirely distinct simply because habits may become conventions and conventions may become rules. Thus, it could become a convention never to ask for a window to be opened directly, but always to achieve that end by saying *It's hot in here*. Similarly, it could be that one day *Can you pass the salt?* will have entirely lost its literal meaning and will be the normal form of the imperative.

Where there is a conventional implication, the assumption is that we can see how the basic meaning is used to imply the conventional one. They are in some way related so that it becomes reasonable, but not necessary in any logical sense, to see one meaning as an extension of, or derivation from, the other. But just as the two meanings are not logically related, it is also a mistake to think that the hearer arrives at the implied meaning by a process of reasoning. Fraser (1973: 305) considers *Should you be doing that?* said by a man to a teenager decorating a car with a paint spray. He offers seven

steps in the reasoning by the hearer which lead him to the conclusion that
the speaker is suggesting that he should stop painting:

[i] The speaker has inquired if it is appropriate for me to be painting this
car.

[ii] We both recognize that it is not appropriate and we both recognize that
the other is aware of this.

[iii] Thus, the speaker cannot be seriously asking me the apparent question
and the question is only rhetorical.

[iv] Rhetorical questions should be reinterpreted as the statement of the
same proposition but with a polarity change (positive questions become
negative statements and negative questions become positive statements).

[v] Thus, the speaker is really 'saying' *You shouldn't be painting that car.*

[vi] The sentence *You shouldn't be painting that car* has the force of a
suggestion to cease the painting.

[vii] Thus, I infer that the speaker is suggesting that I stop my painting.

But the hearer does not reason in this way at all. He knows from
experience that a question of this kind is to be taken as a negative command.
Should you . . . is meant to say 'You shouldn't . . .' and *Must you* . . . 'You
mustn't . . .'. There is no direct line of reasoning. (Fraser himself notes 'one
large jump in the reasoning, namely, that because the question interpretation
is derived this sentence is interpreted as a rhetorical question'.)

The most we can say of these conventionally derived meanings is (*a*) that
they are conventional, (*b*) that they may or may not be marked formally, (*c*)
that they are related to the basic meaning in a reasonable way. To say 'in a
reasonable way' is to say that we can find general explanations but no logical
rules, and that although there is no need for a particular language to follow
a particular convention, it is not surprising if it does. It is not a matter of
what all languages do or what languages must do, but simply of what they
might reasonably do.

Finally, it should be noted that it is not always possible to decide whether
a meaning is basic or implied. We saw in 4.2.3 that for the CAN of permission
it could be argued either that this is a deontic use of CAN or that it is a
meaning derived by implication from its dynamic use. In general, I would
prefer to reserve the notion of implication to the semi-formulaic conventional
implications that we have been discussing; but there is no clear borderline
between these and other related uses.

9.3 Indeterminacy

It has become increasingly apparent in recent years that there are many
areas of syntax and semantics where no clear, discrete categorization is
possible. This does not invalidate any attempt to categorize; it simply means
that the model must recognize that there are often continua with extremes

that are clearly distinct, but with considerable indeterminacy in the middle. The classic example of this is the attempt by Lees (1960) to demonstrate that there are eight underlying constructions for sentences of the type *It's too hot to eat* and the subsequent demonstration by Bolinger (1961) that not only are there more than eight constructions, but also that there is considerable 'blending' in which one construction effectively blends into another.

It should be a matter of no surprise that there is similar indeterminacy in any categorization of the modals (except a purely formal one, and even then some deliberate arbitrariness is needed).

Let us, then, first identify the places in the description of the modals where indeterminacy is most striking and then attempt to relate it to similar features elsewhere in the grammar.

9.3.1 Kinds of modality

We have seen that of all the kinds of modality only epistemic modality stands out clearly, in both semantic and syntactic respects, from the other kinds. Even so, it is possible to envisage circumstances in which it may not be possible to distinguish epistemic and deontic modality. Consider, for instance, that an imaginary ideal society is being described. If the speaker says what may or must happen in such a society, there is no clear distinction between what he conceptually permits or requires to happen and what will sometimes or always happen in such a society. But this is a fairly academic point; I noted no examples of the lack of a distinction between epistemic and deontic modality in the Survey.

There are, however, some really worrying cases where, for a particular degree of modality, there is no clear distinction between two kinds, such that some examples clearly belong to one kind, some to the other and some fall in between. The problem is most acute in three places in our discussion.

[i] With possibility, it is not always possible to distinguish clearly between neutral dynamic and subject oriented ('ability') modality. CAN may express what is dynamically possible or what the subject has the ability to do, and the distinction has some syntactic validity, yet for many examples it is impossible to draw a clear distinction (5.1.1, 5.1.2, 5.3.4).
[ii] With necessity, it is not always possible to distinguish between deontic and (neutral) dynamic modality with MUST, though HAVE (GOT) TO makes the distinction valid in a negative way, in that it is never deontic (4.3, 6.1, 6.2). In contrast, it is less difficult to distinguish deontic and dynamic possibility.
[iii] It is not always possible to distinguish between the futurity and the volitional use of WILL (7.1.1, 7.2.2).

The first of these, together possibly with the third, relates to a wider phenomenon in language, that of 'personal' and 'impersonal' (or 'transitive' and 'intransitive') constructions and will be discussed in 9.3.2. The second is much more difficult, but clearly relates to a similar problem with performatives.

I do not, however, wish to suggest that, by relating these problems to other areas of English, we can provide a tidy solution. Rather, I suggest that indeterminacy of this kind is a general characteristic of language.

9.3.2 Personal and impersonal

Rosenbaum (1967: 71–9, 121) proposes for a sentence such as *John seems to like it* an analysis in terms of 'subject complementation', *ie* that in deep structure an intransitive verb has as its subject the embedded sentence *John to like it*. Huddleston (1969a: 258–9) points out that such an analysis can be extended to include a very large number of the English catenatives, the crucial argument being whether the verb is voice-neutral or not. He goes on to suggest that many of the modals also are voice-neutral, and that similar arguments may apply. He compares:

His remarks seem to have offended her.
She seems to have been offended by his remarks.

His remarks may have offended her.
She may have been offended by his remarks.

He argues that these pairs differ in exactly the same way, and this can be accounted for if the underlying subject of *seem* and of *may* is not *his remarks,* but *his remarks to have offended her.*

This reasoning has been widely accepted. It was used by Perlmutter (1970) to argue that there are two verbs BEGIN, one transitive and the other intransitive. The basic argumentation is again in Huddleston (1969a: 262), where he compares:

The rain began to destroy the flowers.
John began to read the book.

Only the first is voice-neutral:

The flowers began to be destroyed by the rain.

Yet the solution in terms of subject complementation is a rather curious one and largely forced by the TG model employed; indeed, Garcia (1967: 868) had already thought of it, but dismissed it as 'patently ad hoc'. The essential point is that, with object complementation, it is assumed that the underlying subject of the embedded sentence must be the same as that of the matrix sentence. Thus, *John began to read the book* is interpreted as *John began [John to read the book]*, just as *John wanted to read the book* is seen as *John wanted [John to read the book]*. The subject of the embedded sentence is deleted 'under identity' to give the required sentence. But if the embedded

sentence is passivized its subject will no longer be the same as that of the
matrix and the identity deletion cannot take place. If, however, the
embedded sentence is not the object but the subject of the matrix, the same
problem does not arise. There is no deletion under identity; rather the
subject of the embedded sentence is raised to become the subject of the
sentence in surface structure. This is possible whether the embedded
sentence has been passivized or not; indeed, it will actually ensure that the
active or passive subject of the embedded sentence becomes the subject in
surface structure, which is what is required. Thus, [*The rain to destroy the
flowers*] *began* will be transformed into *The rain began to destroy the flowers,*
and [*The flowers to be destroyed by the rain*] *began* into *The flowers began to be
destroyed by the rain.*

Garcia's remarks are justified when it is shown that this is not the only
solution even within TG terms. It is perfectly possible to achieve the same
ends with object complementation, provided that after the identity deletion
there is 'complement raising', which essentially forms the two verbs into a
single verb. For the purpose of the passive transformation, then, *began to
destroy* would be a single verb allowing *The rain began to destroy the flowers*
to be directly transformed into *The flowers began to be destroyed by the rain.*
With *John began to read the book* such complement raising will not take
place.

A similar argument for the modals and the other auxiliaries becomes
necessary only if they are treated as full verbs – the issue to be discussed in
9.4. But for the moment, let us assume that this is the correct way of
handling the modals.

The question we must ask is whether they are, in underlying structure,
intransitive with subject complementation, or transitive with object
complementation. This is to state the issue in the simple terms in which it
was first seen; more complex problems have been raised, and more complex
solutions offered since (see *eg* Radford 1977: 31–40 for a brief account of
some of the issues). Although there may be a temptation to argue that the
modals are all transitive or all intransitive, it is clear that the correct solution
must be that some are transitive and some intransitive and that there is also
a great deal of indeterminacy.

In the clearest cases we can see that there will be no voice-neutrality, and
that the modal can be regarded as transitive, where the subject can be
characterized as being 'agentive' (Lyons 1968: 386) or where there is a
'volitional component' (Huddleston 1969*a*: 260). This explains why there is
no voice-neutrality in:

John won't drive Mary.
Mary won't be driven by John.

It is fairly obvious that it is not the same thing to say that John is unwilling
to drive Mary and that Mary is unwilling to be driven by John. By contrast,

there is no similar notion with an epistemic modal and the following two sentences are thus related in terms of voice-neutrality:

John will have driven Mary.
Mary will have been driven by John.

Yet the feature that is involved is rather vaguer than agentiveness or volition. For similar arguments will hold for subject oriented CAN. We would not normally passivize:

John can read Greek.
John can run a mile in four minutes.

It is not always easy to draw a clear distinction between ability in this sense and mere possibility. For ability to act is not isolable from the circumstances in which that ability is exercised. Whether someone has the ability to do something or it is merely possible for him to do that, is not something that can always be clearly determined. For this reason we cannot always distinguish subject oriented and neutral possibility.

The issue is complicated by the fact that we may say:

Greek can be learnt by anyone.

As was noted in 5.3.6 (and there are similar features with DARE – 5.4) passive sentences with what seem to be subject oriented modals (relating to the subject of the active sentence) may occur provided there is no agent or the agent is indefinite. It would seem that with a 'personal' modal, passivization is impossible only if the person involved is actually specified. If, then, there is a personal agent in the passive we can conclude that the modal is not being used in the 'personal', ie subject oriented sense. In all other cases, however, there is no clear test to distinguish subject oriented and neutral possibility.

Similar arguments hold for the indeterminacy between volitional and futurity WILL. For, if futurity WILL is usually conditional, its conditionality will depend in varying degrees upon the volition (or the 'power') of the subject. Indeed volition is, in a sense, no more than personal conditionality.

The distinction between personal and impersonal constructions is not restricted to the types we have considered. There is a very similar problem with:

I persuaded John to come.
I intended John to come.
I ordered John to come.

With PERSUADE John is clearly personally involved as the object, whereas with INTEND he is not. With ORDER he may or may not be, or there may be indeterminacy. What syntactic possibilities there are reflect the absence or presence, or the degree of presence, of this personal involvement (see Palmer

1973 for a detailed discussion). These show that the indeterminacy related to personal and impersonal constructions is a fairly general one.

One might speculate, perhaps, why there is no similar problem with necessity. Indeed, there seems to be no subject oriented necessity at all in the modal system (6.6.1). It is, presumably, because we think of ourselves as being free agents, as having free wills, that we seldom wish to say that someone has the personal characteristics that make an action necessary. These are characteristics of automata rather than human beings. By contrast 'personal possibility' is essentially human.

9.3.3 **Performatives**

Although Austin (1962) established the notion of performative and it is in his sense that I have suggested the deontic modals are performative, he also recognizes (1962: 83) that we can classify similar verbs as 'Explicit performative', 'Not pure (half descriptive)' and 'Descriptive'. One trio is *I apologize, I am sorry, I repent;* another is *I approve, I approve of, I feel approval.* It is not difficult to see that there is a continuum and not a set of discrete classes, *ie* that there is considerable indeterminacy.

It is not surprising, therefore, if there is similar indeterminacy with the performative (*ie* deontic) modals. MUST, quite certainly, has degrees of performativeness and it is often very difficult to decide between a deontic and a dynamic interpretation. The issue is not very different from that of the last section, except that it concerns the personal involvement not of the subject, but of the speaker.

It is curious that there is such indeterminacy with necessity, but almost none with possibility. In most cases it is easy to distinguish between giving permission and saying that something is possible. This may be partly due to the existence of MAY (although it might be argued, conversely, that MAY exists as a deontic modal only because the distinction is clear), but even when CAN is used it is fairly obvious whether it is deontic or dynamic. The most indeterminate example that I have noted is in Ehrman (1966: 15):

'Stop that! You'll wake up the whole building. Wally can't go any place at this hour —'.

This might be interpreted as 'It is not possible for Wally . . .' or as 'I do not permit Wally . . .', or it might be a bit of both, in that the speaker is, to some degree only, making it impossible for Wally to go.

There is, perhaps, an explanation why deontic possibility is so clearly distinct, yet deontic necessity is not. It will be recalled that there is no very close equivalence of deontic 'not-possible' (refusing permission) and 'necessary-not' (obliging not to), even though there are close equivalences with similar epistemic notions (3.5.3). The reason seems to be that permission is only granted or refused where the speaker is known to have authority; by contrast, when he lays an obligation, he usually takes on that authority. Thus, the conditions for granting permission are more established, more easily recognizable; for this reason, it is easier to distinguish giving permission from merely saying that something is possible than to distinguish laying an obligation from saying that something is necessary.

9.4 Modal and main verb

We noted in 1.2 that there are clear formal criteria that allow us to distinguish the modals from other verbs, and to treat them as a subclass of the auxiliaries, the other auxiliaries being the 'primary' auxiliaries BE, HAVE and DO.

Some scholars, however, have argued that the auxiliaries should not be so distinguished and that they are main verbs like all other verbs. The proposal was first made by Ross (1969). Further arguments were provided by Huddleston (1974, 1976a). Jackendoff (1972: 100) offered arguments to distinguish modals from 'true verbs'; these were countered by McCawley (1975). In my own publications I have always argued for the distinction (cf Palmer 1965, 1974), but in his review of the latter book Huddleston (1976b) offers detailed arguments to disprove this. (For an equally detailed counter-reply see Palmer 1979.)

9.4.1 The status of the dispute

Basically what is in dispute is whether, if we draw the distinction between auxiliaries and main verbs, we can properly say that in a sequence containing one or more auxiliaries but only one main verb, we have a 'simple' verb phrase in which there is no subordination, no sentence (or clause) embedding, and that, in contrast, sequences of main verbs, can only be handled in terms of 'complex' phrases in which each phrase except the first, is subordinated to, or embedded in, another. (I use the term verb phrase in its traditional sense, to refer to the purely verbal element of the sentence, and not in the sense of Chomsky's (1965) VP, which is essentially the predicate, containing objects and adjuncts as well as the verbal element.)

I am not at all convinced that there is a serious issue here. For, if we look in detail at the verbs in question, we shall find that some are more like main verbs than others, or that some are like main verbs in some respects and others like main verbs in other respects. The task of the descriptive linguist is complete if he points out these characteristics, and little is to be gained by demanding that the auxiliaries 'really' are or 'really' are not main verbs. There are, however, two arguments that we should first discuss and dismiss.

[i] Many of the arguments depend essentially on the requirement of the linguistic model employed, in all cases one form or other of a model within

the transformational-generative school. It is, in fact, significant that Ross's (1969) article contains ten arguments to show that auxiliaries are verbs and not that they are main verbs, and only two, one from German and one from universal considerations, to show that they are main verbs. The reason is that he was arguing against the proposals in Chomsky (1965), where the auxiliary does not seem to be a verb at all, since it is not part of the VP. Moreover, Ross actually proposes the recognition of a constituent containing both [+V] and [+Aux] (1969: 78).

It is also very significant that McCawley (1971: 97) sees his paper as arguing 'that the traditional term *auxiliary verb* is syntactically justified', yet offers for *John had been smoking pot* the analysis (99):

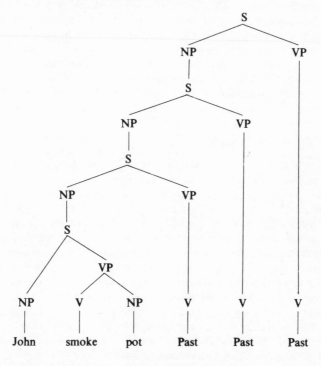

This analysis, which treats tense as well as the auxiliaries as an underlying main verb with no less than four underlying sentences, is clearly not based upon the syntactic behaviour of the auxiliaries, but solely upon a decision to treat all the grammatical-semantic features in this way. The question is begged as it is by Huddleston (1969: 780), who openly states that, if a sentence contains 'incompatible specifiers' (*ie* distinct indications of tense), he would 'assume' that they must be associated in deep structure with

different verbs (see below 9.4.4). If one adopts a model which must by its
nature treat auxiliaries as main verbs, there is little point in arguing whether
they are or are not. What one ought to do is to decide the issue independently
of any model as far as this is possible, and to modify or reject the model if it
fails to account satisfactorily for what has been decided.

[ii] Associated with this argument is the argument that no clear line can be
drawn between auxiliaries and main verbs and that, therefore, they are not
distinct; for a generative model cannot satisfactorily deal with indeterminate
categorization. Thus, Huddleston (1976b: 361–2) argues that there is 'a
considerable variety of restrictions on the structure of the complement', but
that to say that we have a single clause (ie to accept the notion of auxiliary
and simple phrase) 'leads to loss of generality and arbitrary divisions'. But
the absence of generality and the arbitrariness of the divisions is essentially
a feature of the language (as it is of all languages), and nothing is gained by
disguising it or pretending that it is not there. There are similar features
elsewhere in experience. Unless we make some arbitrary divisions, we
cannot establish colours, since one colour shades into another, and there are
plenty of arbitrary decisions in zoological or botanical classifications.

9.4.2 The 'NICE' properties

We saw in 1.2 that what Huddleston (1976b: 333) calls the 'NICE' properties
may be used to distinguish the auxiliary verbs.

Huddleston (1976a: 213) objects to the use of these properties as criteria
on the grounds that 'the differences on which the classification is based are
very much idiosyncratic to English' and that 'classes defined on this basis
can hardly claim to be universal'. He also notes that 'we do not find
equivalent irregularities associated with what are traditionally regarded as
auxiliary verbs in other languages' (1976b: 334). I fail to see the point of this
argument. Languages are idiosyncratic in the way in which they mark their
grammatical categories. But that in no way invalidates the categorization.
Of course, sometimes languages have some purely morphological classes
that have no further significance; the Greek verbs in -mi have little else in
common with each other except that they are very common verbs. But the
situation is not like that with the modals since:

[i] there are no less than four 'NICE' properties, and that can hardly be
insignificant or a coincidence;
[ii] the verbs marked by these properties have much in common grammatically and semantically – they are not an 'accidental' lexical set. (In
particular, the modals have modality in common.)

Most importantly, there are, as we have seen and shall see, some
reasonable grounds for wanting to draw the distinction between auxiliary

and main verb; yet there is no clear dividing line between them if we rely on semantics or many of the grammatical characteristics. It is, then, perfectly reasonable to adopt the purely formal characteristic of the 'NICE' properties to divide the dubious, indeterminate cases and to use it to determine otherwise important but 'fuzzy' distinctions. In this sense, the 'NICE' properties are not the basic reasons for distinguishing auxiliary and main verb; these are to be found elsewhere. But they clearly provide the final test for the decision.

One of the arguments used against the classification is that some verbs seem to belong to both classes. Thus, Ross (1969: 90–3) suggests that treating auxiliaries as main verbs will account for the alternation between *needn't* and *doesn't need*. But this argument can be stood on its head: we can account for these forms by saying that NEED functions both as an auxiliary and as a main verb. After all, the fact that COOK is both a noun and a verb does not invalidate the distinction between nouns and verbs.

Huddleston (1976b: 334) was also worried by the well-known fact that main verbs BE and HAVE have the 'NICE' properties. It was for this reason that H. E. Palmer (1939: 122–5) talked of the 'anomalous finites'. But this seems to me to raise no difficulty. BE and HAVE often behave in an idiosyncratic way in languages; it should be no surprise if, even when they are main verbs, they adopt the formal characteristics of the auxiliaries. (Moreover, when it is a main verb, HAVE often does not have the 'NICE' properties – *doesn't have* can only be a form of the main verb and never the auxiliary.)

The most difficult problem for those who argue that auxiliaries are main verbs is the status of DO. This occurs only where there is one of the 'NICE' properties and there is no auxiliary verb available:

I like it.
I don't like it.
Do I like it?
I like it and so does John.
I dó like it.

To treat DO as a main verb is odd, because:

[i] it is semantically quite empty;
[ii] in a generative grammar it must either be inserted under the 'NICE' conditions or deleted when these conditions do not apply. Either seems entirely artificial and implausible.

9.4.3 The paradigm

In both books (Palmer 1965, 1976) I spoke of sequences of auxiliary and main verb as 'forms' of the verb. Thus, *would have been taking* is treated as a form of TAKE, just as Latin *amavisset* is a form of AMO. The point being made is that the sequence of the auxiliaries is relatively fixed, and that, while we can say *has been talking,* we cannot say **is having talked,* and that there is no possible sequence in which the modal does not occur first. Instead, therefore, of dealing with these sequences in terms of a syntactic process such as subordination, I preferred to treat them as not wholly separable units, and as members of a paradigm.

Against this McCawley (1971: 102) argues that the non-occurrence of **is having* is explained by saying that HAVE is a stative verb and that no stative verbs may be preceded by BE. Thus **is having* is ruled out by the same considerations as **is resembling.* Emonds (1976: 209–10) further argues that perfective HAVE cannot occur after any verb of temporal aspect. We cannot say **John began/continued/resumed having said* .... This restriction equally applies to BE and to HAVE, and is explained in terms of a general consideration that involves other verbs as well as auxiliaries. But both McCawley and Emonds are wrong in not recognizing that forms of the **is having* type are completely ruled out and totally ungrammatical, whereas there is some doubt about **is resembling* and **began having* and it would be possible to find contexts in which they might occur. The point is, as Huddleston (1976b: 338) says, 'the blocking BE *having* V-*en* seems to be more fully "grammaticalized"'. Indeed, it is fully grammaticalized, whereas the other restrictions are not. Of course, we can explain them in similar ways, as McCawley and Emonds have done, but there are two kinds of explanation: in one kind we give a plausible reason for an absolute grammatical rule, whereas in the other we state conditions under which restrictions will apply. **Is having* is ruled out grammatically, and should be accounted for in a different way from **is resembling* and **began having.*

The fact that modals may only come first in the sequence is explained by McCawley (1975: 597) and Huddleston (1976b: 338) by saying that the modals have a defective morphology; since they have only finite forms, they can occur only in this position. But would it not be equally reasonable to argue that they have no non-finite forms because their proper place of occurrence is at the beginning of the phrase? It is a chicken-and-egg problem. It is curious that the modals have a defective morphology. Why has English no **to can,* **canning* (except, of course, with a quite different verb)? If there had been a real need for them, it is, surely, likely that such forms would have existed. This strongly suggests that the absence of non-finite forms is no accident, but a result of their places in the paradigm.

9.4.4 The TNP tests

Huddleston (1976b: 340) also refers to the 'TNP tests' (tense, negation, and passivization). I shall deal in detail only with the first.

Huddleston (1969a: 780, 1976b: 341) argues that we ought to treat in a similar fashion both:

Yesterday John intended to come tomorrow.

Yesterday John was coming tomorrow.

He suggests that as we have two 'tense selections', we ought equally to say that we have two main verbs, in both examples. I recognize that modals may be independently marked for tense and in this respect are more like main verbs. But this is far less true of BE and HAVE and I can, therefore, still argue that the auxiliaries are not main verbs.

The main objection to Huddleston's argument is that there may be more time markers than there are verbs available. Thus, a simple past tense form may be used with double tense marking as in:

They had to leave early as they started work the next day.

Started, here, indicates both the past time at which the statement was valid and the future time at which the action took place. But there are not two verbs here as there would have been if *were starting* had been used. Since double time marking does not necessarily imply two verbs, it cannot rightly be used as an argument to prove that there are two main verbs in *was coming*.

Huddleston's only reply is to recognize an 'abstract verb' (1976b: 345) to account for the second tense. This is, of course, question begging and not a serious contribution to the argument. It is, however, in keeping with arguments in generative semantics (cf McCawley 1971: 99, where all tenses are underlying verbs). (For a much more detailed argument see Palmer 1979.)

There are also difficulties with the analysis of the present perfect. For how can we analyse *I have seen him* in such a way that HAVE is an independent verb with its own specific meaning? Huddleston (1976b: 342) admits that there are problems in treating it as 'past in present'. Indeed, I see no plausible way in which semantically past and present can be assigned separately to HAVE and SEE. Moreover, if they are so assigned it is difficult, if not impossible, to account for the fact that we do not normally say *I have seen him yesterday,* for if *have* indicates past here, such a sentence would appear to be normal. Surely the proper solution is that HAVE is a marker of the perfect, which has a fairly complex meaning that is not divisible simply into two 'tenses'. That is precisely what we would expect on a paradigm interpretation.

On negation there are two points to be made. First, with BE and HAVE it is not possible to negate the auxiliary and the main verb independently. We cannot normally say *He isn't not coming* or *He hasn't not come*. This strongly supports the simple phrase analysis. (Huddleston's arguments to disprove this in terms of the scope of negation are mistaken – Huddleston 1976b: 348–51, Palmer 1979.)

Secondly, we have seen that, with tag questions, the tag is determined grammatically and not semantically (2.3.3[iv]), so that we may say:

He mustn't come, must he?

Semantically *come* not *must* is negative, so that we might have expected ... *mustn't he?* like:

He decided not to come, didn't he?

Clearly, the modal differs in this respect from the catenative and the negation belongs grammatically to the modal, even though it belongs semantically to the main verb ('event'). This points to a clear difference between modal and catenative.

There is little to be said about passivization. The facts are that there is voice-neutrality with BE, HAVE (and DO), and that there is voice-neutrality with some of the modals in some of their uses. There are some catenatives, *eg* SEEM and HAPPEN that also exhibit voice-neutrality. Voice-neutrality is not, therefore, a defining characteristic. But there is significance in the fact that CAN is often voice-neutral (5.3.6), and surprisingly, so is DARE (5.6), even though the semantics make this most unlikely. This is yet another indication of the auxiliary nature of the modals.

9.4.5 Two final arguments

One argument that has been proposed for auxiliaries as main verbs is that what follows them is a constituent that is a sentential complement. Ross (1969: 82–3) considers:

They say that Tom may have been singing and so he might have been.
                                                                might have.
                                                                might.

So replaces *singing, been singing* and *have been singing,* all of which are thus, it is argued, embedded sentences.

There are, however, two good reasons for not accepting this 'sentential complement' argument. First, the catenatives do not always permit similar constructions. We cannot, for instance, say:

*They said that Tom kept lying and so he did keep.

The constructions offered by Ross are, then, especially typical of the auxiliaries; replacement of sentential complement by *so* is not freely permissible with catenatives. Secondly, if we treat the Ross examples in terms of a syntactic process of deletion we entirely disguise the fact that 'code' (see 1.2) is a kind of pro-formation – 'pro-verbalization'. We ought, surely, to treat pro-verbalization in the same way as pronominalization. What we need to say is that a pro-form contains the minimum amount of information that is needed for identification. Pronouns indicate only sex and number, while the pro-verbs used in code indicate only the auxiliary elements of the verb phrase. In neither case is there any indication of the lexical features. It is, therefore, reasonable to handle both pro-formations in the same way, and this can only be done if the auxiliary (non-lexical) element is clearly distinguished from the main verb, which carries all the lexical information. Precisely how this is done will depend on the model used, but whatever the model, it is essential to distinguish between auxiliary and main verb.

The second argument in favour of making the distinction is related to the first. It is the main verb that is essentially the head of the verb phrase. It contains the lexical information and very largely determines the selectional restrictions with the heads of the noun phrases (lexical nouns). Thus we may compare:

The tree broke the window.
The old tree may have broken the large window.

The addition of 'modifiers' – adjectives and auxiliaries – does not affect the selectional restrictions. There are some exceptions, but in general this point is true and the auxiliary–main verb distinction is paralleled by that of adjective–noun.

I will end as I started by commenting that I am not sure that the argument is a very important one, though it may seem important to scholars, who have restricted themselves to a very tight 'rigorous' model. But it has been argued so fiercely that it cannot be ignored.

In practical terms we need to distinguish auxiliaries from main verbs, and, indeed, to distinguish the modals from the other auxiliaries. For me the distinction has the added attraction that without it it would not have been possible to write this book.

References

ANDERSON, J. (1971) 'Some proposals concerning the modal verb in English', in Aitken, A. J., McIntosh, A. and Pálsson, H. (eds) *Edinburgh Studies in English and Scots*. London: Longman, 69–120

AUSTIN, J. L. (1962) *How to do things with words*. London: Oxford University Press

BINNICK, R. I. (1971) '*Will* and *be going to*'. *Papers from the 7th Regional Meeting, Chicago Linguistic Society*, 40–52
(1972) '*Will* and *be going to* II'. *Papers from the 8th Regional Meeting, Chicago Linguistic Society*, 3–9

BOLINGER, D. L. (1961) 'Syntactic blends and other matters'. *Language* 37, 366–81

BOUMA, L. (1973) *The semantics of the modal auxiliaries in contemporary German*. The Hague: Mouton
(1975) 'On contrasting the semantics of the modal auxiliaries of German and English'. *Lingua* 37, 313–39

BOYD, J. and THORNE, J. P. (1969) 'The semantics of modal verbs'. *Journal of Linguistics* 5, 57–74

CALBERT, J. P. (1971) 'Modality and case grammar'. *Working papers in linguistics* (Ohio State University) 10, 85–132
(1975) 'Towards the semantics of modality', in *Aspekte der Modalität: Studien zur deutschen Grammatik I* (ed Abraham, W. *et al*). Tübingen: Gunter Narr, 1–70

CHOMSKY, N. A. (1957) *Syntactic structures*. The Hague: Mouton
(1964) *Current issues in linguistic theory*. The Hague: Mouton
(1965) *Aspects of the theory of syntax*. Cambridge, Mass: MIT Press

CHRISTOPHERSON, P. and SANDVED, A. O. (1969) *An advanced English grammar*. London: Macmillan

CLOSE, R. (1977) 'Some observations on the meaning and function of verb phrases having future time reference', in Bald, W. and Ilson, R. (eds) *Studies in English usage*. Frankfurt: Lang, 125–56

CURME, G. O. (1931) *A grammar of the English language*, vol III *Syntax*. New York: D. C. Heath

DIVER, W. (1964) 'The modal system of the English verb'. *Word* 20, 322–52

EHRMAN, M. E. (1966) *The meanings of the modals in present-day English*. The Hague: Mouton

EMONDS, J. (1976) *A transformational approach to English syntax: root, structure-preserving and local transformations*. New York: Academic Press

FRASER, B. (1973) 'On accounting for illocutionary forces', in Anderson, S. R. and Kiparsky, P. *A festschrift for Morris Halle*. New York: Holt, Rinehart & Winston, 287–307

FRIES, C. C. (1925) 'The periphrastic future with *shall* and *will* in modern English'. *Proceedings of the Modern Language Association* 40, 963–1024
(1927) 'The expression of the future'. *Language* 3, 87–95

GARCIA, E. C. (1967) 'Auxiliaries and the criterion of simplicity'. *Language* 43, 853–70

GORDON, D. and LAKOFF, G. (1971) 'Conversational postulates'. *Papers from the 7th Regional Meeting, Chicago Linguistic Society*, 63–84

GRICE, H. P. (1968) 'Utterer's meaning, sentence-meaning and word-meaning'. *Foundations of Language* 4, 225–42

HALLIDAY, M. A. K. (1970) 'Functional diversity in language as seen from a consideration of modality and mood in English'. *Foundations of Language* 6, 322–61

HINTIKKA, J. (1973) *Time and necessity in Aristotle's theory of modality*. Oxford: Clarendon Press

HOCKETT, C. F. (1968) *A course in modern linguistics*. New York: Macmillan

HONORÉ, A. M. M. (1964) 'Can and can't'. *Mind* 73, 463–79

HUDDLESTON, R. D. (1969a) 'Some observations on tense and deixis in English'. *Language* 45, 777–806
(1969b) Review of Ehrman (1966). *Lingua* 23, 165–76
(1971) *The sentence in written English: a syntactic study based on the analysis of scientific texts*. Cambridge: Cambridge University Press
(1974) 'Further remarks on the analysis of auxiliaries as main verbs'. *Foundations of Language* 6, 322–61
(1976a) *An introduction to English transformational syntax*. London: Longman
(1976b) 'Some theoretical issues in the description of the English verb'. *Lingua* 40, 331–83
(1977a) 'Past tense transportation'. *Journal of Linguistics* 13, 43–52
(1977b) 'The futurate construction'. *Linguistic Inquiry* 8, 730–6

JACKENDOFF, R. S. (1972) *Semantic interpretation in generative grammar*. Cambridge, Mass: MIT Press

JACOBS, R. A. and ROSENBAUM, P. S. (eds) (1970) *Readings in English transformational grammar*. Waltham, Mass: Ginn

JENKINS, L. (1972) *Modality in English syntax*. MIT dissertation (distributed by the Indiana Linguistic Club)

JESPERSEN, O. (1909–49) *A modern English grammar*, I-VII. Heidelberg: Karl Winter, Copenhagen: Einar Munksgaard, and London: Allen & Unwin

JOHANNESON, N-L. (1976) *The English modal auxiliaries: a stratificational account*. Stockholm: Almquist & Wiksell International

JOOS, M. (ed) (1958) *Readings in linguistics*. New York: American Council of Learned Societies

JOOS, M. (1964) *The English verb: form and meanings*. Madison and Milwaukee: The University of Wisconsin Press

KARTUNNEN, L. (1972) 'Possible and must'. *Syntax and semantics I*. New York: Seminar Press, 1–20

KATZ, J. J. and POSTAL, P.M. (1964) *An integrated theory of linguistic descriptions*. Cambridge, Mass: MIT Press

KLIMA, E. S. (1964) 'Negation in English', in Fodor, J. A. and Katz, J. J. (eds) *The structure of language: readings in the philosophy of language*. Englewood Cliffs, N. J.: Prentice-Hall, 246–323

KRUISINGA, E. and ERADES, P. A. (1911) *An English grammar*. Groningen: Nordhoff

LAKOFF, R. (1972a) 'The pragmatics of modality'. *Papers from the 8th Regional Meeting, Chicago Linguistic Society*, 247–58
(1972b) 'Language in context'. *Language* 48, 907–27

LARKIN, D. (1969) 'Some notes on English modals'. *Phonetics Lab. Notes* (University of Michigan) 4, 31–6

LEBRUN, Y. (1965) *'Can' and 'may' in present day English*. Bruxelles: Presses universitaires de Bruxelles

LEECH, G. N. (1969) *Towards a semantic description of English*. London: Longman
(1971) *Meaning and the English verb*. London: Longman

LEES, R. B. (1960) 'A multiply ambiguous construction in English'. *Language* 36, 207–21

LYONS, J. (1968) *Introduction to theoretical linguistics*. Cambridge: Cambridge University Press
(1977) *Semantics*. Cambridge: Cambridge University Press

MCCAWLEY, J. D. (1971) 'Tense and time reference in English', in Fillmore, C. J. and Langendoen, D. T. (eds) *Studies in linguistic semantics*. New York: Holt, Rinehart & Winston, 96–113
(1975) 'The category status of English modals'. *Foundations of Language* 12, 597–601

MCINTOSH, A. (1966) 'Predictive statements', in Bazell, C. E. *et al* (eds) *In Memory of J. R. Firth*. London: Longman, 303–20

MARINO, M. (1973) 'A feature analysis of the English modals'. *Lingua* 32, 309–23

MATTHEWS, P. H. (1972) Review of Jacobs and Rosenbaum (1970). *Journal of Linguistics* 8, 125–36

PALMER, F. R. (1965) *A linguistic study of the English verb*. London: Longman (1973) 'Noun phrase and sentence: a problem in semantics/syntax'. *Transactions of the Philological Society* (*1972*), 20–43 (1974) *The English verb*. London: Longman (1977) 'Modals and actuality'. *Journal of Linguistics* 13, 1–23 (1978) 'Past tense transportation: a reply'. *Journal of Linguistics* 14, 77–81 (1979) 'Why auxiliaries are not main verbs'. To appear in *Lingua*

PALMER, H. E. and BLANDFORD, F. G. (1939) *A grammar of spoken English on a strictly phonetic basis*. Cambridge: Heffer

PERLMUTTER, D. M. (1970) 'The two verbs *begin*', in Jacobs and Rosenbaum (1970), 107–19

PULLUM, G. and WILSON, D. (1977) 'Autonomous syntax and the analysis of auxiliaries'. *Language* 53, 741–88

QUIRK, R., GREENBAUM, S., LEECH, G. and SVARTVIK, J. (1972) *A grammar of contemporary English*. London: Longman

RADFORD, A. (1977) *Italian syntax: transformational and relational grammar*. Cambridge: Cambridge University Press

ROSENBAUM, P. S. (1967) *The grammar of English predicate constructions*. Cambridge, Mass: MIT Press

ROSS, J. R. (1969) 'Auxiliaries as main verbs', in Todd, W. (ed) *Studies in philosophical linguistics*. Evanston, Ill: Great Expectations Press (1970) 'On declarative sentences', in Jacobs and Rosenbaum (1970), 222–272

SADOCK, J. M. (1974) *Towards a linguistic theory of speech acts*. New York: Academic Press

SAPIR, E. (1925) 'Sound patterns in language'. *Language* 1, 37–51. Reprinted in Joos (1958)

SCHEURWEGHS, G. (1959) *Present-day English syntax: a survey of sentence patterns*. London: Longman

SEUREN, P. A. M. (1969) *Operators and nucleus*. Cambridge: Cambridge University Press

STRANG, B. M. H. (1962) *Modern English structure*. London: Edward Arnold

TRUBETSKOY, N. S. (1939) *Grundzüge der Phonologie*. Prague: Cercle linguistique de Prague. (Trans into French by Cantineau, J. *Principes de phonologie*. Paris: Klincksieck)

TWADDELL, W. F. (1960) *The English verb auxiliaries*. Providence: Brown University Press (1965) *The English verb auxiliaries* (2nd edn). Providence: Brown University Press

ULTAN, R. (1972) 'The nature of future tenses'. *Working papers in language universals* (Stanford University) 8, 55–100

WEKKER, H. (1976) *The expression of future time in contemporary British English*. Amsterdam: North-Holland

(1977) 'Future reference in adverbial clauses'. *Interlanguage studies bulletin* (Utrecht) 2, 64–77

WHORF, B. L. (1956) *Language, thought and reality: selected writings of Benjamin Lee Whorf* (ed Carroll, J. B.). New York: Wiley

VON WRIGHT, G. H. (1951) *An essay in modal logic.* Amsterdam: North-Holland

ZANDVOORT, R. W. (1962) *A handbook of English grammar,* (2nd edn). London: Longman

Indexes

Author index

Anderson, J. 40, 102, 129
Aristotle 8
Austin, J. L. 3, 14–15, 36, 177
Binnick, R. I. 108
Bolinger, D. L. 173
Bouma, L. 10, 12–13, 43, 69, 94
Boyd, J. and Thorne, J. P. 14–16, 120, 156
Calbert, J. P. 13
Chomsky, N. A. 9, 12, 178–9
Christophersen, P. and Sandved, A. O. 113
Close, R. 118
Curme, G. O. 6
Diver, W. 12
Ehrman, M. E. 10–11, 20, 40, 60, 72–3, 80, 90, 129, 151, 155, 177
Emonds, J. 182
Fraser, B. 168–9, 171
Fries, C. C. 5, 112
Garcia, E. C. 174–5
Gordon, D. and Lakoff, G. 166–8
Grice, H. P. 165
Halliday, M. A. K. 19, 35, 43, 52, 54–5
Hill, A. A. 74
Hintikka, J. 8
Hockett, C. F. 4
Honore, A. M. M. 85
Huddleston, R. D. 8–10, 35, 42, 60, 118, 120, 138, 143–4, 154, 174–5, 178–83

Jackendoff, R. S. 178
Jakobson, R. 10
Jenkins, L. 10, 35, 119, 132
Jespersen, O. 1–2, 63, 108, 115, 118
Johanneson, N-L. 10, 18, 60, 74, 156–7
Joos, M. 6, 10, 12–13, 25, 42–3, 74, 121
Kartunnen, L. 43, 157
Katz, J. J. and Postal, P. M. 15
Klima, E. S. 26
Kruisinga, E. and Erades, P. A. 161
Lakoff, R. 69, 169–70
Larkin, D. 94
Lebrun, Y. 14, 60
Leech, G. N. 11, 13–14, 42, 130, 152, 154
Lees, R. B. 173
Lyons, J. 3–6, 8, 38, 55, 67, 106, 164, 175
McCawley, J. D. 123, 178–9, 182–3
McIntosh, A. 108, 121
Marino, M. 13–14
Matthews, P. H. 15
Oxford English Dictionary 5
Palmer, F. R. 8–9, 11, 26, 30, 32, 35–6, 38, 40, 43, 47, 72, 85, 100–1, 109, 111, 118, 124, 137, 141, 144, 176, 178, 181, 183
Palmer, H. E. 8, 181
Perlmutter, D. M. 174
Pullum, G. and Wilson, D. 90

Verb index

Subject index